Pricing the Planet

Economic Analysis for Sustainable Development

Pricing the Planet

Economic Analysis for Sustainable Development

*Edited by Peter H. May and
Ronaldo Serôa da Motta*

COLUMBIA UNIVERSITY PRESS

NEW YORK

HC
79
E5
P68
1996

Columbia University Press
New York   Chichester, West Sussex
Copyright © 1996 Columbia University Press
All rights reserved

Library of Congress Cataloging-in-Publication Data
Pricing the planet : economic analysis for sustainable development /
edited by Peter H. May and Ronaldo Serôa da Motta.
    p.   cm.
    Includes bibliographical references and index.
    ISBN 0-231-10174-0
    1. Environmental policy—Economic aspects.   2. Sustainable
development.   3. Economic development—Environmental aspects.
    I. May, Peter Herman.   II. Motta, Ronaldo Serôa da.
HC79.E5P68   1996
333.7—dc20   95-42200
∞   CIP

Printed in the United States of America

c 10 9 8 7 6 5 4 3 2 1
p 10 9 8 7 6 5 4 3 2 1

Contents

Acknowledgments

The presence of hundreds of environmental specialists during the United Nations Conference on Environment and Development (UNCED) in June 1992, arose as a unique opportunity to organize technical gatherings. Aware that a number of environmental economists and ecologists would be converging on Rio de Janeiro at this time, we determined to open space on the agenda of events at UNCED for a forum that would enable these analysts to share their thinking on paths toward sustainable development. This meeting took place on June 2, 1992, during the Symposium and Exhibit of Environmental Technologies (ECOTECH), sponsored by the State Government of Rio de Janeiro. At this gathering more than 150 persons were present, among whom were academics, environmental managers, government technicians and students. The papers presented in this volume reflect the exposition by each speaker during the ECOTECH meeting, which was entitled "Economic Analysis for Sustainable Development."

The Symposium and Exhibit of Environmental Technologies was organized at the initiative of the Rio de Janeiro State Secretariat of Industry, Commerce, Science, and Technology. We express our appreciation to then-Secretary Luis Alfredo Salomão and subsecretary Eduardo Costa for having responded favorably to our idea for a meeting of this kind. We extend this appreciation to the organizer of technical events at ECOTECH, Marília Pastuk, who contributed to make the symposium an intellectually stimulating event.

The current collection represents a selection from seminar proceedings published initially in Portuguese in a book entitled *Valorando a Natureza*

(Rio de Janeiro: Editora Campus, 1994) under the auspices of Brazil's National Economic Research Program (PNPE) with support from the Food and Agriculture Organization of the United Nations and the Italian Ministry of Foreign Relations (Italy-FAO-PROCAPLAN). Most contributions constitute original papers presented for the first time at the ECOTECH Panel during UNCED. Several were previously published in journals (Costanza and Daly) or constitute reports of research undertaken at the request of the UNCED secretariat (Parikh and Margulis). Post-UNCED review of these papers by their authors was complemented by two additional papers by the editors (May and Serôa da Motta) reflecting their work to clarify options for economic analysis in the new and growing realm of international environmental policy. The collection thus offers a current perspective from both developing and industrialized countries.

Above all, we want to express our appreciation to our speakers, not only for the quality of their presentations but, principally, for having enthusiastically responded to our invitation to the meeting that gave rise to this book. The success of the ECOTECH panel during UNCED in Rio de Janeiro where these papers were presented, and frequent citation to the book among readers of the Portuguese version lead us to believe that it offers a unique opportunity to better understand the potential and limitations of economic analysis for global environmental management. In this sense, it can assist in defining models for economic development that are at the same time more environmentally sound and socially equitable.

Pricing the Planet

Economic Analysis for
Sustainable Development

Introduction

Peter H. May and Ronaldo Serôa da Motta

The 1992 United Nations Conference on Environment and Development (UNCED) in Rio de Janeiro definitively ushered the objective of sustainable development onto national and international policy agendas.

Although myriad definitions exist for sustainable development, in Rio, delegates and civil society focused upon their increasing concern with current economic growth patterns, and the troubling notion that human life may one day be threatened by the very prosperity such growth has engendered. The debate was particularly heated when participants discussed the possibility that planetary ecological limits may not permit that consumption patterns enjoyed by rich nations be attained by humanity at large.

Two years beyond UNCED, despite the redirection of negotiators' concerns toward related issues of population management and social inequities, global environmental problems remain daunting and inadequately confronted at a national or international level. The United Nations Commission on Sustainable Development created in the wake of UNCED has made little progress in defining the specifics of a global partnership to manage common threats to resource integrity. For this reason, many of the challenges voiced at Rio continue to absorb the attention of scholars who hope to better articulate the complex issues at stake.

At UNCED, a number of difficult questions were brought to the table. Among them: How far can economic growth go without stretching the limits of an ever more finite planet? What are the potentials for adaptation to these limits using alternative technologies and policies? Are the guiding principles and tools used by economists today up to the task? This book unites studies prepared in the context of UNCED, revised in the light of further developments, that seek answers to such questions.

In an overview of issues repeated throughout the book, Peter May suggests that progress toward sustainable development will depend on policies adopted not only by nations acting in concert but also, and perhaps more compellingly, by policies and actions adopted within national borders. To assist in redirecting development paths, he compares approaches that have come to be labeled "weak" and "strong" versions of sustainable development at the level of national accounts estimation and in evaluation of projects or policies. In the "weak" version, economists adopt the assumption that natural capital may be infinitely substituted by man-made capital, whereas under "strong" sustainability, there are distinct ecological limits to capital substitution. These assumptions affect how environmental costs and services are treated in monetary terms, thus influencing the outcomes of accounts and project feasibility studies. The need to specify biophysical limits to the nature and extent of economic expansion, and uncertainties about the interactions between the economy and the environment brings these issues into the realm of public debate in the search for balance among facts and values.

Among the issues that have drawn significant attention since UNCED are the usefulness of market-based instruments and incentives to encourage internalization of environmental costs, and the perspective that redirecting international trade may be one means to adjust economic activities to reflect such costs. As in other areas, economic analysis derived from mainstream views would leave as much as possible up to market forces, whereas other perspectives, notably those stemming from ecological economics, promote institutional restructuring and would steer clear of excessive reliance on the market. Economic analysis of global environmental policy options, stemming from alternative interpretations, compels negotiation among stakeholders in the international arena.

Among issues that stirred debate at UNCED, the question of "who's to blame?" for global environmental problems was most polemical, due to differing perspectives from North and South. A review of distributive issues in global environmental management is provided by Jyoti Parikh, who suggests that it is the wealthy nations with their privileged consumption patterns that generate the lion's share of global environmental degradation. Parikh analyzes these consumption patterns and their environmental implications. A considerable share of world commodity consumption (50 to 90%) takes place in industrialized nations, where only one quarter of the world's population lives. Reflecting this disparity, these same nations are responsible for nearly 70% of annual CO_2 emissions.

Nevertheless, when one considers environmental control, the roles are inverted. Cities in the richer nations have been able to reduce concentrations of atmospheric pollutants, for example, through technologically sophisticated control policies, whereas the poorest still suffer from health damages associated with pollution. In the case of rural areas, Parikh shows that the use of dung and other biofuels for cooking is a principal cause of respiratory disease. She concludes that the wealthy nations have the greater responsibility to ensure changes in consumption patterns and to finance sustainable development in the poor nations. In the control of global environmental problems, due to their minor share of responsibility for cumulative emissions, the poor nations should be benefited instead of suffering restrictions on their growth.

These assessments by Jyoti Parikh confirm that it will only be possible to balance problems such as global warming if each country carries out changes in its economic activities so as to reduce the emissions of gases causing the greenhouse effect. Defining criteria for distributing the onus that must be incurred among different nations is an equity question, and as such is difficult to resolve consensually.

Adam Rose discusses exactly this equity question in defining allocative criteria between countries for the control of emission of greenhouse gases, through application of a mechanism such as tradable emission certificates. He recognizes that there are innumerable candidate criteria and no consensus regarding which should be used, principally owing to the basis for calculation adopted, and the form in which or indeed whether one is to consider historical emissions as a contributing factor. Still, the choice of one criterion or another will definitively influence the costs and benefits that will be incurred by each country involved in such an accord. Rose discusses ten criteria and their allocative functioning. Further, he introduces dynamics into the question when he considers past and future emissions. The study compares conditions that show which nations might win and those which might lose as a result of the choice of different criteria. The results demonstrate that those criteria which introduce past emissions and industrialization levels into the calculus to define rights for future emissions are those which would most favor poor nations.

Besides the complexity of resolving global questions pointed out by Rose, individual nations must define priorities for environmental policies so as to move toward more sustainable forms of development. One example of how this might be carried forward regarding the Mexican case is discussed by Sergio Margulis. The objective is to establish environmental policy priorities in this country on the basis of costs associated with the use of water, air and soil resources.

In the case of water and air pollution, Margulis estimates the related health costs. For atmospheric pollution, American dose-response functions were used, that correlate levels of pollutant concentration with morbidity and mortality indices. On this basis, Margulis determined the number of deaths, workdays lost, and school absences, for Mexico City, valuing these losses on the basis of an average industrial worker's salary. In the case of water pollution, he considered the number of deaths resulting from intestinal infection and valued them on the same basis as for atmospheric pollution, estimating also the cost of avoidance of death with the general application of oral rehydration therapy. For water resources, he also accounted for marginal costs of potable water delivery should the current sources be lost due to exhaustion or pollution and due to subsidies offered for irrigation water use. Finally, in the case of soil, environmental costs were estimated as the losses in agricultural productivity due to erosion.

The values estimated by Margulis suggest that the costs associated with water pollution—$4.76 billion—are most severe. Those relative to soil and air account for losses on the order of $1 billion each. Margulis recognizes that these estimates are quite approximate, but believes that such calculations may serve to direct Mexican environmental policy toward identification of investment priorities, by defining economic values for each major source of degradation.

The analysis conducted for the case of Mexico is paralleled by contemporary studies accomplished in Brazil. Ronaldo Serôa da Motta and Ana Paula Mendes provide a summation of analyses concerned with costs provoked by Brazilian urban air pollution. The objective of the study was to investigate the relationship between emission abatement indicators and urban epidemiological conditions associated with respiratory sickness. This analysis served as the basis for estimation of environmental externalities from declines in economic performance due to sickness and death. Finally, the relationship between these negative externalities and the costs of providing treatment for these wastes was estimated. The medical costs and lost work days associated with air pollution related sickness and death are valued, as in the Mexican case, on the basis of average industrial workers' salaries. The costs of treatment would exceed these costs under most scenarios considered, suggesting that preventive health measures may be the most cost effective way for Brazil to cope with its inadequate investment in air pollution control facilities.

Even if priorities can be defined as in the studies by Margulis and by Serôa da Motta and Mendes, the implementation of environmental policies requires the definition of clear and consensual criteria as well as of efficient instruments. For this purpose, the use of economic incentives or market mechanisms, such as charges and certificates, is the most efficient means to "set the right price" on natural resources, and by so doing internalize ecological losses in production and consumption decisions. However, the correct and just determination of charges and the creation of marketable pollution emission certificates is not always as simple from a political or social perspective.

Tom Tietenberg discusses in detail how these principles and incentives might orient the economic use of natural resources within nations. The first principle presented is that of "total cost," equivalent to the polluter pays principle, that should be applied to all producers and consumers. The idea is to eliminate subsidies over use of environmental goods and services (intrinsic in an economy that places no price on these values) and ensure that consumers and producers pay the total cost of this use. Tietenberg discusses some of the means in which this principle could be implemented, such as through charges, judicial penalties, reduction of incentives to polluting activities, and environmental insurance coverage by corporations.

The second principle is based more on ecological interactions than on economic premises. This is the carrying capacity principle, related with the limits to assimilation and restoration of natural resources. Thus, in cases such as fisheries emphasized by Tietenberg, it is necessary to adopt practices for resource utilization based on resource carrying capacity. This principle can be adopted with the help of economic incentives, such as quota certificates or license fees for fishing rights. Nevertheless, Tietenberg demonstrates that these incentives should be applied cautiously to avoid the domination of specific interests, generating inequities.

He suggests that economic incentives can serve equally well as a means to relieve global problems such as greenhouse warming. In this sense, he also discusses the proposal for international greenhouse gas emissions certificates. Finally, the relative merit of economic instruments is tempered with the need for political action. The participation of NGOs and communities in the monitoring of environmental policy implementation is the best means to ensure its efficacy. For developing countries, this is one means to overcome difficulties encountered in governmental environment management.

As Tietenberg observes, ecological limits must be integrated with economic analysis. Furthermore, it is becoming imperative to rethink the technological optimism that has been the foundation for the world's economic growth model. These premises represent the grounding of a new scientific approach denominated "Ecological Economics," discussed by Robert Costanza.

First, Costanza defines ecological economics (EE) as a new transdisciplinary field that studies the relations between ecosystems and economic systems. In this sense, EE differs from traditional approaches in both economics and ecology that do not emphasize these relationships. Second, EE does not accept faith in technological advance as the only solution for future problems. Some physical and biological limitations will not be removed through such advances. Constanza also discusses the conflict between short-term individual objectives and long-term goals for planetary sustainability.

He goes on to propose a research agenda for EE, beginning with the need to advance in efforts toward valuation of natural capital, whether based on monetary or energy values. Once resource and sink functions are more adequately valued, national accounts can be adjusted to incorporate environmental questions so that these then become more valuable planning instruments. Also proposed is the use of analytical models based on input/output matrices where natural resources and transformation processes are represented in terms of energetic content. Constanza recognizes that such a model requires information still unavailable, and hypotheses regarding certain relationships that are as yet unknown. Nevertheless, it is proposed that such models be developed to assure greater transparency in the consideration of interactions between resource stocks and flows and the services derived from these, with the related economic activities.

With respect to environmental policy, Costanza defends the imposition of charges for environmental goods and services and, in agreement with Tietenberg, also suggests the creation of assurance bonds held in escrow as a guarantee against future environmental risk. Such bonds would be reimbursed to the insured firms upon demonstration that risk abatement technology had been adopted. Another mechanism that should be adopted is that of pollution certificates for international control of greenhouse forcing gases. In summary, Costanza favors the adoption of prudent development policies that assure the maintenance of natural capital stocks at their current or superior levels, for the benefit of future generations.

The importance of these principles of ecological economics toward realizing sustainable development trajectories is exemplified with great clarity by Herman Daly. He presents two case studies employing the concept of carrying capacity to guide development policies. The identification of carrying capacity seeks to limit economic activities consonant with physical ecosystem restrictions. The first case described is that of the Ecuadorian Amazon, in the process of being occupied through the advance of regional colonization. The development model adopted for regional occupation has not heeded the fact that the ecosystem is fragile and does not represent an inexhaustible source of wealth and fertility. Furthermore, inequalities in income distribution and land tenure have not been corrected and resources derived from petroleum exploitation have not been directed toward incentives for sustainable economic activities. This erroneous vision, according Daly, has been the fault not only of the Ecuadorian government but also of international agencies that finance development projects in the region. Finally, the national labor surplus, due to lack of resolution of distributional questions, ends up forcing colonization of the Amazon, suggesting the need for long-range family planning efforts.

Daly's second case is that of the Paraguayan Chaco, a vast region today occupied by only 6,650 persons engaged in agricultural activities. A regional development project for the Chaco foresees a population of nearly 5 million persons. In the same way discussed in the Ecuadorian case, this proposal ignores ecosystem capacity to support the projected economic activities. Daly emphasizes that, without considering the environmental carrying capacity, development projects in fragile regions end in failure thereby perpetuating poverty.

We observe in Daly's paper that devising planning instruments to guide development in more sustainable directions has become a major priority. One of the mechanisms that has engendered much discussion of late, as is evident from proposals made by the contributions to the present volume, is that of preparation of national environmental accounts that would take into consideration the environmental losses generated during production and consumption activities. For this purpose, it would be necessary to adjust the current macroeconomic indicators so as to internalize ecological questions. This theme is amply discussed by Peter Bartelmus and by Ronaldo Serôa da Motta and Peter May.

Bartelmus first presents the system of environmental accounts integrated with the economic accounts as proposed by the United Nations Statistical Office (UNSO). This system was developed by the UNSO with assistance from numerous specialists and has been tested to date in Mexico and Papua New Guinea, and has also been applied recently in Thailand. Bartelmus discusses the difficulties of attributing monetary value to natural resources. The valuation alternative adopted in the proposed system treats environmental costs as equivalent to the costs of control that a society would have to incur to attain satisfactory environmental standards. Whether a given nation decides to fully integrate environmental values in its current accounting framework, or adopt so-called "satellite accounts" is left to internal decisionmaking. The author concludes by conducting a broad discussion regarding the necessity for definition of stipulable environmental standards, taking into consideration the individual distributive, cultural, demographic and political characteristics of nations adopting environmental accounts.

In contrast to the general theoretical treatment offered by Bartelmus, Serôa da Motta and May discuss in detail the measurement of natural capital consumption for inclusion in the System of National Accounts (SNA). They present theoretical justification for such adjustment, given the lack of accounting for natural resource exhaustion in the traditional SNA. In this respect, Serôa and May focus on use of natural resources that due to excessive exploitation tend toward depletion over time, thus eliminating natural capital stocks accessible to future generations. They compare two measurement techniques discussed in the literature: net price and user cost methods. In the net price method, the entire net receipt generated through production of exhaustible resources is treated as depreciation of natural capital. In the user cost approach, only the present value of this receipt discounted over the period required to exhaust the resource is considered to represent depreciation. The theoretical and methodological distinctions between these methods are enormous, as Serôa and May demonstrate, since estimates they generate result in extremely divergent values, as shown in case studies they present for mineral and forest resources in Brazil.

According to Serôa and May, these discrepancies cannot be understood only in the light of the theoretical approach adopted, but also due to their implicit hypotheses related to the sustainability of income generated by exhaustible resource exploitation. As initially proposed by Peter May in the first paper in this book, these principles suggest different prospects for substitution between natural and manmade capital. In the net price case, considering the entire receipts generated today as a cost imposed on future generations, it is assumed that financial flows derived through the appropriation of natural resources cannot be used to augment capital stocks that would compensate such losses. That is, natural capital consumption would make inviable any future economic growth based on the income generated from these resources. In the case of user cost, on the contrary, the other extreme is adopted, in which financial flows from natural resource use can be used to finance capital accumulation in any productive sector, to compensate natural resource losses. This approach thus allows for full substitution between natural and man-made capital. For Serôa and May, it is essential to define whether natural capital may or may not be substituted, in order to adopt the appropriate accounting methodology. This question requires the specification of ecological limits, thus reinforcing the concept of carrying capacity.

This book, therefore, is a response to a number of issues that arise in considering prospects for sustainable development. In what form can economic analysis contribute to such development? What are the distributive questions that need to be considered, between nations (North and South), and between generations alive today and those as yet unborn? What planning instruments should be devised to ensure efficient environmental management? What research agenda should be followed by economists and natural scientists to expand the growing interface between these fields?

The reader will find that economics must advance considerably in the comprehension and assimilation of ecological perspectives to be able to offer a response to society's demands that development processes be more sustainable. The studies presented in the chapters that follow represent initial efforts to overcome a grave oversight on the part of the economics profession: the need to adequately account for environmental change as an integral part of the development process.

ONE

Sustainability: Challenges to Economic Analysis and Policy

Peter H. May

The legacy of the United Nations Conference for Environment and Development (UNCED) has been to make economy and the environment inseparable in international debate regarding the agenda for development. In consequence, the effects of economic, trade, and infrastructure policies on global and local environments and their peoples have come under increasing scrutiny. It has become imperative to change the way development economists and policymakers perceive the world.

Sustainable development, variously defined, seeks to guarantee the welfare of future generations without jeopardizing that of those alive today. This simple formulation masks complex equity issues that were only too clear during UNCED: between North and South, and between elites and the poor majority. Economists worry that if we reduce the pace of resource exploitation to ensure future availability of raw materials and protect the global environment, we may prejudice an economic growth whose rising sea could sustain all ships. On the other hand, growth that benefits some at the expense of others and further undermines natural environments cannot be viewed as sustainable. The distributional effects of global commitments to constrain resource use, the methods of accounting for change in stocks and for the services proffered by the natural environment in absorbing human residuals, and the reorientation of policies to reflect this guidance are important areas as yet only beginning to be addressed in development work.

Environmental problems arise in part because those responsible are not made to pay the costs of prevention. Theoretically, an unfettered market could enable economic actors to internalize environmental costs through the price mechanism. Under clear liability rules, it is thus conceptually possible to resolve externalities by negotiated compensation. The inadequacy of market solutions in practice, however, has forced nations to rely on regulatory mechanisms. Recently, there has been burgeoning interest in use of market-based instruments as part of a strategy for environmental control, since markets are often extraordinarily efficient in allocating resources. Success in such strategies depends on the capacity of public agencies to assess marginal costs, impose charges or devise marketable permits, and monitor compliance by polluters. Knowing what instruments are available and when and how to use them means strengthening governments' analytical capacities to consider where economic incentives may perform best.

While environmental economists see the market as capable of signaling necessary shifts in resource use and rewarding innovation to solve environmental problems, those who espouse ecological economics are not so optimistic about technological solutions. Instead, they argue, policy choices affecting the environment should be taken only once ecosystem limits are identified and boundaries placed on the expansion of scale in the human economy. The definition of ecosystem thresholds and opportune social development paths stems from an ethical regard for other species and a healthy skepticism about technological progress in light of manifest uncertainty. Ecological economics advocates transparent negotiation among stakeholders rather than the invisible hand of the market to resolve socio-environmental conflict. This does not by any means rule out the appropriate use of market mechanisms when they are seen to get the job done. It does, however, imply a more pluralistic and flexible approach to rule-making within the framework of a continuum of property regimes, conscious of institutional failures and threats to ecological resilience that may arise from human interaction with the biosphere.

Among areas in which the difference between a conventional economic approach and an ecological economic approach is evident is that of trade, adjustment and environment. In the former perspective, the environmental effects of trade liberalization are perceived as being positive, since there would be greater allocative efficiency. Trade policy would not be used as an arm to reduce the pace or techniques of resource exploitation, which could be constrained by domestic policy mechanisms that engender full-cost accounting where externalities arise. From the ecological economics viewpoint, in contrast, sustainable trade rules become essential in an era of footloose financial capital that will locate where environmental and labor costs are lowest. Trade policies should not only internalize environmental costs in the price of products but also harmonize environmental restraint among trading partners and reward sustainable production practices.

A strategy to make development policy harmonious with sustainability objectives must be sensitive to the surfeit of reliable information on ecosystem-economic interactions. There is an immediate need to encourage and coordinate efforts of the few groups in developing nations working to value natural resource rents and environmental services to advise policymakers. Furthermore, it will be important to provide tangible evidence of the benefits of adopting sustainable development policies. Policy options should address the potential economic and employment opportunities and beneficial ecosystem effects obtainable in productive sectors through recycling, energy conservation, watershed management and biotechnologies.

To implement agreements adopted at UNCED, national efforts must cumulatively build toward global solutions. To test applicability of sustainability principles to developing nations, no better base can be found than Brazil, whose self image of limitless frontiers has in the past decade begun to be tempered with realistic perspectives on interdependence and resource limitations. Policymakers from participating nations should be attracted to define a mission for sustainable development studies to ensure commitment toward its goals and to channel findings to assist in decision making toward a more sustainable future.

DEVELOPMENT, EQUITY, AND THE ENVIRONMENT

Agenda 21—the basic accord shaped through deliberations at UNCED in Rio de Janeiro in June 1992—is laced through with reference to the need for "internalization" of environmental costs in the prices of commodities, land and common property resources. If internalization is desirable, externalities or "spillovers" must be present: environmental economists define these as indirect effects of individual actions on the well-being of others.

Among such indirect environmental effects of development processes may be enumerated the increased combustion of fossil and ligneous fuels, contributing to air pollution and consequent respiratory disease, crop and forest damage, and the greenhouse effect; disposal of sewage and chemical wastes to waterways at a rate superior to their absorptive capacity, thus imperiling potable supplies and aquatic life; and the encroachment of mechanized agriculture and extensive pastures on native forests, exacerbating soil erosion, upsetting the hydrologic balance, and despoiling diverse plant and animal biomes.

Such perverse effects of economic development are often difficult to trace due to multiple sources, obscure pathways and ambiguous interactions. The role of collective decision-making regarding the future of the planet would be to ensure that indirect costs of development are identified and reduced, and that those whose consumption demands result in pollution pay the price for prevention.[1] But for global negotiations to succeed requires that people hold similar values, agree on the extent and nature of these losses and are willing to make compensatory adjustments in their behavior or transfer payments to ameliorate environmental costs. These conditions rarely hold.

In the developing world, in particular, exercise of sovereign rights to exploit and degrade resources is often conceived as essential for peoples to strive toward the quality of life enjoyed by industrialized nations. Any move to curtail such rights through global compact may be interpreted as a mechanism to ensure that the poor stay poor.

The Brundtland Report (WCED 1987) argued that it would be unimaginable to stabilize consumption while citizens of developing countries barely survive at per capita incomes five percent those of the North. Instead, the Report argued, a "transition" period during which global development would accelerate from to five to ten times current production levels would be necessary before society could complacently halt growth and "sustain" development. Goodland et al. (1991) in a response to this proposition, argue that the globe may already be nearing the limits to growth in economic "scale," and propose that a more rational policy would be for Northern countries to halt growth immediately, while the South struggles to reduce the welfare gap by curbing population growth and investing in environmentally benign development projects.

Insistence at UNCED on the need to restrain population growth and carbon emissions while at the same time promote use of tropical biological diversity was taken as an indication that poor nations were being asked to "sell cheap" their compliance with global restraint (Martinez-Alier 1994). In fact, there has been a tendency in discussion of environment-development problems to blame the victims: poor farmers who must slash and burn forests to scratch out a living because there is no land available to them elsewhere, urban migrants who are forced to occupy hazardous slopes thus causing floods, and whose untreated sewage chokes water supplies (Pastuk and May 1994).

Although the poor have been pressed toward the margins of habitable space, thus inflicting environmental hazards upon themselves and others, they cannot be made to bear the brunt of global problems. According to studies conducted for the UNCED Secretariat, on the contrary, up to 75 percent of global carbon emissions are due to energy consumption in the North, where per-capita use of most raw materials is far higher than in the South (Parikh et al. 1992). So there may be a case for an "environmental debt" to the nations whose resource base has been pillaged over the past five centuries to satisfy the unquenchable demands of the North.

Sustainable development that would ensure future generations have at least the same opportunities as the present one for welfare improvement (WCED 1987) should not necessarily be a win-lose situation. Negotiations at UNCED reflected the concerns of the poorest nations in declaring as a basic principle the "right to development" (UN 1992a). The equity effects of alternative policies toward the global environment must be maintained at the forefront in discussions of sustainable development.

In many cases, however, despite the threat of climate change, acid rain and other transboundary problems, the most serious environmental and distributional effects of economic behavior are experienced within and not yet between nations. Achievement of the mandate of Agenda 21 and associated international environmental conventions will depend initially on the adoption of sustainable development strategies at a national level. The next sections explores some of the instruments available to meet this mandate and debate regarding their relative effectiveness.

MARKET MECHANISMS FOR ENVIRONMENTAL QUALITY

As a specific response to UNCED's concern for the need to integrate environment and development into decision making (chapter 8 of Agenda 21), States have been urged to make "effective use of economic instruments and incentives" (ICED 1992). Adoption of appropriate economic incentives would help to ensure the diffusion of environmentally sound technical and institutional innovations. Many economists argue that emerging environmental problems stem from the misallocation of resources and the inadequacy of the unfettered market to reflect the costs incurred. Transaction costs between source and recipient have made theoretically optimal market solutions unattainable (Coase 1960). For this reason, governments have sought through command and control strategies to regulate their way out of environmental dilemmas. But such tactics are often perceived as inefficient and costly to administer.

In theory, externalities and "commons" tragedies could be remedied by eliminating market imperfections, removing distorting subsidies and imposing taxes or charges that would let the market seek an "optimal pollution" level, equating marginal costs to society and benefits to the polluter. Pollution taxes are by no means a recent concept; taxation of externalities to optimize social welfare was proposed by Pigou in the 1920s, but has since been elaborated as a theory of environmental control (Baumol and Oates 1988). Finding the right tax that would adjust producer costs to meet these conditions is by no means trivial, however, demanding that environmental administrators have access to detailed information regarding the marginal costs of pollution control and of the biophysical and economic effects of abatement.

Developed nations have had considerable experience in using emission charges, taxes or negotiable pollution permits for industrial environmental control (Panayotou 1994), while these mechanisms are nearly unknown to the South (Serôa da Motta and Reis 1994). Charges are generally applied on inputs to production (e.g., leaded fuel is priced higher than regular) in efforts to dissuade their squandering, while taxes are placed on the pollutants themselves. The latter would serve as an incentive for firms to adopt pollution abatement technology as long as the tax were set at a level high enough to guarantee change in behavior, while generating revenues needed to assure adequate enforcement of the applied standards.

The procedures for adoption of a tax system are as follows: (1) a local or regional ambient standard is established, specifying permissible pollutant emissions within a specific air or water basin, for example, generally related to the proportion of emissions controlled, or the concentration of pollutant loads, with reference to an identified biophysical absorption capacity and the technical-financial viability of control by firms in the area; and (2) a tax is imposed on pollutants discharged above the volume deemed to lie within environmental absorption capacity. As long as the marginal cost of pollution control remains below that of the tax, the infractor is motivated to adopt technology in order to avoid payment; when the cost exceeds the tax, it is rational to pay. Because control technologies tend to be bulky investments, there would be discontinuity in such response.

A more recent innovation on this theme is to create new markets for tradable "pollution rights" or licenses to use resources. In such a scheme, a marketable instrument is created, giving the holder the right to emit a certain volume of pollutants or to extract a given quantity of fish or wood. These volumes, related to firms' current or historic emission or use levels, would be determined so as to sum to a pre-established regional or resource-related limit. Those firms whose costs of control exceed those of others would then pay the latter to sell them their pollution or extraction quotas. New polluting industries only would be permitted to enter in the controlled region if they were able to purchase existing pollutant or use rights. To improve environmental quality over time, the total volume of emissions permitted would be gradually decreased.

The concept of negotiable permits has been extended to the issue of global sustainability as a mechanism for compensating nations that adjust their economic behavior to reduce emissions of greenhouse gases. This concept is considered to be an efficient mechanism for the implementation of global climate change accords. Due to the relatively less costly carbon sequestration in forest conservation and recuperation of degraded lands, tropical nations could obtain "credits" paid by those nations desirous of reducing their net contribution to global warming, but unwilling to pay the high price of reducing fossil fuel emissions. These credits could be negotiated for investments in other sectors, or go toward compensating the costs of resource conservation. (See Rose and Stevens in this volume.) Although this form of tradable license has not yet been implemented at a global level, there are already cases of Northern firms transferring resources to tropical nations toward reforestation as an "offset" to polluting activities.

In a recent summary of work in this area, Schneider (1993) suggests that the value of carbon sequestration based on taxes recently established on CO_2 emissions in Scandinavian nations, could lie between US$600 and $7,000 per hectare of native dense forest retained. As land prices in tropical forests are situated well below this value, it would be more advantageous economically to use these lands for carbon sequestration (with the added benefit of biodiversity conservation and other indirect values) than convert them to agropastoral uses. This premise is valid, however, only if those who control land use are effectively coerced to manage their land in this fashion, and those who would pay feel secure these lands will in fact be allocated as carbon stores.

Such mutual assurance problems confound many efforts to achieve environmental objectives, since it is often in the interest of economic actors to "free-ride" in the hopes that others will observe the behavioral changes desired. The result is that no one changes and the status quo reigns. Policy failures of this nature threaten the prospects for market-based instruments to fulfill their promise, urging a new look at institutions and assumptions.

CHANGING THE RULES OF THE GAME

Economists tend to apply an analytical focus and indicators which reveal facets important to their clients (King 1994). In the case of productive enterprises this means profits and financial rates of return, whereas for governments, employment and growth in GNP are key measures of economic health. For neoclassical economists, these indicators and their maximization objectives are mutually consistent: individual profit maximization favors national income growth and full employment of productive resources including labor.

On the other hand, the financial rate of return desired by private enterprise may not lead to sustainable rates of growth, due to exhaustion of the resource base and clogging of the sink capacities of the natural environment. Traditional measures of economic product treat resource extraction as income without compensating for the drawdown on natural capital, and expenditures on pollution control and waste cleanup are likewise bundled together with gross product. While mobile capital gravitates toward its more profitable application, investors may be thereby seeking opportunities to undercut labor remuneration and avoid pollution control costs, so maintaining competitiveness at the expense of workers and the environment.

Many believe that standard neoclassical precepts of market equilibrium and consumer sovereignty provide ample grounds for adjusting prices and accounts to reflect environmental externalities (Tietenberg, in this volume). Furthermore, they believe that the question of sustainability may be subsumed under this same theory by applying the "right price" to discount the future. Neoclassical allocation theory presupposes that natural and manmade capital may be infinitely substituted for one another. Underlying this belief is a fatalistic optimism that technological progress will overcome whatever limits to growth may arise due to resource scarcity. The price mechanism which allocates resources to their most efficient end will see to it that emerging scarcities are adequately signalled, guiding appropriate adjustments in the mix of resources and products to reflect the quest for new materials. More efficient extraction and industrial recycling processes will further extend the availability of dwindling resources beyond their predicted point of exhaustion.

Yet, given the absence of either fully functioning democratic institutions or consumer sovereignty in today's interdependent oligopoly markets, decisions regarding development-environment tradeoffs may be misguided by neoclassical precepts. The current global pursuit of liberal trade regimes within a private property context is likely to make collective decisions at a national level to protect common pool resources all the more difficult.

Public management, on the other hand, is under fire for "government failure" (Opschoor 1994); environmental mismanagement arises because governments pay little heed to the welfare of large unorganized groups and future generations (Andersson 1991). In addition to environmental spillovers, government failure is evident in the absence of suitable mechanisms for adjusting policy outcomes to ease the plight of the poor. When lumped together with bureaucratic inefficiency, rent seeking behavior and corruption, such failure encourages skepticism that public institutions can manage resources wisely or allocate them equitably. For a growing number of scientists and concerned laymen, therefore, further reliance on either market mechanisms or today's governance framework to resolve environmental problems will be insufficient to cope with looming ecological catastrophe. A change in the direction of economic development, they feel, will require a more substantial "paradigm shift."[2]

THE EMERGENCE OF ECOLOGICAL ECONOMICS

Ecological economics[3] seeks a precautionary approach to natural resource utilization and exploitation, that adequately considers the potential needs of future generations. This approach assumes that limits to growth founded in natural resource scarcity and carrying capacity are real and not necessarily overcome through technological progress. That is, besides the traditional mechanisms of allocation and distribution considered in economic analysis, ecological economics would add the concept of "scale," referring to the sheer physical volume of matter and energy that is converted and absorbed in an entropic process of economic expansion. Sustainable scale is such that environmental carrying capacity is not eroded over time. Far from assuming technological impotence, this strategy requires adapting technologies to reduce "throughput"—resources used to satisfy human needs (Daly 1992).

There are at least three essential ways in which ecological economics differs from conventional economics in the treatment of environmental concerns:

1. Environmental problems as externalities to otherwise efficient market functions vs. economy as intrinsic to and bound by ecological processes.

In conventional economics, environmental problems constitute "market failures" external to otherwise efficient exchanges, to be adjusted by "getting the price right" and adjusting supply of goods or bads accordingly. In the ecological economics approach, the economy is not separate from the environment. Rather, productive interchanges occur within a hierarchy of human influenced ecosystems which possess unique dynamics and limits. Because intact natural systems are fairly stable, providing crucial life support functions that benefit humans and other organisms, the expansion of the human economy must be guided by and respect ecosystem functions and limits. The intrinsic resilience of natural systems, which has encouraged human societies to expand their use of the source and sink functions of the environment is currently under strain, as evidenced in such transboundary problems as global climate change, oceanic contamination and acid rain.

2. Technological optimism vs. prudent pessimism.

Conventional economics assumes that advances in technology will overcome emerging limits to expansion in the scale of human use of the physical environment. From this perspective, there is no evidence that the scope of growth will be limited by scarce fuels or materials, since the costs of extraction that signal scarcity have been historically declining. However, ecological economists suggest that it would be prudent to be skeptical regarding unlimited prospects for technical innovation. Market prices have not adequately signaled the need to adjust raw material and fuel usage to imminent shortage, or share technologies among an ever more interdependent global society. Other measures are needed to indicate when extraction rates exceed the capacity of renewable resources to recuperate, and when exhaustible resources are declining at a pace which may preempt future options. Operational definitions for sustainability with regard to natural capital substitution must be negotiated.

3. Disciplinary compartmentalization and ideological hegemony vs. transdisciplinary integration and humility.

Conventional economics has dominated post-war development policy and planning, heeding concerns raised by the natural sciences and humanistic fields in an only parenthetical fashion. Ecological economics would revamp this disciplinary hegemony by (a) seeking to identify biophysical limits to economic expansion, (b) promoting a socially just distribution of wealth and, only finally, (c) adjusting market or command mechanisms within the economy to allocate productive activities and goods more efficiently (Daly 1992).

Ecological economics is thus not simply an "add-on" or afterthought to conventional economic evaluation of investment options. Rather, it advocates a modification in both the measurement and planning of development to achieve sustainability. Ecological economists do not claim to dominate techniques necessary to plumb uncertain values, but rather seek to extend knowledge regarding previously omitted concerns and, above all, admit uncertainty. In this sense, there is no claim to creating a new discipline that could supplant conventional economics, but rather the admission of different perspectives on the conditions for sustainability. Ideally, this approach would promote more complete societal participation in the identification and choice among development options. Where uncertainty reigns and there is no fundamental agreement among stakeholders on the facts or values affecting a decision, not only good science, but political consensus building and extended peer review (Funtowicz and Ravetz 1993) become essential.

What is the relevance of this perspective to the developing world? Developing nations increasingly perceive that subordination of development policy to conventional economic precepts has put both people and the environment after assuring free trade, GNP growth and unbridled capital investment. For example:

- Structural adjustment has wittingly cut salaries and public expenditures and fortified resource extractive export sectors, marginalizing those outside markets and eliminating social safety nets.
- Multilateral infrastructure investments justified by the internal rate of return to market inputs and outputs have endangered fragile unpriced ecosystems and native peoples while further indebting nations now unable to make good on more than project interest payments nor to even maintain the facilities they have built.
- Less-developed countries (LDCs), out of desperation with their faltering economies, open the doors to Northern manufactures in the hopes that in return they will obtain preferential access for primary product exports. The result is that the LDCs have been pitted ruthlessly against each other in a battle over the limited market for similar resource products, rather than seeking solutions through South–South cooperation (more detail is provided on trade and environment themes, below).

These tendencies suggest that not only are current trade, project analysis or adjustment policies inappropriate, but the underlying rationale for their adoption may be unfavorable to the aspirations of developing nations. Ecological economics would involve efforts toward full pricing of environmental and social effects in the evaluation of projects, policies and the growth process itself. Indicators of progress toward sustainable development would furnish more appropriate planning instruments than the conventional measures of income. Policy analysis would encourage a precautionary approach corresponding to uncertainties regarding the character, incidence and timing of socioenvironmental effects.

At the same time, however, ecological economics for equitable development recognizes the fundamental right to development. Rather than putting a brake on development processes, this would imply the need to adapt technologies to cope with environmental problems through a more adequate distribution of resources and knowledge. It would suggest the need to direct energy policy toward conservation methods and use of renewable sources (e.g., biomass fuels, small-scale hydropower, etc.) that can increase employment today, rather than draw down nonrenewable natural capital stocks to the detriment of future generations. Development cannot become sustainable if human welfare does not improve within ecological limits.

Although ecological economics only recently received formal recognition (establishment of an international society and a scholarly journal devoted to the subject occurred in 1989), the concepts which underlie its critique of neoclassical theory have a longer history. Kenneth Boulding conceived of an economy adapted to the limitations of the "coming spaceship Earth" (1968). Ciriacy-Wantrup (1952) proposed "Safe Minimum Standards" as criteria for the level of protection to be afforded critical resources. Nicholas Georgescu-Roegen (1971) applied the Second Law of Thermodynamics to the problem of energy flow in the human economy, suggesting that increasing entropy would impose limits to growth. Herman Daly's steady state economics (1974) derived fuel from the same principle. Neo-malthusian alarm over the capacity of the Earth to absorb a demographic explosion in the poorer nations (Ehrlich and Ehrlich 1970; Meadows et al. 1972) was rekindled in the late 1980s after a decade of technological complacency when global climate change emerged as a focal point for debate on the transition to sustainable development (Goodland et al. 1991).

By necessity, the estimation of ecosystem limits and the valuation of environmental costs and benefits of alternative development paths require interdisciplinary collaboration, predictive modelling and scenario building skill.[4] To be effective, ecological economists must have access to the policy maker's ear and be open to political negotiation. Good science is rarely sufficient to cope with the rapid resource degradation and imminent environmental catastrophe experienced in the wake of development processes (Viederman 1992).

TOOLS FOR DECISION MAKING[5]

For ecological economics to be effective, therefore, it is imperative that decisions regarding resource use be couched in policy relevant analysis. There have been two broad methodological alternatives proposed for research and policy analysis using ecological economics as a tool for decision making. The first would expand the framework for traditional benefit-cost analysis toward a more thorough quantification of interactions between economic activity and ecological functions. The primary difference between this approach and traditional wisdom would be the elucidation of causal chains that affect broader ecosystem functioning. Relying heavily on ecosystem models, this would engender translating emissions and withdrawals into measures of environmental risks and health effects. These could then be converted to costs and benefits using nonmarket valuation methods.[6] Such an approach would make explicit the interactions between withdrawals, emissions, market and nonmarket costs and benefits and final effects on distributional equity and socioeconomic goals.

The principal difficulty in such analysis is the tremendous degree of uncertainty prevalent in the numerous estimates that must be obtained. Uncertainty exists because "physical, biological, chemical and economic phenomena are difficult to measure, do not always take place in predictable ways, and have unstable lag structures" (King 1992). That uncertainty prevails should not necessarily paralyze analysis, but tends to subject the testing of parameter variations to "extended peer review," and the determination of public policy to "communication wars" (Funtowitcz and Ravetz 1991).

A second alternative, that recognizes the imperfect capacity of modern science to elucidate such complex ecosystem flows with any measure of certainty would establish limits to economic encroachment on natural ecosystems. This approach inverts the analysis, by considering the cost-effectiveness of alternatives constrained by limits on resource use, rather than the alternative that demonstrates highest net economic return after environmental costs are deducted. Recognizing the enormous empirical burden that would be required to adequately expand the frontiers of benefit-cost analysis, this process also heeds the necessity for societal participation in policy choices where there are differences in values and uncertainty over the veracity of the facts. Although scientifically less "robust," such an approach may in the end be more appealing to economists frustrated with lack of definition of the environmental effects of human activities.

External specification of limits by ecological or political processes would facilitate the definition of subsequent growth paths. King (1992) suggests that particular ecosystems exhibit different gradations of fragility and importance, and that informed societal establishment of normative principles for access and use of these environments could serve as a basis to develop sustainably. Some resources are so fragile that only total protection is justifiable, whereas the resilience of other biomes is such that unfettered market mechanisms may be relied upon to regulate user access, as long as environmental costs are internalized in the price structure. Between these extremes lie a range of situations in which socially agreed upon limitations to the rate and volume of extraction and disposal must be defined through quotas, minimum size limits, engineering and performance standards, seasons and areas, etc. (figure 1.1). Aggregate indices of ecosystem health or

IMPORTANCE

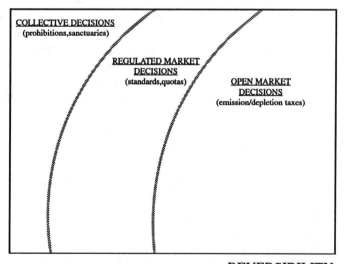

REVERSIBILITY

FIGURE 1.1. Public intervention to protect natural capital (based on King 1994:336).

integrity may serve as a basis for measuring importance, and the technical and economic feasibility of restoring lost ecological functions to measure the relative reversibility of human induced modifications. Just how the lines are drawn to demarcate the boundaries of ecosystem fragility and importance for application of different rules must rely on societal negotiation regarding the facts and values at issue, i.e., politics.

The comparison between extended benefit-cost analysis and imposition of ecosystem limits echoes in many respects debate over different measures for adjusting national accounts to reflect resource exhaustion and environmental services. In environmental accounting, there are also two disparate approaches. Their differences rest on divergent perspectives regarding the relative validity of substituting natural for man-made capital in the search for sustainable development. That their results sometimes diverge by enormous magnitudes suggests that debate over the appropriate use of indicators to measure sustainable development is not a trivial matter.

A "weak sustainability" approach assumes that capital substitution possibilities exist in a broad sense. Sustainable income in this view represents the amount that can be consumed so that "at the end of the day" one is equally well off as at the beginning, a concept derived from John Hicks' (1946) definition of "income" (Hartwick 1977), referring to exhaustible resources, provides that one must reinvest rents (called "user costs") from exploitation of natural resources so as to achieve constant real consumption over time.[7] Where one reinvests the proceeds from resource exploitation is determined by the neoclassical precept that one puts one's money where it earns the best return. There is no constraint in this approach that one must dedicate part of this rent to cleaning up the mess that was caused by the exploitation in question, and there is no particular incentive in the structure of user costs that would motivate a change in the rate or form of exploitation.

Although various gradations may be foreseen for "strong sustainability"[8] a simplified version of this argument suggests that substitution prospects are not at all infinite, and that a desirable rule for evaluating whether development is sustainable would be a situation in which there is no change in some kinds of ecosystems. These include those which provide "life support" functions, such as maintenance of carbon balance, hydrologic cycles, and nutrient flux (Pearce and Atkinson 1992). This perspective does not prohibit resource exploitation, but suggests instead that there should be investment of resource rents in natural capital, so that the net change in these resources would be greater than or equal to zero.[9]

Not only is there an alteration in the direction of the proceeds, but the net rent magnitudes measured for strong sustainability tend to be significantly larger when compared with the user cost approach. This is so because, instead of assuming prospects for reinvestment in other capital assets, the strong sustainability argument assumes that what you exploit today is gone for good. The net rent derived from resource removal is thus charged in its entirety against the sector responsible for the damage.[10]

In summary, the methods chosen for assessing movement toward sustainable development and appraising specific courses of action in this direction are far from neutral, and depend very much on one's perception of just what sustainability implies for the natural resource base. In order to determine how much of a given ecosystem should remain intact to maintain vital physical survival functions and also economic well-being in the long term, it may be possible to devise intricate models of economy-environment interaction. On the other hand, where agreement on the facts is impossible owing to uncertainty, and where the relative desirability of substituting ecosystem functions for material well being is controversial due to differences in peoples' underlying values, there is often need for negotiation in political arenas. Here the ecological economist can do little more than offer plausible and lucid suggestions regarding the probable outcomes of particular decisions. The rest depends on political mobilization and informed rule making. The importance of these different perspectives is particularly evident in the case of trade issues.

TRADE AND ENVIRONMENT ISSUES

The doctrine of free trade has dominated international relations in the post-War years and was the hallmark of the Bretton Woods agreements that created the World Bank and the International Monetary Fund. Free trade policies including, inter alia, the removal of tariff barriers to permit broader access to markets, are seen to be generally beneficial to global society, in that expanded markets would allow for the greatest exercise of comparative advantage with respect to individual nations' resource endowments. The result of trade liberalization is thus a general growth in economic output, creating new jobs and, it is hoped, greater welfare. Protectionism, on the other hand, usually benefits specific interests at the expense of consumers. Progress toward eliminating such barriers in trade between states has been the modus vivendi for the General Agreement on Tariffs and Trade (GATT).

Despite the generally favorable macroeconomic results predicted to derive from the overall neoliberal trend in commercial relations, institutional adaptation and producer adjustment may be unnecessarily painful in some cases. Privatization of marketing boards, elimination of subsidies and restraints on credit has left developing nations, many of whom are dependent on exports of primary products for foreign exchange, far more vulnerable to declining relative commodity prices resulting from the collapse of economic clauses of international trade agreements. Increased producer vulnerability in commodity production can be shown to provoke serious socioenvironmental costs (UNCTAD 1993).

Patterns of trade and production expansion in developing nations are closely linked with macroeconomic conditions and can have serious consequences for the natural resource base. During the 1960s and '70s throughout Latin America, for example, the drive toward import-substituting industrialization relied upon exploitation of natural resources—treated as inexhaustible sources of materials—to fuel the expansion in reproducible capital stocks. The "conservative modernization" of agriculture, which stressed mechanization and agrochemicals applied to large-scale export monocrops to rapidly expand production, without a commensurate effort to distribute land, resulted in massive rural-urban exodus, slum proliferation and income concentration (Altieri and Masera 1993).

In the 1980s and early '90s, the debt crisis and the inflationary spiral led to a strategy of structural adjustment and trade liberalization, eliminating selective subsidies to export crop production. The slowing of horizontal expansion in agriculture during the 1980s is ambiguous from an environmental standpoint: it is often suggested that the recession may have been environmentally benign, due to reduction in the pace of resource extraction and conversion (FOE/GTA 1994). Nevertheless, a liquidation of natural capital to counter imbalance in prices, and the social costs of producer dislocation have been severe. In the specific case of coffee and cocoa in Brazil, for example, a loss in financial viability led to disinvestment in agroecosystem maintenance and industrial control technology, substitution of environmentally amenable crops with less appropriate land uses, and widespread rural unemployment (May 1993).

In response to these unanticipated side-effects of trade liberalization, there are a number of environmentally related concerns that have arisen during the final years of the Uruguay Round of negotiations to revise the GATT, that is expected to lead to creation of a new World Trade Organization (WTO). Among other mechanisms, the GATT has sought to combat discrimination in trade on grounds of production processes used in the country of origin. The use of import restrictions against products whose origins are considered unsustainable would thus represent a transgression of GATT principles. Contests to such restrictions, that have been accused of serving as protectionist nontariff barriers having few concrete environmental objectives, would engage the WTO in environmental disputes for which it was not devised, and for which it lacks expertise (Ekins 1994).

On the other hand, sustainable trade would benefit from implementation of targeted measures which reward producers who seek to minimize polluting production and processing technology and reduce energy consumption, use biodegradable packaging materials and encourage materials recycling. Targeted mechanisms for the internalization of environmental costs in commodity prices include the certification of sustainable sources ("green labeling") and "international commodity related environmental agreements" (ICREAS). A number of recent studies suggest that these instruments could serve as the backbone of consumer-based determination to pursue sustainable trade (Low 1992; Kox 1994). Product certification and consumer boycotts may lead to efforts on the part of producers to alter practices, but unless these efforts are remunerated by price differentiation or improved market scope, they will not be adopted widely, nor will they engender significant environmental improvement.

Consumer insistence on product quality can be a two-edged sword for environmental sustainability. An informed consumer community aware of environmental consequences of product demand can help to motivate adoption of less aggressive technologies. For example, having enough flexibility to accept slightly discolored tropical products grown using integrated pest management and mechanical rather than water-polluting processes could make a significant difference in the direction of producer expenditures (May 1993). It may therefore become necessary to devise new classification criteria through the WTO, with the purpose of encouraging methods of cultivation used by sustainable producers. Without consumer action to insist on such classification, environmentally more appropriate production techniques will not be able to affirm themselves as a viable option.

The question is whether market segmentation alone can serve as a means to promote improved environmental standards in commodity production. Local instruments establishing new property arrangements over lands in threatened biomes and their redistribution to smaller producers or extractivist cooperatives who commit themselves to manage forests may be part of a solution that, besides being environmentally appropriate, may also be socially just. Financing such a transition would require access to capital of considerable magnitude, possibly obtainable through debt swaps or new biodiversity funding arrangements being considered by the International Finance Corporation to complement the Global Environment Facility.

TOWARD SUSTAINABLE DEVELOPMENT: THE CASE OF BRAZIL

What is the potential that the tools and principles discussed here might be of use to developing nations in their search for sustainable paths to development? Although undeniable that resource limits and environmental hazards exist, their observance is placed secondary to economic growth, deemed necessary to assure progress in improving standards of living and to meet nationalistic aspirations. Nowhere is this so true as in Brazil, whose national self image was nurtured in the past in its pride for expanding frontiers and unlimited natural resources.

Owing to its continental scale and abundant mineral, water, land and human resources, Brazil was able for many years to pursue a fairly autarchic economic development posture. Transfers from extensive export-oriented agriculture financed the core of a substantial industrial sector based on subsidized hydroelectric power, nationalized steel and petroleum production, and a cheap well-disciplined labor force. By 1980, Brazil's population was already predominantly urbanized and had a large and growing auto industry geared to the domestic market. To fuel the fleet, it was pumping large volumes of pure ethanol from expanded sugarcane plantations subsidized by taxes on gasoline, the latter distilled mostly from imported petroleum. To release the pressure valve of regional inequalities, and to offer yet another symbol of national manifest destiny, the government built a new planned capital at Brasília in the heart of the central savanna, and later cut new highways and railroads for agricultural settlements and mines deep into the dense Amazon forest. Dependent development in Brazil, serving the interests of a triple alliance among multinational, state, and local capital (Cardoso and Faletto 1979; Evans 1979), was very much driven by this conscious self image of unlimited potential.

In the 1980s, with the debt crisis and second oil price shock, Brazilians were rudely awakened to the perception that they were not immune to international interdependence or resource limits. While the country grappled with four-digit inflation and wage earners' buying power declined to their 1970 levels, the failure of the prior decades' strategy to grow out of underdevelopment was matched with increasing poverty and environmental crises.

Unlimited horizons and inadequate heed to environmental costs resulted in a history of major infrastructure projects that placed Brazil among the ranks of the most severely indebted nations while at the same time nourishing environmental controversy. Among recent policy disasters were those related to the expansion of Amazonian hydroelectric generation, whose immense reservoirs flooded out indigenous groups and diverse tropical biomes. The Polonoroeste land settlement scheme in Rondônia and neighboring Mato Grosso also garnered international acrimony as its herringbone-aligned roads were shown to be stimulating deforestation and soil degradation at a rapid pace, as placer miners and lumber mills encroached upon indigenous and biological reserves. Generous subsidies and tax exemptions for beef ranching expansion helped to provoke further destruction, and were shown to be justifiable neither economically nor environmentally (Browder 1988). Dams, roads, nuclear and chemical hazards, and misdirected government subsidies abound in other parts of the nation, but the Amazon emerged as cause celebre. These concerns redirected social movements to successfully establish the environmental agenda as a force to be reckoned with in public policy (FOE/GTA 1994).

Despite the global appeal to save tropical forests and their indigenous inhabitants, for the majority of Brazilians, the environment remains a question of poverty. Over 40 percent of the national population now earns less than what is necessary to fill a minimal market basket, most homes lack sewage collection or treatment, and infant mortality at 57 per 1000 is still unacceptably high. How can the needs and aspirations of these multitudes be met while remaining within ecological limits? Here lies a dramatic test of the options for sustainable development.

Prior to the emergence of environmental crises, development decision making in Brazil was strongly centralized, with rare opportunities for affected communities to be heard. The economic considerations Brazilian policymakers relied upon to arrive at decisions were drawn from mainstream public finance concepts, while welfare economics criteria have only been considered when international lending agencies insist. As elsewhere, political factors guide the allocation of public resources far more than rational economic criteria. Environmental issues have until very recently been marginalized in policy/decision making.

In 1985, partly as a result of international pressure on multilateral lending institutions, Brazil enacted fundamental environmental legislation, creating a national Environmental Council (CONAMA) with nongovernmental representation. As its first act, CONAMA established norms for the preparation of environmental impact statements (RIMAS), whose contents were to be generally accessible and subject to public hearings. Although there are some cases in which impact assessment has led to reformulation of project siting decisions (Pastuk 1992), in general RIMAS aim to rubber stamp decisions already taken through political bargaining. And many "urgent" projects have evaded the requirements altogether.

Although in the early 1970s as a result of exposure to the international environmental movement, environmental economics (Nusdeo 1975) and the notion of "eco-development" (Sachs 1980) caught the imagination of a small group of Brazilian scholars, economic analysis of environmental problems has only recently become of interest in Brazil.[11]

The rejoining of environment and development issues in the discussions leading up to UNCED stimulated widespread attention to these issues. An economic-ecological zoning exercise was promoted in response to international outcry over Amazon devastation. And most international lending institutions have begun also to insist on at least a partial valuation of environmental benefits and costs in economic appraisal of development projects (IDB 1990), creating new demand in training institutes. At the same time, ecologists who have grown frustrated in presenting their case from a purely scientific perspective have begun to look upon valuation of environmental functions and services as an additional means to justify conservation efforts, and are actively seeking economist collaborators.

The legacy of the "lost decade" has been increasing realism; although Brazil has not ceased to consider itself a country of the future, its perception of unlimited frontiers has been at least temporarily curbed. Many now hunger for a more complete vision of development and environment. Their hunger is echoed by concerned scientists, organizations and leaders throughout the developing world. Environmental restraint represents no threat to sovereignty, but instead can be part of the means to guarantee that states maintain their footing in international markets while improving domestic welfare consistent with goals of social justice.

A Strategy to Encourage Research on Sustainable Development

Brazil is not alone in seeking institutional capacity to resolve socioenvironmental conflicts. While a number of centers in the North have shown capability to respond analytically to discussion of urgent global challenges,[12] there is no comparable capacity in the developing world. This must be remedied. In this conclusion, we enumerate some of the priority targets for capacity development in the South.

The strategic points of entry for studies of sustainable development involve first recognizing the surfeit of accessible information that can serve as a basis for development decision making. Provision of comparable indicators, dose-response functions and model parameters regarding the ecological consequences of similar decisions elsewhere could generate information where today there are only impressions. A number of institutions in Brazil and elsewhere are now engaged in efforts to define and operationalize Indicators of Sustainability through transdisciplinary dialogue. This would not overcome the generalized failure to make use of informed analysis in the development policy process but could ensure that dependable information is available for those willing to use it.

Second, the joint coherence of environmental, development and equity objectives must be more adequately demonstrated. Accelerated economic growth is perceived in many development circles to be the only available means to improve broad popular welfare. Yet, distributive policies may be more effective in offering sustainable options for development.

Analysis and demonstration of the potential economic and employment opportunities and net ecosystem benefits obtainable in productive sectors through recycling, energy conservation, watershed management, and biotechnologies, for example, could amplify arguments in favor of such options.

Third, due to the dispersed and limited number of trained professionals available particularly in the developing world, it is important to acknowledge and stimulate incipient efforts at local and national levels, while channeling their output to meet concrete demands from policymakers. A reference point in the South is needed for those dispersed groups who desire to share their efforts in environmental valuation, resource accounting and ecological-economic models. In this sense, the activities of these groups could be better linked, and methodological problems shared, while a concerted effort be launched to strengthen academic credentials and knowledge of methodological advances.

Finally, leading policymakers from developing nations must assume the responsibility to guide research on sustainable development. This represents a crucial part of a strategy to ensure their commitment toward these goals, and to channel analytical findings to aid legislators and governments in making the necessary decisions toward a more sustainable future.

Acknowledgment: This paper was presented at the Workshop to Create an International Center for Studies of Sustainable Development, Getúlio Vargas Foundation, Rio de Janeiro, November 28, 1994.

NOTES

1. To resolve externalities usually costs money, affecting the producer's supply price. To achieve their amelioration, production levels may decline, resulting in a general loss of welfare measured by the limited yardstick of efficiency.

2. The concept of *paradigm,* or dominant world view, was originally presented by Kuhn (1962), in his treatise on scientific revolutions. It is still somewhat early and may be somewhat immobilizing to suggest that a closer articulation between economics and natural sciences would constitute a paradigm shift (Daly and Cobb 1989).

3. Ecological economics refers to collaborative efforts "to extend and integrate the study and management of "nature's household" (ecology) and "mankind's household" (economics)" (Costanza 1989). The two words share the same Greek stem, *oikos*—household. The word *oikonomikos* means stewardship, which suggests ecological economics should be directed toward better management of the interactions between man and the environment so as to entrust resources to future generations.

4. In some analyses involving ecological economics, the numeraire by which alternative choices are evaluated is revised to remove the distorting effect of markets. A valuation system based on energy flow (Odum 1983) has been devised and made commensurable with monetary values for comparative evaluation.

5. This section draws on proposals in Costanza (1992), Daly (1991), King (1992), and Pearce and Atkinson (1992), among others.

6. There is a large and growing literature on the estimation of nonmarket benefits and costs regarding environmental spillovers (see Dixon and Huffschmidt 1986; Barbier et al. 1990; Pearce and Turner 1991). These range from measures derived from productivity differentials (e.g., fertility loss due to erosion); preventive expenditures (health and pollution treatment costs); hedonic pricing (e.g., property values affected by proximity to hazards or scenic beauty); travel costs (as a proxy for demand for recreational facilities); to contingent valuation (survey based measures of demand for unpriced goods). In contingent valuation—the only means to reflect the subjective value of having the option to use resources at a future time, bequeath such resources to others or obtain

satisfaction from the sheer existence of ecosystems or species—these measures are obtained through the creation of "surrogate markets" for environmental goods and services. Through survey research, actual or potential consumers are elicited to determine the maximum amount of their income they would be willing to pay to ensure continuing availability or, on the contrary, the minimum they would be willing to accept to go without the goods and services in question.

7. The user cost measure was refined by El Serafy (1988) to represent the amount one should reinvest in each period such that, at the end of the lifetime of the resource in question, the amount one has saved is sufficient to generate an equivalent income flow in perpetuity (assuming constant real interest rates). With finite resources near exhaustion, this method generates impressive values, but for resources with considerable and sometimes expanding reserves (mineral exploration, forest regeneration and reforestation), the period to exhaustion may be so far in the future that user costs in the present are very small. For example, May (1994) evaluates the user cost of Amazon deforestation for agricultural purposes at close to nil from 1971 to 1985, due to the immensity of the area still remaining intact. When disaggregated for specific resources nearing extinction, and when geographical limits to human expansion are proscribed, the user cost would increase.

8. Turner (1992) discusses a gradation from "very weak" to "very strong" sustainability. The former was described by Daly (1991) as referring to a "Disneyland effect" in which perfect substitution exists between natural and man-made capital, and society is forever equally happy as this substitution takes place. In the "very strong" version, Turner (1992) adds "cultural capital" to natural capital in defining limits to substitution. This would include the preservation of indigenous knowledge and cultural diversity. Finally, Goodland and Daly (1994) provide for an even more extreme case— "absurdly strong sustainability"—in which nothing could ever be depleted, and mankind would have to survive on the "ecological product" of renewable climax ecosystems (Leff 1994).

9. The importance of this assumption to developments in this field is evident from the theme of the 1992 post-UNCED meeting in Stockholm of the International Society for Ecological Economics: "Investing in Natural Capital." It is also evident from the emergence of companion fields of ecological engineering and ecosystem health and medicine (Costanza et al. 1992).

10. In the case of Costa Rica (Solórzano et al. 1991) and Brazil (May 1994), for example, the net rent valuation of merchantable timber lost due to deforestation yields magnitudes approaching the entire gross national agricultural product. With the user cost approach, on the other hand, the values obtained for Brazil verged on just half of one percent of the agricultural product.

11. Few academic institutions offer courses in this area, and although several interdisciplinary graduate programs in environmental subjects have recently emerged, there is no officially recognized graduate concentration in environmental or resource, not to mention ecological economics. Attention should be drawn to a recently created doctoral program in ecological economics that involves faculty associated with the University of Brasília, along with collaborators in Chile, Scotland, and Sweden. A similar program is under consideration in Curitiba. The Federal Rural University of Rio de Janeiro has also

established a chair in ecological economics within its graduate program in agricultural development, whose first occupant is the author of the present paper.

12. These include the International Institute for Environment and Development, the World Resources Institute, Center for Socio-Economic Research on the Global Environment, the Beijer Institute for Ecological Economics, Maryland International Institute for Ecological Economics, and a range of Northern universities.

REFERENCES

Altieri, M. and O. Masera. 1993. "Sustainable Rural Development in Latin America: Building from the Bottom-Up." *Ecological Economics* 7:93–122.

Andersson, T. 1991. "Government Failure—the Cause of Global Environmental Mismanagement." *Ecological Economics* 4:215–236.

Barbier, E., A. Markandya, and D. Pearce. 1990. "Environmental Sustainability and Cost-Benefit Analysis." *Environment and Planning* 22:1259–1266.

Baumol, W. and W. Oates. 1988. *The Theory of Environmental Policy.* 2d. ed. New York: Cambridge University Press.

Boulding, K. 1968. *Beyond Economics.* Ann Arbor: University of Michigan Press.

Browder, J. 1988. "Public Policy and Deforestation in the Brazilian Amazon." In R. Repetto and M. Gillis, eds., *Public Policies and the Misuse of Forest Resources,* pp. 247–297. Cambridge: Cambridge University Press.

Cardoso, F. H. and E. Faletto. 1979. *Dependency and Development in Latin America.* Berkeley: University of California Press.

Ciriacy-Wantrup, S. 1952. *Resource Conservation: Economics and Policies.* Berkeley: University of California Press.

Coase, R. 1960. "The Problem of Social Cost." *Journal of Law and Economics* 3:1–44.

Costanza, R. 1989. "What Is Ecological Economics?" *Ecological Economics* 1:1–8.

——— 1992. "Ecological Economics: A Research Agenda." *Environmental Management* 10:252–286.

Costanza, R., ed. 1991. *Ecological Economics; The Science and Management of Sustainability.* New York: Columbia University Press.

Costanza, R., B. Norton, and B. Haskell, eds. 1992. *Ecosystem Health; New Goals for Ecosystem Management.* Covelo, Calif.: Island Press.

Daly, H., ed. 1973. *Toward a Steady State Economy.* San Francisco: W. H. Freeman.

Daly, H. 1991. "Sustainable Development: Some Basic Principles." Washington, D.C.: World Bank. Mimeo.

Daly, H. 1992. "Allocation, Distribution, and Scale: Towards an Economics That Is Efficient, Just, and Sustainable." *Ecological Economics* 6:185–193.

Daly, H. and J. Cobb. 1989. *For the Common Good: Redirecting the Economy Towards Community, the Environment, and a Sustainable Future.* London: Green Print.

Dixon, J. and M. Huffschmidt. 1986. *Economic Valuation Techniques for the Environment; A Case Study Workbook.* Baltimore: Johns Hopkins University Press.

Ehrlich, P. and A. Ehrlich. 1970. *Population, Resources, Environment.* San Francisco: W. H. Freeman.

Ekins, P. in press. "International Trade at a Crossroads." In O. Segura and R. Costanza, eds. *Getting Down to Earth: Practical Applications of Ecological Economics.* Covelo, Calif.: Island Press.

El Serafy, S. 1988. "The Proper Calculation of Income from Depletable Natural Resources." In Y. Ahmad et al., eds. *Environmental and Resource Accounting and Their Relevance to the Measurement of Sustainable Development.* Washington, D.C.: World Bank/UNEP.

Evans, P. 1979. *Dependent Development: The Alliance of Multinational, State and Local Capital in Brazil.* Princeton: Princeton University Press.

FOE/GTA (Friends of the Earth/Grupo de Trabalho Amazônico). 1994. *Sound Public Policies for the Amazon Region.* São Paulo: Friends of the Earth International Amazon Program.

Funtowicz, S. and J. Ravetz. 1991. "Three Types of Risk Assessment and the Emergence of Post-Normal Science." In D. Golding and Skrimsky, eds., *Theories of Risk.* Westport, Conn.: Greenwood Press.

Georgescu-Roegen, N. 1971. *The Entropy Law and the Economic Process.* Cambridge, Mass.: Harvard University Press.

Goodland, R., H. Daly, and S. El Serafy. 1991. *Environmentally Sustainable Economic Development: Building on Brundtland.* Washington, D.C.: World Bank.

Goodland, R. and H. Daly. in press. "The Universality of Environmental Sustainability." In O. Segura and R. Costanza, eds., *Getting Down to Earth: Practical Applications of Ecological Economics.* Covelo, Calif.: Island Press.

Hartwick, J. 1977. "Intergenerational Equity and the Investing of Rents from Exhaustible Resources." *American Economic Review* 66:972–974.

Hicks, J. 1946. *Value and Capital.* 2d ed. Oxford: Oxford University Press.

ICED (Inter-Parliamentary Conference on Environment and Development). 1992. *Draft Final Document.* Brasília: Inter-Parliamentary Union.

IDB (Inter-American Development Bank). 1990. "A Note on the Treatment of Environmental Protection Costs in Economic Project Evaluation." Washington, D.C.: IDB Operations Evaluation Office. Mimeo.

King, D. 1994. "Can We Justify Sustainability? New Challenges Facing Ecological Economics." In A. Jansson, M. Hammer, C. Folke, and R. Costanza, eds. *Investing in Natural Capital,* pp. 323–342. Covelo, Calif.: Island Press.

Kox, H. 1994. "The International Commodity-Related Environmental Agreement: Background and Design." Amsterdam: Free University.

Kuhn, T. 1962. *The Structure of Scientific Revolution.* Chicago: University of Chicago Press.

Leff, E. 1994. *Producción Ecológica.* México: Siglo XXI.

Low, P., ed. 1992. *International Trade and the Environment.* Washington, D.C.: World Bank.

Martinez-Alier, J. 1992. "Distributional Obstacles to International Environmental Policy (the failures at Rio and prospects after Rio)." Paper presented at the Second Meeting of the International Society for Ecological Economics: Investing in Natural Capital, Stockholm, Aug. 3–6.

May, P. H. 1993. "Reconciliation of Trade and Environmental Policies; Coffee and Cocoa Production and Processing in Brazil." Geneva: UNCTAD.

May, P. H. 1994. "Measuring Sustainability: Forest Values and Agropastoral Expansion in Brazil." In F. J. Duijnhouwer et al., eds., *Sustainable Resource Management and Resource Use: Policy Questions and Research Needs,* pp. 139–164. Netherlands Advisory Council for Research on Nature and the Environment, RMNO Publication no. 98.

Meadows, D., D. Meadows, J. Randers, and W. Behrens III. 1972. *The Limits to Growth.* New York: Signet.

Mishan, E. 1982. *Cost-Benefit Analysis.* London: Allen & Unwin.

Nusdeo, F. 1975. *Desenvolvimento e Ecologia.* São Paulo: Saraiva.

Odum, H. 1983. *Systems Ecology.* New York: Wiley.

Opschoor, J. in press. "Institutional Change and Development Towards Sustainability." In O. Segura and R. Costanza, eds., *Getting Down to Earth: Practical Applications of Ecological Economics.* Covelo, Calif: Island Press.

Panayotou, T. 1994. "Economic Instruments for Environmental Management and Sustainable Development." Cambridge, Mass., Harvard University. Draft paper prepared for the United Nations Environmental Programme's Consultative Expert Group Meeting on the Use and Application of Economic Policy Instruments for Environmental Management and Sustainable Development, Nairobi, August 10–12 1994.

Parikh, J. et al. 1992. "Consumption Patterns: The Driving Force of Environmental Stress." Bombay: Indira Gandhi Institute for Development Research.

Pastuk, M. 1992. "EIA in Brazil: Some Political Aspects." Paper presented at the Conference of the International Association for Impact Assessment, World Bank, Washington, D.C., August 19, 1992.

Pastuk, M. and P. May. 1994. "Valuing Social Sustainability: Conceptual Issues Applied to Favela Hillsides in Rio de Janeiro." Paper presented at the III Meeting of the International Society for Ecological Economics, San José, Costa Rica, October 24–28.

Pearce, D. and G. Atkinson. 1992. "Are National Economies Sustainable? Measuring Sustainable Development." London and East Anglia: Center for Social and Economic Research on the Global Environment (CSERGE), CSERGE Working Paper GEC 92–11.

Pearce, D. and R. Turner. 1991. *Economics of Natural Resource Use and the Environment.* Baltimore: Johns Hopkins University Press.

Pezzey, J. 1989. "Economic Analysis of Sustainable Growth and Sustainable Development." Washington, D.C.: World Bank, Environment Department Working Paper 15.

Randall, A. 1972. "Market Solutions to Externality Problems: Theory and Practice." *American Journal of Agricultural Economics* 54:175–183.

Sachs, I. 1980. *Strategies de l'Écodeveloppement.* Paris: Editions Ouvrières.

Schneider, R. 1993. *The Potential for Trade with the Amazon in Greenhouse Gas Reduction.* Washington, D.C.: World Bank, LATEN Dissemination Note #2.

Serôa da Motta, R. and E. J. Reis. 1994. "The Application of Economic Instruments in Environmental Policy: The Brazilian Case." Workshop on the Use of Economic Policy Instruments for Environmental Management, OECD/UNEP, Paris, May 26–27, 1994.

Solórzano, R. et al. 1991. *Accounts Overdue: Natural Resource Depletion in Costa Rica.* Washington, D.C.: World Resources Institute.

Turner, R. K., P. Doktor, and N. Adger. 1992. "Sea Level Rise and Coastal Wetlands in the U.K.: Mitigation Strategies for Sustainable Management." In A. Jansson, M. Hammer, C. Folke, and R. Costanza, eds., *Investing in Natural Capital,* pp. 266–290. Covelo, Calif.: Island Press.

UNCTAD. 1993. *Experiences Concerning Environmental Effects of Commodity Production and Processing: Synthesis of Case Studies on Cocoa, Coffee and Rice.* Geneva: UNCTAD Secretariat.

UN (United Nations). 1992a. *Rio Declaration on Environment and Development.* Geneva: United Nations Conference on Environment and Development Secretariat (as adopted by UNCED Plenary in Rio de Janeiro, June 13, 1992).

UN. 1992b. *Agenda 21.* Geneva: United Nations Conference on Environment and Development Secretariat.

Viederman, S. 1992. "Public Policy: Challenge to Ecological Economics," In A. Jansson, M. Hammer, C. Folke, and R. Costanza, eds., *Investing in Natural Capital,* pp. 467–478. Covelo, Calif.: Island Press.

WCED (World Council on Environment and Development). 1987. *Our Common Future.* Oxford: Oxford University Press.

TWO

Consumption Patterns: The Driving Force of Environmental Stress

Jyoti Parikh

The present patterns of development pose serious threats to the global ecosystem. The compulsions of poverty force the poor to live off the natural resources of the land and their environment. On the other hand, the insatiable desires for ever-increasing material comforts of the economically affluent also lead to severe stress on the environment. While the consumption patterns of the poor are insupportable in terms of land-use and cause degradation of the village commons, those of the rich are unsustainable in terms of use of nonrenewable resources, deterioration of the global commons, as well as pressure on land resources. Together, they stress the carrying capacity of the earth—at present and in the future.

Far too many persons suffer from poverty and deprivation. The sufferings of the poor cannot be relieved without economic development. Such development needs to be sustainable development in which the growth of the "goods" needed for improving the welfare of mankind is not constrained by the environmental "bads" or by the availability of required resources.

The environmental stress of underdevelopment as well as affluence is studied here in terms of consumption patterns, demographic pressures, rural-urban divide, and urbanization.

Here, per capita and aggregate consumption levels and the environmental consequences of population growth and urbanization in selected developed and developing countries are quantified. The resource needs for overall economic development, the consequences of continued poverty and the trade-offs and priorities among local, regional and global environmental problems are examined. Finally, some policy options to promote sustainable development in an equitable way at both the national level of developing countries and the global level are discussed.

CONSUMPTION PATTERNS AND POPULATION GROWTH

The developed countries (DVLPD) have only 24% of the world population, but their share in global consumption of various commodities ranges from 50% to 90%. As table 2.1 shows, even for the products that fulfill basic needs, like cereals, milk, and meat, the consumption of the developed countries constitutes 48% to 72%. The consumption shares of the DVLPD for other products are: 60% for fertilizer, 81% for paper, 86% for copper and aluminum, 80% for iron and steel, 85% for chemicals, and 92% for cars. This also means that their per capita consumption is as high as 3 to 8 times that of the developing countries for items of basic need and 20 times and more for items like chemicals and vehicles. The share of energy consumption is 75% for the developed world. Obviously environmental stress is proportional to these consumption levels. The developed world is responsible for about 70% of the annual total carbon dioxide (CO_2) emissions and 77% of cumulative emissions over 1950–1988. The per capita carbon emissions from the rich countries are 7 times that of the developing countries. Regional details against the world average can be seen in figure 2.1. Thus, it is the consumption pattern of the developed countries that has led to global environmental stress.

The per capita elasticity of carbon dioxide emission with respect to GNP per capita is 1.20; i.e., for every 1 percent increase in per capita GNP the increase in CO_2 emissions is 1.2 percent. This implies that if populations in poor countries were half of what they are now with aggregate GNP remaining the same as at present, their per capita income levels would have been doubled and consequently their consumption would have been higher by a factor greater than two. In fact, with lower population they would have had much higher rates of economic growth and their per capita income levels would have been still higher. Thus, population growth retards development in poor countries which possess a labor surplus and hence retards consumption levels.

This is illustrated in table 2.2. The first row in the table shows the base year population, GNP, GNP/cap., CO_2/cap., and total CO_2 emissions by a

TABLE 2.1
Consumption Patterns for Selected Commodities: Distribution Among
Developed and Developing Countries.

Category	Products	World Total (MMT)	Share Dvlpd.	Share Dvlpg.	Per Cap (KG. or M^2) Dvlpd.	Per Cap (KG. or M^2) Dvlpg.	Dvlpd/ Dvlpg	USA/ India
Food	Cereals	1801	48%	52%	717	247	3	6
	Milk	533	72%	28%	320	39	8	4
	Meat	114	64%	36%	61	11	6	52
Forest	Round wood	2410	46%	55%	388	339	1	6
	Sawn wood	338	78%	22%	213	19	11	18
	Paper etc.	224	81%	19%	148	11	14	115
Industrial	Fertilisers	141	60%	40%	70	15	5	6
	Cement	1036	52%	48%	451	130	3	7
	Cotton & wood fabrics	30	47%	53%	15.6	5.8	3	6.4
Metals	Copper	10	86%	14%	7	0.4	19	245
	Iron & steel	699	80%	20%	469	36	13	22
	Aluminium	22	86%	14%	16	1	19	85
Chemicals	Inorganic chemicals	226	87%	13%	163	8	20	54
	Organic chemicals	391	85%	15%	274	16	17	28
Transport vehicles	Cars	370	92%	8%	0.283	0.012	24	320
	Commercial vehicles	105	85%	15%	0.075	0.0006	125	102
Fuel and electricity	Solid	2309	66%	34%	1278	199	6	14
	Liquid	2745	75%	25%	1720	175	10	61
	Gas	1611	85%	15%	1147	61	19	227
	Electricity	343	81%	19%	230	17	13	46
	Total energy	7009	75%	25%	4376	453	10	35
Global CO_2 emissions	Total emissions	5723	70%	30%	3.36	0.43	8	27
	Comulated emissions (50–88)	112060	77%	23%				

SOURCE: Parikh et al. 1992

hypothetical country. If the population of the country doubles in 30 years
and the total GNP also doubles during this period the per capita GNP and
CO_2/cap. remain the same, but if the population of this country doubles,
total CO_2 emissions also double. However, in scenario B, the population of
the country remains at 100. the per capita GNP now has increased by 100%

TABLE 2.2

Hypothetical CO_2 Emissions and Population Growth

Year	Population	GNP	GNP/capita	CO_2/capita	CO_2
1990	100	100,000	1,000	C	100C
Scenario A: High population growth					
2000	200	200,000	1,000	C	200C
Scenario B: No population growth					
2020	100	200,000	2,000	2.2C	220C

SOURCE: Parikh et al. 1992

and with the elasticity of 1.20, CO_2/cap. emission would increase by 120%. The total CO_2 emissions are now 220 C, which is greater than 200 C of scenario A when the population is twice as much.

However, we point out that in addition to curbing unsustainable consumption patterns, it is also necessary to contain population growth because, although in the short run population growth retards growth of per capita consumption and thereby generates less greenhouse gas (GHG) emissions, a larger global population will eventually make it more difficult to reach a steady sustainable state.

URBAN ENVIRONMENT

To what extent are urbanization and big cities responsible for the environmental degradation? These questions were examined in an econometric framework in Parikh et al. (1992), where it is concluded that the levels of overall emissions are largely the result of economic growth associated with urbanization rather than urbanization *per se*. It is observed that large cities experience greater pollution and health related problems as a result of a greater concentration of industrial activities. Pollution abatement in urban areas is an answer to this problem.

For developing countries, the adverse effects on health from local pollution represent serious problems.[1] For example, ambient air quality in cities of developing countries have very high level of concentration of particulate pollutants (a daily mean of 200 and above $\mu g/cm^3$ compared to 100 and below for cities in the developed countries). Air quality in the cities of developing countries has deteriorated whereas improvements are evident in the cities like New York and Tokyo that could afford pollution abatement costs.

Nevertheless, estimated greenhouse effects do appear to be related to countries' urbanization levels, due to high per capita commercial energy consumption in urban areas. This does not vary dramatically either with characteristics of urban distribution in very large cities or with other variables studied.

Reduction in environmental pollution is best undertaken with a variety of economic instruments designed to deal with specific polluting sources in a technologically appropriate manner rather than curbing urbanization, since restraining the pace of urbanization would go against overall developmental goals. Such actions might include a greater emphasis on mass transit in large cities of developing countries than what many developed countries have seen fit to accord.

RURAL ENVIRONMENT

The rural populations of developing countries face serious health hazards associated with the use of biofuels. A major part of the domestic energy (as much of 73% of which is devoted to cooking) is provided by biofuels that emit various kind of pollutants like particulates, oxides of sulfur and nitrogen, carbon monoxide, hydrocarbons, etc. The concentration of these pollutants inside the kitchen is several times the maximum recommended by the World Health Organization. This results in respiratory problems and other diseases, specially among the rural women who are directly exposed to these pollutants in the kitchen.

LOCAL AND GLOBAL POLLUTANTS

A variety of pollutants and effluents are generated due to various activities. Some have local effects, and some have global impacts. The "local pollutants" are oxides of sulfur (SOx) oxides of nitrogen (NOx), particulates (TSP), carbon monoxide (CO), etc., whereas global pollutants are carbon dioxide (CO_2), methane (CH_4), and chloroflurocarbons (CFCs). Many local pollutants have severe health effects. They enter through skin, lungs, and eyes. Some local pollutants associated with biofuels are carcinogenic and some of these cause and aggravate cardiovascular and respiratory diseases if they exceed certain threshold levels. The health effects result from the total exposure (obtained by multiplying the amount of pollutants, the number of hours of exposure exceeding the threshold level, and the number of persons exposed). The health effects for women and children from cooking with biofuels are substantial.

SOCIOECONOMIC TRADE-OFFS AND ENVIRONMENTAL PRIORITIES

Environmental priorities have to be set depending upon the consequences of the various environmental effects, urgency with which compensation measures are required, the extent of the population involved, the costs to be incurred and whether it is the present or the future generation that is affected. These trade-offs are present at all stages:

* trade offs among environment and development;
* among the local pollutants and the global pollutants; and
* among greenhouse gases, i.e., among the socioeconomic
* activities that cause equivalent greenhouse effect.

In addition to these there are further trade-offs:

* among the regions of the world and
* among the present and the future generations.

Trade-Offs Among Activities

To illustrate the question of trade-offs, let us take the case of greenhouse gases. What are the socioeconomic trade-offs in reducing greenhouse gas emissions? What does a reduction of 1,000 tons (t) of carbon mean in terms of curtailing socioeconomic needs in the developing countries as opposed to the developed countries? 1,000 t of carbon emissions represent fuel wood consumption for cooking by 2000 poor households. A reduction of 1000 t of carbon equivalent from methane emissions can be attained by reducing rice production (a staple food for the poor) by an amount that is enough for

12,000 persons, or by reducing cattle stock by 4,000 head depriving more than a 1,000 households of a part of their food and fuel requirements. Alternatively, it could be achieved by reduced electricity production by an amount that would be enough for 2,700 to 4,600 households. It is clear that to meet developmental needs, emissions from developing countries are bound to increase in near future. On the other hand, the same reduction in GHG emission can be attained by burning less gasoline, say by having 800 fewer cars in the United States.

Trade-Offs Among Regions

How much reduction would have to be accomplished by others when some of the low-income developing countries move closer to the world averages? As a simple exercise, we take India and China. We assume that global CO_2 emissions in 2025 should not be more than the 1986 level (i.e., 5.7 billion t C).

We assume that per capita incomes increase modestly to US$796 in 2025 from $249 in 1985 for India and $2,000 in 2025 from $310 in 1985 for China. Furthermore we consider a low emissions scenario. Even then the aggregate emissions of these two countries increase by 21% of the gross GHG emissions of the world in 1986. This implies that, to stabilize aggregate emissions, the emissions of the developed world have to be reduced by 30% just to provide for modest increases by India and China. It should be stressed that even in 2025, India's per capita emissions, even if they were to be calculated on the basis of India's population in 1985, remains lower than the world average in 1985.

Uncertainties in Estimates of Methane Emissions

The aggregate emission data for developing countries include methane emissions from paddy rice and livestock. There is a lot of uncertainty about coefficients of methane emissions from the above sources and reliable data are not available. In fact, even the factors on which these depend are yet not properly understood. Therefore, these data and their use to attribute methane emissions to different countries have to be interpreted with caution. Uncertainties on methane emissions are too large to make it a basis for international negotiations.

CO_2 from Deforestation

The same uncertainty applies to data on deforestation. The data available are not reliable and indicate unrealistic consumption patterns for fuel wood. Even the areas deforested appear to be unrealistic. These anomalies in the data seriously affect the estimate between estimated gross emissions and measured increase of carbon in the global atmosphere. The sink capacity is high, if estimates of emissions are inflated, and low if these are corrected. Thus, based on CO_2 concentrations increase in atmosphere and two sets of data: ORNL (1989) and WRI (1990, 1992) on emissions, the sink capacity could be anywhere between 1.8 to 4.7 billion tons of carbon. Even fossil fuel emissions by India are 15% less when grade-wise coal production is considered, which means less CO_2 for low grades of coal. Thus, a more thorough analysis of CO_2 emissions is needed.

THE MAIN MESSAGE

We conclude that economic growth is desirable not only to mitigate the sufferings of the poor and raise their living standards, but also to reduce environmental degradation that is exacerbated by poverty. The present patterns of consumption of the rich are unsustainable with currently available technology and hence this trend needs to be altered to limit environmental degradation. Population growth also needs to be controlled to be able to achieve a steady state sooner and at a higher sustainable consumption level.

The important question that arises is how the global environmental can be preserved at least cost. Cooperation of the rich and the poor is essential. A fair allocation of emission rights, that would allow development for the poor and adjustment to a sustainable pattern of consumption for the rich is a major requirement. Under the "Polluter Pays Principle" the nations above the world average should pay those below average (see figure 2.1). Through a fair allocation of rights and marketable permits, the poor would also be able to set their own environmental priorities and through prudent behavior be able to secure the capital necessary for development. Besides economic development, reduction of local pollution is also necessary for the developing world.

Specific policy actions such as fuel substitution in favor of cleaner fuels like natural gas, energy efficiency improvements, promoting use of

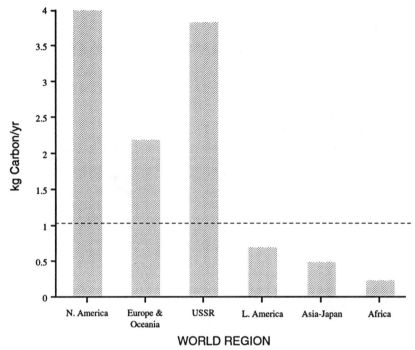

Figure 2.1.   Per-capita CO_2 emissions (from fossil fuels and cement). Source: ORNL (1989).

renewable sources of energy, and appropriate pricing of fuels (including internalizing the environmental costs wherever necessary) can help in achieving the goals of reduction in environmental degradation and sustainable development. Mechanisms such as afforestation in third world countries, debt-for-nature swaps and so on, can also be helpful if the conditions surrounding such arrangements are fully transparent and the overall impacts of these fully understood by all.

There are many things we can do to reduce if not eliminate danger to the earth' environment. If we act well and wisely, and with charity, opportunities are at hand that we can seize to green the earth. For Earth's sake let us do that.

Acknowledgment: This paper is based on the Executive Summary to a study by J. Parikh et al. (1992), prepared at the request of the UNCED Secretatiat.

NOTES

1. For examples, see the studies by Margulis and Serôa and Mendes in this volume.

REFERENCES

ORNL (Oak Ridge National Laboratory). 1989. *Estimates of CO₂ Emissions from Fossil Fuel Burning and Cement Manufacturing Data.* Environmental Sciences Division, Publication no. 3176.

Parikh, J., K. Parikh, S. Gokam, J. P. Painuly, B. Saha, and V. Shukla. 1992. "Consumption Patterns: The Driving Force of Environmental Stress." Bombay: Indira Gandhi Institute for Development Research.

WRI (World Resources Institute). 1990. *World Resources 1988–89.* Washington, D.C.: WRI.

—— 1992. *World Resources 1990–91.* Washington, D.C.: WRI.

THREE

A Tradable Carbon Entitlements Approach to Global Warming Policy: Sustainable Allocations

Adam Rose and Brandt Stevens

Any successful policy to deal with global warming must have several attractive features. Given the potentially immense sums that may have to be spent on abatement, it is important that the policy be cost-effective. Given the magnitude of the costs and the variation in both costs and benefits across countries, it would be desirable that the policy be equitable, or fair.[1]

Equity considerations are usually accorded a secondary role in most economic policy-making, but, in the case of global warming, there are reasons why they may be paramount. First, there is no supranational institution that can force a greenhouse gas (GHG) agreement; hence, volunteerism is of great importance. Second, appeals to economic efficiency will not be sufficient to rally countries together, given the wide disparities in their current welfare and of welfare changes implied by efficient policies.

Thus, over and above the usual role of equity in promoting fair policy outcomes, this criterion might serve as a unifying principle in forging a greenhouse warming agreement. A global problem requires a global solution and hence as many participants as possible. The public good nature of GHG abatement means it is prone to free rider problems. At the moment, a few countries may be responsible for most of the emissions of CO_2 and other GHGs, but, as development proceeds, the number of large contributors will increase. Greater cooperation is likely to be forthcoming if the policy process and policy outcomes are perceived to be fair.

A tradable entitlements, or marketable permits, approach to greenhouse gas mitigation has several attractive features (see e.g., Barrett et al. 1992). Coase (1960) was the first to point out that a system of exchangeable property rights yields an efficient outcome to an externality problem irrespective of who receives the rights. Thus, we are not faced with the usual equity-efficiency tradeoff that plagues many policy decisions. In this case, any tradeoff would be between various equity principles and the degree of comprehensiveness that they can inspire.[2] Some compromises could arise to bring more countries into the fold to share the cost burden. That is, some countries may shift to an equity principle other than their first choice in order to lower their own cost of abatement, even if the result is a less pleasing overall distribution of net welfare changes.

One significant problem arises with respect to equity, however. Unlike efficiency, there is no universal consensus on the best definition on either the international or interpersonal level. Until recently, in-depth analysis was rarely undertaken, even in the context of global climate change, which has been a subject of economic inquiry for twenty years.[3] Many policy pronouncements include ambiguous or erroneous definitions of equity, and empirical estimates of equity implications are rarely offered.

The purpose of this paper is to analyze equity aspects of a tradable entitlements approach to CO_2 mitigation, with special reference to sustainable allocations, both in regard to industrialized and developing countries and transfers between the two. We begin with a detailed analysis of 10 equity principles, including their transformation into operational rules for global warming policy in general and tradable entitlements in particular. We then proceed to discuss alternative reference bases and match them with equity principles. Finally, we explore the implications of the various criteria in terms of who gains and who loses, both before and after trading.

Sustainable development calls for the simultaneous pursuit of economic growth and a clean environment (see, e.g., Pearce 1989). A tradable entitlements policy for CO_2 mitigation can help promote this dual outcome. Inherently, it reduces pollution, thereby improving the overall allocation of resources, both conventional and environmental. The tradability feature also provides for transfers between nations. This is the standard outcome that results when the marginal GHG abatement cost functions of some countries (typically considered to be the industrialized ones) are steeper than those of others (typically developing countries). But these transfers can be accentuated or diminished according to initial assignments of entitlements. Motivations for fine-tuning the allocations include: making it feasible for poorer countries to participate in an agreement, bringing more countries to the bargaining table, and using the entitlements as a conduit for foreign aid in general. Our focus will be on *sustainable allocations* of entitlements. These allocations are defined as avoiding net cost commitments on the part of the developing countries that would seriously detract from their future economic development and avoiding assignments that would result in massive and long-term aid flows from industrialized nations that would be politically infeasible, both of which would undercut a global agreement. We will show below how entitlement allocations based on equal proportional CO_2 reduction requirements may violate the first of these requirements and how assignments based on population may violate the latter.

INTERNATIONAL EQUITY CRITERIA

Equity represents a normative evaluation, or value judgment, of the social desirability of economic and noneconomic disbursements, both positive and negative. The concept has been a major focus of philosophers since ancient times and has been the implied or explicit concern of monarchs and politicians for at least as long. The vast majority of attention has been devoted to the distribution of well-being among individuals, but when gains and losses transcend political boundaries, the unit of analysis enlarges accordingly. Below, we offer several equity principles applicable to global warming policy. In most cases, we begin with the more typical interpersonal context and then show how the concept can be extended to the international arena. The equity principles, a general operational rule emanating from each, and a rule applicable to the allocation of tradable entitlements for CO_2 emissions are summarized in table 3.1.

Before proceeding to our analysis, we point out a confusion in the literature arising from the failure to distinguish between fundamental equity criteria and what we will term "reference bases." The former refer to general concepts of distributive justice or fairness and the latter to specific measures or indices to which the equity principles can be applied according to the policy issue under examination. It is not surprising that many analysts emphasize the latter. Reference bases are more concrete and less controversial than ethical principles.[4] On the other hand, their equity implications are often ambiguous or not really what is claimed. Examples (to be discussed in detail below) are population, which is consistent with several conflicting equity criteria (e.g., egalitarian, sovereignty, consensus), and land area, which is at best only weakly related to some criteria. In addition, there are dynamic versions of these reference bases, relating to past (cumulative) and

TABLE 3.1
Alternative Equity Criteria for Global Warming Policy

Criterion	General Operational Rule	Operational Rule for CO_2 Entitlements
Horizontal	Equalize net welfare change across nations (net cost of abatement as proportion of GDP equal for each nation)[a]	Allocate entitlements to equalize net welfare change (net cost of abatement as proportion of GDP equal for each nation)[a]
Vertical	Progressively share net welfare change (net cost proportions inversely correlated with per capita GDP)[a]	Progressively distribute entitlements (net cost proportions inversely correlated with per capita GDP)[a]
Ability to pay	Equalize abatement costs across nations (gross cost of abatement as proportion of GDP equal for each nation)[b]	Allocate entitlements to equalize abatement costs (gross cost of abatement as proportion of GDP equal for each nation)[b]
Sovereignty	Cut back emissions proportionally across all nations	Allocate entitlements in proportion to emissions
Egalitarian	Cut back emissions in proportion to population	Allocate entitlements in proportion to population
Market justice	Make greater use of markets	Auction entitlements to highest bidder
Consensus	Seek a political solution promoting stability	Distribute entitlements so (power weighted) majority of nations are satisfied
Compensation	Compensate net losing nations	Distribute entitlements so no nation suffers a net loss of welfare
Rawls' maximin	Maximize the net benefit to the poorest nations	Distribute large proportion of entitlements to poorest nations
Environmental	Cut back emissions to maximize environmental values	Limit entitlements associated with vulnerable ecosystems (e.g., forests)

[a] Net cost equal to the sum of mitigation benefits–abatement costs + permit sales revenues–permit purchase costs.
[b] Gross cost refers to abatement cost only.

future (development-related) emissions, the damage they incur, and the cost of mitigating them.

There is also the question of the object of equity analysis, or what exactly is being distributed. The most straightforward consideration is the cost of mitigation. From a more comprehensive perspective, however, we would consider the net welfare change, or net cost. The net cost is equal to the sum of mitigation benefits and permit sales revenues minus abatement costs and minus permit purchase costs.[5] There is a temptation to simplify the analysis and merely confine it to abatement costs, but for the purpose of achieving an agreement one cannot ignore the magnitude and variations across nations of benefits from avoiding global warming damages. Even if the scientific community feels these benefits can never be accurately measured, nations are likely to have strong perceptions of their magnitude, a factor that will influence their negotiating position. Thus, while we can simplify the analysis of tradeable entitlements from the efficiency side by resorting to cost-effectiveness analysis (i.e., simply assuming a given CO_2 reduction level and examining whether it can be attained at least cost), we do not necessarily have this luxury from an equity standpoint.

Note again that we are focusing on equity criteria, but are not suggesting that other considerations are not important. We have avoided the usual discussion of equity-efficiency tradeoffs, because they detract from our main theme. Also note that there are considerable conflicts between our several equity principles themselves. Although references to equity are typically vague in most contexts, it is extremely important to clearly define which variant of the concept is being proposed in global warming policy.[6]

REFERENCE BASES

We will now examine alternative reference bases to which equity criteria can be applied. These bases are essentially indices against which to gauge the equity implications of policy designs. We will distinguish between operational bases, those that can be utilized with data currently at hand, and ideal measures, those that require further conceptual refinement and/or data gathering in order to more accurately reflect the intent of underlying equity principles. Also, we will distinguish between static measures, which pertain to a given point in time (including a future target date), and dynamic measures, which refer to a series of past or future levels of some of the measures. Reference bases, their applicability and their measurement are summarized in table 3.2.

Note two points of emphasis. Some equity criteria can have more than one reference base. Moreover, several reference bases are consistent with more than one criterion. This raises a concern about the ambiguity of many previous policy proposals, a concern our categorization hopes to clarify. At the same time, the lack of unique correspondence between criteria and measures may actually be a policy-making plus, in that it allows for more flexibility and the possibility of satisfying more countries.

The fact that GHGs are stock pollutants has important implications for the intergenerational allocation of resources forward in time, in terms of the usual issues relating to discounting (see, e.g., Nordhaus 1989; d'Arge 1989). Going backward in time, in the sense of cumulative emissions, also

TABLE 3.2
Static Reference Bases for CO_2 Tradable Entitlements

Reference Base	Applicability to Equity Criteria[a]	Operational Measure	Ideal Measure
Economic welfare	Horizontal, Vertical, Ability, Compensation, Maximin	Per capita gross domestic product (PC GDP)	PC Augmented GDP[b] (adj. for purchasing power parity)
Population	Egalitarian (Consensus)	Population	Population (adj. to discourage growth)
Land area	(Horizontal, Vertical, Environmental)	Square miles	Square miles (adj. for travel costs)
Energy use	(Vertical, Environmental)	Btu's (adj. for carbon equivalence)	Btu's (adj. for carbon equivalence & fuel efficiency)
Energy reserves	(Horizontal, Vertical, Compensation)	Btu's (adj. for carbon equivalence)	Btu's (adj. for carbon equivalence & fuel efficiency)
CO_2 emissions	Sovereignty, Environmental (Horizontal, Vertical)	Emissions (adj. for carbon equivalence)	Emissions (adj. for carbon equivalence & fuel efficiency)

[a] Parentheses indicate applicability is weak.
[b] Refers to GDP enhanced by non-market goods and services, primarily environmental.

has important implications for the specification of abatement requirements. In terms of efficiency, policy instruments should be applied only to current and future emissions, since built-up GHGS are analogous to sunk costs. From an equity standpoint, however, the stock nature of GHGS does matter. Industrialized nations have developed by abusing the global commons with little or no penalty. Ignoring the past build-up and simply basing reduction requirements on subsequent emissions would be equivalent to penalizing developing countries for their progress, when no such penalty was imposed on industrialized countries. Since the efficiency and equity aspects of tradable entitlements are generally separable, we can thus address the latter without wasting resources.

Most of the equity criteria presented in the previous section can be reinterpreted in terms of cumulative emissions. One way of incorporating this feature into equity analysis is to think of it as affecting a country's GHG "rights" or "responsibilities" where these are relevant. The consideration of rights arises in the context of sovereignty and the egalitarian ethic. Responsibility is not explicitly related to any of the criteria except sovereignty and the environmental ethic, and possibly rather weakly to consensus. Otherwise, it is simply compatible with all other criteria except market justice and one rigid form of egalitarianism.[7]

There are two straightforward ways of operationalizing past actions as a reference base. One is to consider cumulative CO_2 emissions minus an adjustment for absorption and decay over time. Another is to use cumulative emissions minus any absorption at time of release only. The latter would in effect be a measure of any instantaneous damage. This might not have been significant until recently, if at all, but is likely to be an increasingly important consideration when policy is being discussed in future years.

How would the other reference bases noted in table 3.2 be affected? In most views they would not be. For example, policymakers are likely to evaluate the vertical or horizontal equity of abatement, even if the level is related to cumulative emissions, in terms of *current* economic welfare (per capita GDP), *current* energy reserves, etc. There is the option of adjusting the various operational measures, other than emissions, to past levels, but there would seem to be little justification to do so. Finally, we note that two reference bases are in effect applicable in nearly all cases—implicitly (past) carbon emissions are combined with per capita GDP, population, land area, etc.

The effect of including the cumulative emissions consideration in an adjustment of the reference base against which to measure equity is to alter abatement requirements or permit allocations accordingly. This then would affect the cost side of the ledger. Some climate engineering alternatives may in the future allow for differential adjustments on the benefits side. It may be surprising to some, however, that the cumulative emissions reference base would not change the distribution of the CO_2 cost burden dramatically. Smith et al. (1991) estimates the split between industrialized and developing nations as 60:40 on a current basis and 70:30 on a cumulative one.

The stock nature of GHGs, as well as the potential for them to be emitted at significantly higher rates as population grows and economic development spreads, justifies special concern over future emissions. We will discuss these emissions both in terms of the simple case of current emissions at some future time and the dynamic case of trade-offs over a time horizon.

In the former case, the focus is on the fact that the contribution of developing countries to CO_2 emissions is likely to rise from 30–40% of the world total currently to 60 + % in perhaps the next 30 to 40 years. As such, the pressure will mount to raise emission limits or reduce emission entitlements (or at least the surplus entitlements) for these countries. While there has been a big emphasis on the low cost of achieving emission reductions in the third world, especially if technology transfer takes place, there is also the prospect of implementing costly policies. One example is a policy to discourage coal use or to institute an outright ban. Under these circumstances, it may be legitimate to include the opportunity cost of devalued resources. In countries like China, these costs could be huge. Their inclusion into the net welfare calculus would put such countries in a position to receive extra entitlements under criteria like vertical equity and Rawls' Maximin principle.

In the dynamic case, it must be emphasized that currently undertaking CO_2 abatement diverts resources from investment needed to stimulate economic development. Thus, while this abatement reaps future benefits, it also imposes costs on current and future generations in terms of both stock and flow measures of well-being. Thus, the opportunity cost extends beyond the partial equilibrium aspects associated with fossil fuel reserves, and includes the general equilibrium lost surplus measures from foregone economic growth and development. The result is problematic in two regards. First, these nations are especially needy and, according to some specifications of welfare functions and views of equity, suffer more from a comparable decrease in the rate of economic growth than industrialized nations. Second, it breeds resentment in the third world, especially in the face of sizable cumulative emissions by industrialized nations (see, e.g., Agarwal and Narain 1991).[8] This situation is likely to have some significance for the utilization of criteria like consensus equity.

Future emissions also have some dimensions of rights and responsibilities discussed in the context of historical emissions, though typically to a weaker extent. Most obvious is that costs must be incurred now for the sake of providing benefits to future generations. Of course, these expenditures do impose a cost on future generations in terms of lower productive capacities. Also, some ethical systems have very strong beliefs about intergenerational equity that need to be considered.

To avoid confusing many important issues we have thus far refrained from discussing time discounting. However, one of the most frequently used approaches for evaluating policy impacts on future generations is to convert them to present value terms. This involves considerations of the discount rate that are beyond the scope of this paper. We should note, however, that the choice of the discount rate implicitly or explicitly implies some value judgment about intergenerational equity (see, e.g., Nordhaus 1990). It also spills over onto issues of international equity in that some cultures (e.g., Moslem-based) and some ideologies (e.g., socialism) have strong convictions about the appropriate level of interest rates that differ from much of the rest of the world (see d'Arge 1989).

The policy analysis of future emissions may differ from that of cumulative emissions in terms adjustments to other reference bases. That is, policy-makers may not wish to confine their attention to the current generation. Modifications are relevant to all reference bases except land area. Note, as in the previous subsection, emissions considerations would, in most cases, be combined with another reference base for the implementation of the various equity criteria. In addition, factors like the change in value of reserves would enter into the cost-benefit calculus of welfare changes. Other options would be to also include consideration of necessary and unnecessary emissions. In this case, as in others, there is nothing wrong with using a combination of ethical judgments.

The effect of including future dynamic elements would likely shift the allocation of entitlements in favor of developing countries. Again, most of the influence is through the cost-side of the ledger. In cases like consensus equity, however, this result is attributable to the rising relative political and economic stature of the third world.

WELFARE ANALYSIS

In this section, we estimate the welfare effects on eight major countries and world regions of three equity criteria for allocating entitlements: Sovereignty, Rawlsian, and Egalitarian. The criteria are examined in terms of current reference bases only. Among the goals for mitigating greenhouse gas emissions, a 20% reduction in projected CO_2 emissions in the year 2000 is one of the most widely discussed.[9] In our simulations, we assume this goal has been specified by a treaty protocol, thus fixing the global supply of CO_2 entitlements at 80% of projected 2,000 emissions. We realize that this approach only pursues cost-effectiveness, but, given the tenuous nature of data at this time, believe it is impossible to identify a totally efficient outcome. Initial entitlement assignments, to be discussed further below, are presented for each of three criteria in table 3.3.

The empirical analysis employs a nonlinear programming model in which the initial allocation of entitlements can be changed in accordance with different equity rules (see Rose and Stevens 1993a and 1993b, for more details of the theoretical and empirical models). We examine net

TABLE 3.3
Initial Entitlement Allocations And Final Trades
(in thousands of tons of carbon)

Country (Area)	Sovereignty		Rawlsian		Egalitarian	
	Entitlement assign-ments	Entitlement trades[a]	Entitlement assign-ments	Entitlement trades[a]	Entitlement assign-ments	Entitlement trades[a]
United States	1,213,334	109,267	1,130,111	192,490	406,156	916,445
Canada	108,124	11,192	100,708	18,609	42,348	76,968
Western Europe	780,165	84,398	726,653	137,910	501,266	363,297
C.I.S.	1,080,110	−160,044	1,080,110	−160,045	465,510	454,555
Brazil	55,633	−16,513	55,632	−16,512	252,646	−213,526
Central Africa	4,426	−114	5,256	−944	140,812	−136,500
Indonesia	31,228	−9,269	37,084	−15,124	305,646	−283,687
China	733,150	−18,918	870,615	−156,383	1,891,785	1,177,553
Totals[b]	4,006,170	204,857[c]	4,006,170	349,009[c]	4,006,170	1,811,265[c]

[a] Positive entries represent entitlement purchases; negative entries represent entitlement sales (cost offsets).
[b] Totals may not add up due to rounding.
[c] Sum of absolute value of either entitlement purchases or sales.

welfare changes (benefits minus costs plus or minus entitlement sales or purchases) when CO_2 entitlements are not transferable and when entitlements can be bought or sold. When entitlements cannot be traded, the allocations determine each country or region's CO_2 reduction. Individual country benefit and cost functions are used to estimate the net welfare impacts of the protocol (note that since mitigation of greenhouse gases is a global public good, each country's benefit is determined by the 20% global emission reduction of CO_2 irrespective of who undertakes the abatement). When entitlements can be traded, gross benefits will be identical to the first case, but trading will alter the net welfare impacts of a protocol because of the effect of trading on abatement costs and permit sales revenue or expenditures.

Empirical Results

Our analysis is undertaken for the eight countries or country groupings listed in column 1 of table 3.4, representative of various levels of development as denoted by their GDP in column 2. Columns 3 and 4 list estimates of benefits (environmental damage avoided) from mitigation of 20% of CO_2

TABLE 3.4

Changes in National Welfare Due to Static Sovereignty Entitlement Assignments
(20% abatement level)

Country (Area)	Per Capita GDP[a]	(All Cases) Benefit	(Without Trading)		(With Trading)		
			Cost	Net change	Cost	Trading	Net change
United States	$20,725	$16.98	$ 9.13	$ 7.85	$ 3.64	$4.19	$ 9.15
Canada	18,648	1.07	.89	.18	.30	.43	.34
Western Europe[b]	14,322	10.27	6.67	3.60	2.08	3.24	4.95
C.I.S.	3,491[c]	2.28	2.90	− .62	7.72	− 6.14	.70
Brazil	2,167	1.52	.10	1.42	.53	.63	1.62
Central Africa[d]	475	.14	.02	.12	.02	− .01[e]	.12
China	375	5.38	3.03	2.35	3.72	− .73	2.39
Total	——	$38.11	$22.80	$15.31	$18.31	$ 0.00	$19.80

NOTE: All figures in billions of 1990 dollars except Per Capita GDP.
[a] Data for 1989 from World Bank (1991).
[b] Western Europe includes the European Community countries: Belgium, Denmark, France, Germany, Greece, Ireland, Italy, Luxembourg, Netherlands, Portugal, Spain, and the United Kingdom.
[c] Data for 1988 for Soviet Union from Euromonitor (1991).
[d] Central Africa includes: Burundi, Cameroon, Central African Republic, Congo, Equatorial Guinea, Gabon, Rwanda, and Zaire.
[e] Less than .005 billion dollars.

emissions in the year 2000 and the associated costs associated with equal proportional cutbacks, respectively. At this stage of scientific inquiry, the numbers are of course crude, but still are able to indicate the relative policy impacts. For example, benefits are relatively small for Canada and the Commonwealth of Independent States (C.I.S.), since a warming of their climate would increase agricultural productivity and would offset considerably the damage due to sea level rise and loss of recreational benefits and tourist revenues. At the same time, some of the more populated areas of Europe and Indonesia could be inundated by a fairly modest melting of the polar ice caps.

Mitigation costs are evaluated in terms of actual direct expenditures rather than general equilibrium or macroeconomic effects (cf. Manne and Richels 1991). The reliance of China on its coal resources, and the cost of fuel switching, for example, are the main reasons for its relatively high mitigation costs in relation to other developing countries.

Sovereignty Criterion

The net change in national welfare from a 20% global reduction in CO_2 when entitlements are distributed according to the Sovereignty criterion, but before permit trading, is presented in column 5 of table 3.4 as a point of reference. All eight countries/regions would stand to reap positive net benefits except the C.I.S. The sum of net benefits is $15.31 billion.

Our analysis of the Sovereignty principle has not yet included permit trading, which will take place as long as some countries have marginal abatement costs greater than or equal to the world market price of entitlements and some countries have abatement costs less than or equal to this price. It is usually assumed, and generally borne out by the cost studies, that abatement costs are relatively higher in developed countries than developing ones. Trading will thus lower the total costs to the former and provide a transfer to the latter, which in effect also lowers the net abatement costs of developing countries.

The effect of trading, as determined by the nonlinear programming model, is presented in the last three columns of table 3.4. These results indicate that the United States, Canada, and Western Europe would be permit buyers and the other five countries/regions would be permit sellers. Nearly 205 million entitlements would be traded with a total value of $7.86 billion (see table 3.3) at the equilibrium price of $38.35 per ton of CO_2.

The revenues from the sale of entitlements more than offset the increased costs of abatement incurred by the sellers.

Trading has several implications for the sustainability of a treaty protocol, i.e., whether individual countries would find the treaty acceptable enough to sign it and to abide by the protocol's provisions. First, the equalization of marginal costs of abatement saves this global group $4.49 billion, or almost 20% of the $22.80 billion of abatement costs associated with the uniform emission reduction requirement. The net cost savings (including expenditures on entitlements) to the three Western industrialized countries/regions is $2.80 billion, or about 17% of their costs at uniform abatement levels. In addition, trading is estimated to be a source of revenue for developing and transitional economies. In fact, for Brazil and Indonesia, the permit revenues more than offset their total abatement costs. Finally, all of the countries examined receive positive net benefits from a 20% CO_2 emission reduction policy, though it is important to note that the United States and Western Europe received the highest net change overall and the greatest gains from the trading of entitlements. There is, of course, the possibility that some countries not in our sample would have negative net benefits, but they would still be better off than if permit trading were not allowed.

Rawlsian Criterion

This case accentuates the shift of the initial abatement burden to industrialized nations by way of assigning more entitlements to developing countries, in this case the three lesser-developed countries (LDCs) in our sample. The Rawlsian Maximin rule favors the most disadvantaged group, in principle, though there is not specific guidance on exactly how much. Our approximation is to increase permit assignments from 80% of projected year 2000 emissions to 95% for LDCs, or a 5% control requirement. The entitlements assigned to the three Western industrialized nations decrease in number accordingly so as to still attain an exact 20% global reduction (see table 3.3). Interestingly, the initial control requirements for industrialized countries do not increase much (they become 25.8% for the current reference base Rawlsian case).

The net welfare changes of this allocation in the absence of trading are presented in table 3.5. In comparison to the Sovereignty criterion, before trading, control costs do go up dramatically to nearly $31 billion, with

TABLE 3.5
Changes in National Welfare Due to Rawlsian and Egalitarian Permit Assignments
(20% abatement level)

Country (Area)	Rawlsian Current Reference Case					Egalitarian Current Reference Case				
	Without trading		With trading			Without trading		With trading		
	Cost	Net	Cost	Trading	Net	Cost	Net	Cost	Trading	Net
United States	$15.14	$1.83	$ 3.64	$7.38	$ 5.96	$161.17	−$144.19	$ 3.64	$35.15	−$21.81
Canada	1.48	−.41	.30	.71	.06	13.43	−12.36	.30	2.95	−$21.81
Western Europe	11.07	−.80	2.08	5.29	2.90	44.69	−34.42	2.08	13.93	−5.74
C.I.S.	2.90	−.62	7.72	−6.14	.70	38.89	−36.61	7.72	17.43	−22.87
Brazil	.10	1.42	.53	−.63	1.62	.00	1.52	.53	−8.19	9.18
Central Africa	.00[a]	.14	.02	−.04	.15	.00	.14	.02	−5.23	5.35
Indonesia	.00[a]	.46	.30	−.58	.75	.00	.47	.30	−10.88	11.05
China	.18	5.20	3.72	5.99	7.66		5.38	3.72	−45.16	46.82
Total	$30.87	$7.22	$18.31	$0.00	$19.80	$258.18	−$220.07	$18.31	$ 0.00	$19.80

NOTE: All figures in billions of 1990 dollars.
[a] Less than $.005 billion.

global net benefits less than $7 billion. Moreover, all four industrialized nations stand to incur negative net benefits. As in the other cases we examine, trading improves the situation greatly. Entitlements for 350 million tons of CO_2 would be traded with a value of $18.3 billion. Post-trading abatement costs are the same as for the other cases examined (note the $18.31 billion total in tables 3.4 and 3.5). Global net benefits increase dramatically to nearly $20 billion, and all countries receive positive net benefits. China is clearly the largest net winner in this case, and the United States and Western Europe do not fare as well as in the other cases examined.

The Rawlsian case is likely to be acceptable among treaty signatories since all countries experience positive net benefits after trading. Such a distribution of entitlements would also result in a transfer of wealth of roughly $12 billion annually from the United States and Western Europe to China and the C.I.S. The former Soviet republics would only be marginally better off in terms of net benefits, but their abatement costs are still larger than permit sales revenues. China, however, would effectively earn a profit on permit sales of $2.27 billion per year, due primarily to the large quantity of entitlements it is initially allocated.

Egalitarian Criterion

In the Egalitarian case, the global supply of entitlements is distributed according to projected 2000 population in each region. For some LDCs, the initial stock of entitlements substantially exceeds year 2000 emissions. The resulting total trades are much greater (by at least a factor of five) than under the Sovereignty or Rawlsian criteria (see table 3.3), and large monetary transfers from industrialized nations to these LDCs occur.

The net welfare changes of this allocation before trading are presented in table 3.5. The result for the United States is an astounding $144 billion loss (per year!), with abatement costs of $161 billion. The net welfare effects for Western Europe and the C.I.S. are also strongly negative. Trading significantly reduces the negative impacts, though remain in the sizable $20 billion range for both the United States and C.I.S. These large negative net benefits for the industrialized countries even with trading implies the Egalitarian rule is likely to be unacceptable to some potential treaty signatories. It also reinforces the idea that if greenhouse gas mitigation produces positive net global benefits, sustainable permit distributions are those that allow winners to compensate losers, and that net gains even after compensation should be positive.

Discussion of a greenhouse protocol at the international level has focused on several questions, including the distribution of abatement within the international community. Among developing countries, there is a strongly held belief that the world's industrialized nations should bear a greater share of responsibility for curbing greenhouse gas emissions due to relatively high per capita energy usage, now and in the past, as well as higher per capita incomes. Hence, the idea of distributing entitlements on the basis of each nation's current population is attractive to many representatives of these less-developed countries. This type of distribution is well understood to foster transfers from the industrialized to developing countries, and it allows for future growth in greenhouse gas emissions from the latter. Our empirical analysis, however, has uncovered a potential problem that is not apparent when this criterion is presented in the abstract. A distribution of entitlements on the basis of population does increase monetary transfers to developing countries, but the transfers are so large that they are likely to be considered unsustainable by industrialized nations, especially in light of the negative net benefits to them that ensue.

INTERPRETATION OF THE RESULTS

We have obtained several important findings. First, gains from permit trading are likely to be substantial. Abatement cost savings are on the order of 25% for the Sovereignty criterion for example. While there is sizable uncertainty in the data used, the results represent relative improvements and are therefore less susceptible to variations in the data than are absolute levels of cost savings. Also, permit trading will result in transfers in the tens of billions of dollars per year to developing countries.

A definitive finding is that trading substantially erodes the differences in real world implications of some equity criteria. In a comparison of the first two criteria we examined (and several others we do not present for lack of space), there is a striking uniformity in the final outcomes of individual country abatement levels. This is due to the uniqueness of the cost-effectiveness equilibrium. As predicted by the Coase Theorem, no matter how entitlements are assigned, there is a single, least-cost mix of abatement levels between countries. Put another way, this means that post-trading abatement costs will always be the same for any given cost-effectiveness target no matter what the initial allocation of entitlements. Since these abatement costs will be a major proportion of the net costs (including permit transactions), this feature will significantly reduce the variance of net benefits between nations. Only those countries engaging in large permit transactions will have noticeably varying net welfare changes.

The Egalitarian entitlement distribution, however, causes large transfers and results in such large negative net welfare impacts for industrialized nations that the criterion is likely to be "unsustainable," i.e., unacceptable to major parties to a greenhouse protocol. All of this has very important policy implications. It, in effect, narrows the distinct number of equity criteria that may need to be examined, and hence could speed the negotiation process. First, some criteria may be widely unacceptable and will not become the subject of negotiations. Second, among sustainable equity criteria, two countries may differ in their first choice of equity principles to apply to permit assignments, but if the two principles have the same welfare implications, a deadlock can be avoided.

We emphasize that these results do *not* mean that initial permit assignments do not matter or that equity is not an actionable policy criterion. In our empirical analyses, the outcomes for some countries likely to engage in permit trading on a large scale, such as the United States and China, were significantly different across criteria and reference bases. Moreover, relatively high initial permit assignments may give some countries a greater sense of security about this policy instrument, thereby making their participation in an international agreement more likely. What the results do mean are that tradable entitlements have some inherent limitations, if redistribution is a major policy objective. For one thing, no matter how large a revenue gain is forthcoming from the sale of a sizable allocation of entitlements, there is a partially offsetting cost incurred in undertaking the abatement necessary to make the sale legal (moreover, this offset level is constant over all permit assignments).

There are several other important findings. None of the eight countries/regions that we examined would appear to be a net loser in the case of sustainable allocations. In fact, Brazil and Indonesia receive permit revenues in excess of their abatement costs. Even if we have grossly overestimated the benefits for these countries, there is no question that their welfare will be improved as a result of global warming policies like those we examined.

Of course, some of our empirical results might change significantly if we were to have explicitly addressed some other critical issues, such as the free-rider problem. We plan to investigate considerations such as this in future work.[10]

We have performed an analysis of equity aspects of a tradable entitlements approach to global warming policy. We first presented ten distinct international equity criteria and then translated each into an operational rule for the assignment of marketable entitlements . Our empirical analysis involved the application of a nonlinear programming model to analyze the costs and benefits before and after permit trading for three of the criteria.

We found that net benefits are positive for a 20% reduction of CO_2 emissions and on the order of $20 billion for the eight countries/regions and for the three equity criteria we examined. Trading helps arrive at a much more efficient outcome. Trading also involves transfers of tens of billions of dollars towards developing and transitional economies, improving the sustainability of any given assignment emanating from the Egalitarian and Rawlsian equity criteria. Moreover, net benefits of the post-trading outcome are positive for all countries under these allocation criteria. However, such a result does not take place for all criteria. We showed that the outcome of an Egalitarian criterion (associated with a per capita reference base) would lead to an outcome likely to be unacceptable to industrialized nations.

Another important finding is that trading reduces national/regional disparities in the net welfare impacts of a greenhouse protocol among different entitlement assignments. For many equity criteria, the post-trading outcomes are quite similar. The reason is the uniqueness of any efficient equilibrium. Final abatement levels and abatement costs are the same regardless of the initial permit assignment, with only the level of transfers being different. This means that, although some equity criteria would appear to have significant philosophical and political differences, their implications for the welfare of nations may be very similar. This fact should facilitate negotiations by minimizing tensions over the initial assignment of entitlements for CO_2 emissions.

Acknowledgments: This paper represents an extension of a chapter from a UNCTAD *study cited in the references of Barrett et al. (1992).*

The research assistance of Amit Mor and Michelle Leitzinger in earlier stages of research is gratefully acknowledged. We also wish to thank Kjell Roland and Ronaldo Serôa da Motta, and other participants at the UNCTAD Expert Workshop on Tradeable Carbon Emission Entitlements for their helpful comments.

NOTES

1. In this paper the term "equity" refers to the fairness of the distribution of costs and benefits across countries, i.e., "international equity." This differs from dynamic, or intergenerational, equity, which is another major consideration in global warming policy. It is our contention that these two types of equity can be analyzed separately. Some aspects of the dynamics of equity will be analyzed below.

2. Efficiency, in the form of cost-effectiveness, may be affected if countries with the very lowest control costs do not participate.

3. Recent work explicitly dealing with equity includes: d'Arge (1989), Chapman and Drennen (1990), Rose (1990), Bergesen (1991), Burtraw and Toman (1991), Grubb and Sebenius (1991), Solomon and Ahuja (1991), Young (1991), and Rose (1992).

4. Reference bases have the desirable properties of focal points, a term Schelling (1960) coined to represent a key, facilitating feature of negotiation processes. Toman and Burtraw (1991) suggest that "negotiators will seek out rules of thumb," but also note that because of strategic considerations, it is unlikely that "simple rules of thumb alone can successfully guide the negotiation process." They go on to state: "Thus strategic and procedural aspects of negotiation can be viewed as essential to the evolution of a commonly shared standard of equity that must accompany an international agreement" (p. 12). Morrisette and Plantinga (1991) have likewise stated: "Success, however, will depend on how the different stakes of nations can be dealt with in the negotiation process in an equitable manner" (p. 6).

We will give primacy to equity principles in the presentation to follow. If global warming were an uncomplex issue that could be settled in a short time, we would endorse the more pragmatic "rule of thumb" approach. Since the issue is complex, negotiations likely to take years, and to go through several stages, it is imperative that they have a solid foundation. It is our contention that countries of the world are more likely to rally around higher ideals under such circumstances and that these equity principles need to be thoroughly articulated and their full implications understood before a sound agreement can be reached.

5. Note that there are several ways to conceive of abatement costs. As will be discussed below, we prefer general equilibrium effects (interactive impacts on the entire economy), as opposed to partial equilibrium measures (direct costs). In addition, we confine our attention to incremental costs, those over and above the expenditures already being made to explicitly abate CO_2 or that result in abatement in the course of meeting another objective. Note also that benefits should include consumer surplus in a general equilibrium context.

6. Note that our equity criteria are somewhat ethnocentric, i.e., have a Western bias. Criteria based on percepts of Middle-Eastern and Eastern religions should also be considered given the global scale of the issue (see, e.g., d'Arge 1989). Also, we have not considered all possible equity criteria.

7. In addition, there are some equity criteria that are only relevant in the context of historical emissions and very explicitly so. A good example is Young's (1990) "status quo" or "adverse possession" criterion, which stipulates that the current rate of GHG emissions constitutes a "right" legitimized by usage and custom. The latter has been

proposed by Fujii (1990) in terms of every person having an equal emissions quota regardless of his/her location or *generation*.

8. Investments in environmental quality, however, need not necessarily be incompatible with investment in economic growth. In the global warming context, this view has even been espoused by those not typically associated with the sustainable development school (e.g., Brundtland Report 1987; Pearce 1989).

9. A 20% reduction in baseline emissions has been estimated as necessary to avoid a doubling of CO_2 in the atmosphere by the middle of the twenty-first century (even taking into account atmospheric removal rates). Most serious policy pronouncements have not been so rigid as to require a 20% reduction across the board; most policymakers are cognizant of the status of LDCs and simply require some capping of emissions or allowing for modest growth to avoid stifling development. This dichotomy is actually more consistent with vertical equity or the Rawlsian principle. Still, we choose to use the stylized version of the actual policy pronouncement in order to simplify the analysis and to begin with the depiction of the pure Sovereignty case.

10. Note, for example, we have performed an empirical examination of the cumulative reference base versions of the Sovereignty and Rawlsian criteria. Interestingly, we found them to yield outcomes very similar to those reported above (e.g., differences in permit transactions and net welfare changes differed by less than $1.0 billion for each country between the current and cumulative reference base Rawlsian allocations).

REFERENCES

Agarwal, A. and S. Narain. 1991. *Global Warming in an Unequal World.* New Delhi: Centre for Science and Environment.

Barrett, S., M. Grubb, K. Roland, A. Rose, R. Sandor, and T. Tietenberg. 1992. *Combating Global Warming: A Global System of Tradeable Carbon Emission Entitlements.* Geneva, Switzerland: UNCTAD.

Bergesen, H. 1991. "A Legitimate Social Order in a 'Greenhouse' World: Some Basic Requirements." *International Challenges* 11:21–30.

(Brundtland Report). World Commission on Environment and Development. 1987. *Our Common Future.* New York: Oxford University Press.

Burtraw, D. and M. Toman. 1991. "Equity and International Agreements for CO_2 Containment." Discussion Paper ENR 91–07. Washington, D.C.: Resources for the Future.

Chandler, W., ed. 1990. *Carbon Emissions Control Strategies.* Washington, D.C.: World Wildlife Fund and The Conservation Foundation.

Chapman, D. and T. Drennen. 1990. "Economic Dimensions of CO_2 Treaty Proposals." *Contemporary Policy Issues* 8:16–28.

Coase, R. 1960. "The Problem of Social Cost." *Journal of Law and Economics* 3:1–44.

d'Arge, R. 1989. "Ethical and Economic Systems for Managing the Global Commons." In D. Botkin et al., eds. *Changing the World Environment.* New York: Academic Press.

Energy Information Administration. 1988. *International Energy Annual.* Washington, D.C.

Epstein, J. and R. Gupta. 1991. *Controlling the Greenhouse Effect: Five Global Regimes Compared.* Washington, D.C.: Brookings Institution.

Fujii, Y. 1990. "An Assessment of the Responsibility for the Increase in the CO_2 Concentrations and Inter-Generational Carbon Accounts." IIASA Working Paper WP-05-55.

Grubb, M. and J. Sebenius. 1991. "Participation, Allocation, and Adaptability in International Tradeable Emission Permit Systems for Greenhouse Gas Control." Paper prepared for OECD Workshop on Tradeable Greenhouse Gas Permits, Paris, France.

Hahn, R. and G. Hester. 1989. "Marketable Permits: Lessons for Theory and Practice." *Ecology Law Quarterly* 16:361–406.

Kosobud, R. and T. Daly. 1984. "Global Conflict or Cooperation Over the CO_2 Climate Impact." *Kyklos* 37:638–659.

Manne, A. and R. Richels. 1991. "Global CO_2 Emission Reductions: The Impacts of Rising Energy Costs." *Energy Journal* 12:87–107.

Morrisette, P. and A. Plantinga. 1991. "The Global Warming Issue: Viewpoints of Different Countries." *Resources* 103:2–6. Washington, D.C.: Resources for the Future.

Nordhaus, W. 1993. "Rolling the DICE: The Optimal Transition Path for Controlling Greenhouse Gases." *Resource and Energy Economics* 15:27–50.

Pearce, D. 1989. "Sustainable Futures: Some Economic Issues." In D. Botkin et al., eds., *Changing the World Environment.* New York: Academic Press.

Rawls, J. 1971. *A Theory of Justice.* Cambridge, Mass.: Harvard University Press.

Rose, A. 1990. "Reducing Conflict in Global Warming Policy: Equity as a Unifying Principle." *Energy Policy* 18:927–935.

—— 1992. "Equity Considerations of Tradeable Carbon Entitlements." In S. Barrett et al., *Tradeable Carbon Emission Entitlements.* Geneva: UNCTAD.

Rose, A. and B. Stevens. 1993a. "The Efficiency and Equity of Marketable Permits for CO_2 Emissions." *Resource and Energy Economics* 15:117–46.

—— 1993b. "Equity Aspects of the Marketable Permits Approach to Global Warming Policy." Paper presented at the Association of Environmental Resource Economists Session of the Southern Economics Association Meetings in New Orleans, La.

Rose, A., B. Stevens, and G. Davis. 1988. *Natural Resource Policy and Income Distribution.* Baltimore: Johns Hopkins University Press.

Schelling, T. 1991. "Economic Responses to Global Warming: Prospects for Cooperative Approaches." In R. Dornbusch and J. Poterba, eds., *Global Warming: Economic Policy Responses.* Cambridge, Mass.: MIT Press.

Smith, K. et al. 1991. "Indices for a Greenhouse Gas Controlling Regime that Incorporates both Efficiency and Equity Goals." Washington, D.C.: World Bank Environment Department Divisional Working Paper, No. 1991-92.

Solomon, B. and D. Ahuja. 1991. "An Equitable Approach to International Reductions of Greenhouse Gas Emissions." In *Global Climate Change* (forthcoming).

Tietenberg, T. 1985. *Emissions Trading: An Exercise in Reforming Pollution Policy.* Washington, D.C.: Resources for the Future.

Toman, M. and D. Burtraw. 1991. "Resolving Equity Issues: Greenhouse Gas Negotiations." *Resources* 103:10–13, Washington, D.C.: Resources for the Future.

Young, H. 1991. "Sharing the Burden of Global Warming." Equity and Global Climate Change Project, School of Public Affairs, College Park, Maryland: University of Maryland.

FOUR

Back-of-the-Envelope Estimates of Environmental Damage Costs in Mexico

Sergio Margulis

For developing countries budget constraints help set the agenda on mitigating environmental damage, one of the indelible marks of our era. Political considerations often dictate the measures taken. There are no firm analytical formulae to help even environment-conscious policy makers to rank needs and remedies.

A developing country like Mexico—the focus of this paper—cannot afford an in-depth study of every environmental issue. Policy makers need to be provided with rough, "back-of-the-envelope" estimates of the economic costs of various environmental problems. This will allow them to rank the issues—and to act.

In this paper, I applied existing method to estimate the costs stemming from different environmental problems in Mexico. Although the examples are Mexican, the method can be relevant in other developing countries as well. The paper shows how creative use of U.S. and other data can help provide simple estimates of likely costs of soil erosion, air pollution, mining of underground waters, and estimates of the health effects of water and solid waste pollution, lack of sanitation, and ingestion of food contaminated by polluted irrigation. The assumptions in most calculations are conservative.

Table 4.1 summarizes the major problems analyzed, their potential effects, the costs involved, and a summary of the equations and calculations. The second section describes the method and its limitations. Finally, the last section provides details on the cost estimates. (Some environmental

TABLE 4.1
Summary of Major Environmental Costs in Mexico

Problems	Potential Effects production/health	Method/formula	Annual Costs (US$ billions)	Built-in Assumptions
Soil erosion	Loss of agricultural output	Average productivity loss × output (soybeans, maize, sorghum, and wheat) + increased fertilizers	1.20	Application of projected tendency losses in U.S. to perpetuity + 20% for fertilizers.
Health effects from air pollution (Mexico City only)	Particulates: Morbidity (respiratory restricted activity days-RRAD)	ARRAD = 0.0114 × baseline RRAD × (conc. fine particulates-legislation standard)	0.36	Day Lost = US$32. Conc. FP = 119 $\mu g/m^3$. FPStandard = 50$\mu g/m^3$. Baseline RRAD = 3.
	Particulates: Mortality (MR)	ΔMR = 1.69/million × concent. suspended particles	0.48	Conc. SP = 298$\mu g/m^3$. 1 Statistical life = US$75,000.
	Ozone: Morbidity	ΔRRAD = baseline × adult population × exp [(6.88 × Δ ozone) −1]	0.10	50% productivity loss other assumptions as above.
	Lead: Children's treatment for high blood lead levels (BLL)	Population affected × average estimated treatment costs	0.06	Screening if > 25$\mu g/dl$. EDTA test if > 35$\mu g/dl$. 1% require chelation. Hospital cost = 1/15 of U.S. cost.
	Lead: Children's compensatory education	Population affected × education costs	0.02	20% of those > 40$\mu g/dl$. Average education expenditure per child
	Lead: Hypertension in adults	Population affected × average estimated treatment costs	0.01	Δ1$\mu g/m^3$ lead in air = Δ3$\mu g/dl$ in blood. Δ1%BLL = Δ0.8% prob. of hypertension. Lead conc. air = 1.4 $\mu g/m^3$. Average BLL 15$\mu g/dl$.

Excess use of underground waters due to poor pricing (not social costs)	Lead: Myocardial infarctions	As above	0.04	60% occur in hypertense. Costs = 1/2 as in U.S.
	Subsidies to supply water to Mexico City	(Marg.cost-charge) × consumption	1.00	Average price P$2900. Marginal Cost P$4500. Average consumption = 1.8 billion m³.
	Subsidies to irrigation	As above	0.16	Implicit subsidy of US$82/ha/year to 2 million ha.
Diarrheal diseases from water and solid waste pollution; lack of sanitation and foodstuff poisoning	Morbidity	Incidence × average treatment costs	0.03	Children and elderly require treatment, 50% ORT, 20% lab analysis. Adults require treatment and 20% ORT.
	Mortality: Scenario 1-current situation	No. of lives × life expectancy × value	3.60	1 Statistical life = US$75,000.
	Mortality: Scenario 2 -with oral rehydrat. therapy (ORT)	Incidence × average treatment costs	0.00 (US$450,000)	Treatment = US$3, ORT = US$1 + 12 administration.

NOTE: In all cases, the rate of discount is 5%.

damage issues, such as loss of biodiversity, were too complex to permit quantification).

The estimates presented here are conservative estimates of the likely environmental costs of the problems analyzed. Policy recommendations based on these estimates have to be made with extreme caution. A much more detailed analysis of the data provided, as well as of the applicability of the U.S. experience to the Mexican conditions, would have to be made. From the calculations, we draw the following conclusions.

(1) Where human lives are at risk, the costs of environmental problems rise sharply, even attributing the most conservative values to them.

(2) Water- and solid-waste related health problems are significant only if one assumes current diarrheal disease mortality rates, without reference to the potential benefits of oral rehydration therapy (ORT). Guaranteeing water supply, sewage supply, water treatment, and solid and toxic waste disposal are all vital. But given the potential benefits of ORT, the government should urgently promote campaigns to advertise ORT, its proper administration, and its benefits, and attempt to guarantee access of all those at risk to serum ingredients or laboratory compounds.

(3) If diarrheal infant mortality were controlled or significantly reduced, air pollution in Mexico City would be the country's major environmental problem. This would reflect both the large urban population and the incredibly high pollution level.

(4) Particulate matter is Mexico's most damaging pollutant, more dangerous than ozone and lead. Lead should soon cease to be a major health hazard—although the issue of use of leaded and unleaded gasoline in the Mexico City metropolitan area (MCMA), their prices and effects on the use of catalytic converters are still critical issues for government.

(5) Water supply to both Mexico City and to irrigation in agriculture are rarely mentioned as major Mexican environmental problems. But underpricing water has led to overuse. We calculated only the subsidies implicit in the charging systems. Massive pumping underground waters is also causing the terrain to sink, threatening infrastructure. Although the effects of subsidence in Mexico City were not calculated, the cost estimates here suggest that adjustment of pricing is urgent.

(6) Soil erosion is often considered the major environmental problem in Mexico and some Central American countries. The calculations suggest that after water pollution and related problems this could well be the case. We only considered on-farm costs (impaired crop yields and compensatory use of fertilizers), but off-farm costs (siltation of dams, for example) must

eventually be taken into account. Estimation based on the application of U.S. parameters to Mexican soil data may be particularly invalid because the effects of soil erosion are very site specific. Such issues deserve much further analysis.

METHOD AND LIMITATIONS

Ranking Environmental Problems

No unambiguous criterion ranks one environmental problem over another— for instance, making urban water pollution more critical than air pollution, loss of biodiversity, or soil erosion. The issue is complicated by the different nature and effects of the problems. One criterion would be to consider more severe the problem that implies the highest costs—but this would not necessarily indicate which problem must be addressed first. Given the budgetary constraint, even though the costs of water pollution may be higher than those caused by air pollution, it may be more cost effective to control air pollution first, if the control costs are lower.

On a practical level, the above limitation may not be so serious. There is a significant lack of information on the extent of physical problems, on the damages, and on the costs of control. Thus, it would be too grand a goal to make a full benefit/cost analysis of every major environmental problem in a country such as Mexico. This is probably true in most nations. Making rough estimates of damages may be a realistic, less ambitious way to indicate to environmental authorities the relative severity of national environmental problems. This is a necessary first step to defining priorities. The exercise here demonstrates to policymakers that benefits can be estimated with currently available information, so that when full cost-benefit analyses are performed, they already have a place to start, i.e., a very practical (back-of-the-envelope) guide for first cut benefit estimation.

An important additional benefit derives from the quantification of the environmental costs of different problems. Under the laws of most countries, and under the Bank's lending conditionalities, environmental impact assessments (EIA) are now required for different types of investment projects. But economic decisions on the viability of projects are usually independent of EIA since a number of environmental costs are direct costs, there is clear scope for estimates of such costs to be made based on EIA and then incorporated in the economic evaluation of projects. This would allow for

EIA to become a more integral part of project preparation. The economic evaluation would give a more rational ranking of alternatives.

The theoretical literature has recognized that ranking individual projects versus composite of projects can lead to different results, depending on the orientation of a general or partial equilibrium comparison: outcomes can be biased under the second approach. For instance, "in the problem of species preservation, conventional benefit studies demonstrate the nontrivial benefits for each of a limited number of representative species; yet there are hundreds of thousands of species in danger of extinction. Conventional procedures surely overlook the scarce productive capacity and substitutions that it imposes, overstating net benefits" (Hoehn and Randall 1989). In our analyses, the effects of the change in people's willingness to pay and the implicit costs associated with activities that may have interactive effects (e.g., air and water pollution) may be present. Improving our estimates would require estimating changes in individual's surpluses by imposing price changes sequentially: given the back-of-the-envelope nature of the exercise, this is not done here.

Method

Three basic steps help estimate the costs associated with environmental degradation. The first is to measure the level of environmental quality (or degradation). The second is to relate such level of quality to damages—health, productivity, materials. This depends on knowledge of the "dose-response" function, the relationship that associates the incidence of health problems (or other effects) to different levels of environmental quality.[1] The last step then assigns monetary values to the predicted incidence of health problems (or loss of agricultural production, or damage to materials). In the case of the health effects, the monetization approach should determine values according to individual preferences (willingness to pay). As discussed below, this requires data not readily available in Mexico. An alternative, which is adopted here, is to base the estimates on opportunity costs—hospital treatment costs of illness, and the productivity (or human-capital) technique for the value of premature loss of life.

I do not discuss here the pros and cons of assigning monetary values to physical or to health effects from environmental degradation. There is a fairly vast literature on this issue. What is missing are applications of theory, particularly in the context of developing countries. The existing applications have been made almost exclusively for the United States and some European countries. Some methodologies used in the U.S. studies are not readily applicable elsewhere, because of geographic and socioeconomic differences. Even so, in some situations, simple first order estimates of the damage costs can be made by "direct" application of the U.S. experience; that procedure is not new here.

Limitations

This study is limited in several respects. As indicated, dose-response curves are not necessarily applicable to all populations and all regions. In addition, (1) quantification methodologies are still subject to much debate; (2) not all major problems have been considered in this study, and for those problems analyzed, not all the effects have been estimated and a great deal of uncertainty is involved; and (3) in the case of Mexico, there is a paucity of information on parameters. We briefly discuss each of these major limitations.

(1) Estimating the economic effect of environmental improvement (or degradation) has been controversial. In some environmental problems, society incurs in "direct" costs—material damage, loss of agricultural production, and so on. It is necessary to incorporate these costs into decisions on investment projects. The costs associated to the health effects of pollution involve subjective pain, which cannot be readily quantified, as well as direct costs (hospital and treatment cost, loss of productivity). "Much research has been devoted to the area and several health benefit studies on the acute effects and the mortality effects [of air pollution] are now available" (Krupnick and Alicbusan 1990).

Cost studies on the mortality effects of environmental degradation involve estimating the value of life, and there are basically two approaches to do that, neither completely satisfactory. One measures the willingness to pay by an individual for a reduction in his/her probability of dying. The second is the human capital approach, which values an individual's life according to the net present value of his/her earnings. While the first approach is theoretically more adequate, the second requires substantially less data. It can be shown that the human capital approach is a lower bound estimate of an individual's willingness to pay.[2]

(2) Among the major environmental problems in Mexico not included in the analyses are loss of biodiversity and coastal/marine degradation. The main reason is lack of knowledge on the effects of loss of biodiversity (loss of known and unknown pharmaceutical products, soil erosion and so on)

and the extent of coastal and marine pollution. Economic valuations would involve many subjective considerations and great uncertainty. The information available is extremely limited, even for developed countries.

As to uncertainties, "they range from questions about the existence of an effect, to statistical uncertainties about the values of coefficients, to issues about what dollar values should be assigned to various benefit categories" (NERA 1990). "Currently, the usual technique for dealing with uncertainty is sensitivity testing" (Bojö et al. 1990). We think that addressing uncertainties more rigorously would be beyond the purpose here. Most references present sensitivity analyses for major parameters and assumptions. We make a few sensitivity exercises for the discount rate, and concentrate our estimates essentially on mean expected values of the various parameters.

(3) Because it is not possible to make an assessment of environmental costs without information on the levels of environmental degradation, the estimates here are restricted to those problems where data are known or reasonably estimated. As just mentioned, coastal management and deforestation—major environmental problems in Mexico—are not included. And because the effects are largely the same, the environmental costs of water pollution and of solid and toxic waste disposal are not analyzed individually, but together.

I describe in some detail the steps taken in applying the U.S. methodology to the Mexican data. Because data are limited, a few assumptions and simplifications had to be made, and they are explicitly mentioned. We are convinced that the exercise provides a guide for prioritization and could be replicated elsewhere.

Cost Estimates of Major Problems

Damage and Control Costs

In estimating the benefits of improving the level of environmental quality, it is important to distinguish between damage and control costs. In the case of pollution, control costs are located at the source (typically a filter); in the case of erosion, they are the costs of soil conservation practices. Damage includes both mitigation (preventive) costs and costs from the impacts remaining after mitigation and control (typically, the costs from pollution after filters have been installed and medication has been used to treat pollution-related diseases; in the case of erosion, the yield losses after both soil conservation measures have been implemented and compensatory fertilizers have been applied). As discussed previously, we concentrate on damage costs in this exercise.

The estimation of such costs, however, presents complications. For instance, assuming that asthma is the only health effect from air pollution, how to estimate the benefits associated with the reduction of pollution resulting from abatement (or the damage from pollution)? The damage should be given by the opportunity cost to the affected population to avoid and protect itself from pollution. This includes the preventive and defensive measures taken by pollutees, as well as the remaining costs after these measures have been taken—such as work loss days and loss of productivity, and the indirect costs such as suffering and pain. A typical defensive measure in the case of asthma is medication, which costs around US$5 per case, while the work loss day and loss of productivity would run around US$30 per day in Mexico. While suffering and pain may account for a large portion of the damage costs, they are not estimated in this exercise.[3]

Soil Erosion

Soil degradation and its negative impact on water retention, run-off, and aquifer recharge is one of the most serious environmental problems confronting Mexico. A 1988 Bank study stated that 66% of the national area (112.8 million hectares) had moderate erosion and 13% (22.4 million hectares) severe erosion. Comparisons with limited but more detailed aerial photographic coverage indicate that the situation may well be even worse, with some 42% of land totally or severely eroded. At "moderate" levels (in Mexico), losses may be as much as 10 tons of soil per hectare per year; at "severe" levels, such losses are from 10 to 15 tons.

On-farm erosion costs are impaired crop yields, land removed from crop production or used in less productive enterprises, and additional production costs, notably fertilizers to replace lost nutrients. Non-farm losses to erosion are siltation of waterways, dams, and other collection sites. No good evidence exists on these effects in Mexico. Estimates of non-farm costs from research done in other countries are subject to uncertainty because of the local specific interactions between erosion and land use. There is disagreement on the magnitudes of these costs relative to on-farm costs. *The estimates here of the total costs of erosion are based exclusively on reduced yields, thus they are clear underestimates.*

In order to estimate the change in yield in the United States due to erosion, a regression of yield trend values on annual erosion rates was made (Crosson and Stout 1983), using county level data. For the U.S. yield losses to erosion estimated this way range from 1% to 18% of maize yield, with an average loss of 4%; from 2% to 22% of soybean yields, with an average of 4%; and 1% of wheat.[4] These crops represent roughly 65% of the area of annual agricultural crops in Mexico.

Application to the Mexican case was made by estimating the 1965–85 Mexican yield trends and then applying the average U.S. erosion effects above;[5] the resulting estimated yields (with and without erosion) were then compared.[6] The results were the following: losses in wheat on the order of 1% of the value of 1990 output, or US$4.6 million at international prices; average losses to maize 2.9%, or US$38 million, and 0.4% to soybean, or US$0.5 million in 1990. Sorghum, beans, and cotton would be the other annual crops where erosion is intense (the area occupied by these crops is roughly 25% of the total agricultural area), but no studies are available relating erosion rates to yield losses. Only sorghum has shown a decrease in productivity in the last five years; for this crop we assumed that the effects of erosion on yields are the same as for wheat—only 1%—which lead to an estimated loss of US$6 million in 1990.

Total annual estimated losses to erosion were US$50 million. "However, erosion-induced productivity losses are not confined to a terminal year, but accumulate over much or all of the intervening period. Consequently, knowledge of the effect of erosion on costs in a terminal year is incomplete. The way to compensate (for these deficiencies) is to calculate the present value of the annual productivity loss" (Crosson and Stout 1983).

To illustrate this aspect, suppose we have a crop yield of 10 tons/ha without erosion, and that with erosion there will be a yield loss of 1 ton/ha. This means that yield in year 2 will be 9 ton/ha. If, again, on year 3 no preventive measures are taken, productivity will further decline to 8 ton/ha. This could be repeated for 10 years, when productivity would eventually drop to zero. Whichever the decision on year 2, the productivity loss of 1 ton/ha in the first year is perpetual, assuming it is irreversible. Therefore, irrespective of actions taken on subsequent years, the loss per hectare due to erosion on the first year alone is the discounted value of 1 ton of the crop to perpetuity.

The procedure above assumes that losses to erosion are irreversible. Applying the procedure using a 5% value for the discount rate would give an estimated net present value of yield losses caused by one year of erosion in Mexico of roughly US$1 billion.[7] Such cost, however, does not include the increased application of fertilizers to compensate for the loss of nutrients caused by erosion. Such "compensatory" use of fertilizers represents a mitigation cost of the environmental problem (equivalent to the medication costs in the case of pollution previously discussed). For the United States, it has been estimated that such compensatory use of fertilizers represents 20% of the costs of yield losses (Alt et al. 1989). Application to the Mexican case would lead to *an estimated net present value of the costs due to one year of erosion in Mexico of US$1.2 billion.*

Air Pollution in MCMA

Several studies have analyzed air pollution health effects on humans. The costs of such health effects are of three types: medical expenses (prevention and treatment), lost wages, and individual disutility (discomfort, suffering and the opportunity cost of time). Monetary estimates of the first two types of costs are fairly straightforward and are the only costs estimated here. While information on willingness to pay or willingness to accept changes in health status could identify the third type of costs, such data are beyond the scope of this exercise. For the United States, it has been estimated that the ratio between willingness to pay and the costs of illness (in medical expenses and lost wages) is roughly two (Chestnut and Rowe 1988). Additionally, damage costs to material and loss of (agricultural) productivity are not considered here due to lack of information.[8] The numbers presented here underestimate the total costs of air pollution.

Exposure to different air pollutants causes different health effects. This means that the dose-response curves differ between pollutants and that analyses must be made for each pollutant. Moreover, the combined effects of two or more pollutants are usually greater than the "sum" of their contributions. This synergistic effect is complicated and not well understood, mainly because so many factors of atmosphere's chemistry are involved. Such effects are not considered here, again giving conservative estimates.

The three basic procedures in quantifying the health effects of a pollutant are: (1) to determine the ambient concentrations; (2) given the concentration levels and the population age distribution, to use a specified dose-response curve to determine the (incremental)[9] incidence of diseases in the population; and (3) based on the costs associated with each disease (treatment, lost wages or life), to determine the overall costs.

One brief qualification—Dose-response curves. Relations between concentration of pollutants and effects on health are based on both laboratory experiments and epidemiological studies. One interesting aspect is the possibility of threshold levels below which some health effects cease to occur; this would directly affect the benefits (or costs) associated with a change in pollution. There is insufficient evidence for the pollutants analyzed here, except for lead. Thus, the procedure adopted was to consider the legislation standard as the level of air quality associated to "no" deleterious health effects, and zero concentration level in the case of lead.

In MCMA the major health impacts originate from suspended particulate matter (SPM), ozone, and lead. The effects of carbon monoxide and sulphur dioxide are not analyzed here. Oxides of nitrogen and hydrocarbons are precursors in the formation of ozone, so their effects are "captured" in the analysis of the latter.

Suspended Particulate Matter

Morbidity. The major health effects from exposure to particulates are restricted activity and increase in overall mortality rates. Restricted activity means acute morbidity that, in the case of particulates, can be measured in terms of restricted activity days (RAD days), when a respondent was forced to alter his/her normal activity); work loss days (WLD), visits to emergency rooms, minor respiratory disease, and children's chronic cough.

The most relevant (highest cost) morbidity effect from suspended particles relates to respiratory related restricted activity days (RRAD). The dose-response equation used is the following (based in Ostro 1987, and Chestnut and Rowe 1988): [10]

$$(\Delta\text{RRAD})/person/year = 0.0114 \times baseline \text{ RRAD} \times (\Delta \text{ Annual FP}),[11] \quad (1)$$

where (Δ RRAD) is change in respiratory related restricted activity days, baseline RRAD is the average current level of restricted activity days due to respiratory diseases per person per year, and (Δ Annual FP) stands for a change in annual average arithmetic mean concentration of fine particulates;[12] fine particulates are the smaller suspended particles that penetrate deeper into the respiratory tract and cause harm, usually between 30 and 65% (SdeS 1991; Chestnut and Rowe 1988; Kleinman et al. 1989).

The two parameters needed to apply equation (1) to the Mexican conditions are baseline RRAD, which is 3 (SdeS 1991; and personal information), and the change in the annual concentration of FP, which is the difference between the current average levels of FP (119 μg/m^3) and the legislation standard (50 μg/m^3). Substitution of these values in equation (1) leads to a change in RRAD of 2.4. The population in the metropolitan area of Mexico City is not precisely known. We used the round estimate of 17 million in 1990, of which 55% were adults (SdeS 1988a, b). In estimating the monetary value of saving 2.4 restricted activity days per person per year, we assumed that half the cases of RRAD implied a work loss day (this is based on the fact that the elasticity of WLD to pollution was roughly half of that for RRAD). The total number of work loss days saved by bringing the current levels of FP pollution to the legislation standards is thus 11.2 million (17 million $\times$ 0.55 $\times$ 0.50 $\times$ 2.4).

We took the average wage in industry in Mexico City—US$4 per hour—to value each day lost. Excluding all suffering and eventual medication to treat minor RRAD, the morbidity benefits associated with the reduction of the current levels of FP pollution to the legislation standard are estimated at US$358 million.

Mortality. Several studies suggest that there is a significant relation between TSP (total suspended particulates) and mortality rates. The regression estimates of changes in mortality rates (Δ MR) as a function of changes in the concentration of TSP (Δ TSP) are all linear (Δ MR = b $\times$ Δ TSP), with coefficient b varying from 2 to 4.46 per 1 million people (Oskaynak 1985 in USAID 1990; Schwartz and Marcus 1986). We used the value 1.69 per 1 million people (NERA 1990; Evans et al. 1984). Based on the current levels of TSP pollution in Mexico City (annual average concentration of 297.8 μg/m^3 in 1990), Δ TSP is 222.8 μg/m^3 (the standard is 75 μg/m^3), and the estimated total number of (statistical) lives saved would be 6,400—equivalent to 3.8 lives per 10,000 people.

Since older people and those who already have respiratory diseases are more likely to die from pollution-related problems, we assumed an expected life of those who die prematurely from TSP of only 12.5 years (NERA 1990). As discussed previously, in order to place a value on human life we should use willingness to pay. This is impossible to be performed in the case of Mexico due to lack of data. An alternative would be to multiply U.S. figures by the two countries GDP ratio. We use the human capital approach which provides a first cut estimate, which is the purpose here.

Based on the hourly wage, the annual salary is US$7,700. Discounting at 5% per year gives a value of US$75,000.[13] Multiplying the 6,400 lives saved by the value of each gives an estimated saving of US$480 million.

The total annual estimated cost related to particulate matter pollution in Mexico City is US$850 million.

Ozone

Ozone is a pollutant formed in the atmosphere in the presence of hydrocarbons, nitrogen oxides, and sunlight. It is the primary component of photochemical smog and is believed to be irritating to the human respiratory system (Chestnut and Rowe 1988). The major health cost from ozone pollution in Mexico City relates to RRAD. Specific effects such as asthma attacks, eye irritation, mild cough, sore throat, headache, and chest discomfort have been examined in the literature. Because the values obtained were too small compared to those for RRAD—and also due to lack of data—such effects were not considered individually here. The relationship between these effects and RRAD is not clear.

The major study relating RRAD and ozone levels is Portney and Mullahy (1986). It provides a number of alternative specifications that have been adopted throughout the literature. The general specification is the following:

$$No.\ \text{RRAD}/adult = exp\ (Az + b(ozone)^c), \tag{2}$$

where Z stands for other independent variables, *ozone* stands for the maximum daily hour concentration of ozone, measured in PPM, a and b are estimated parameters, and c varies from 0.5 to 2. Variables are measured over a period of two weeks, so that the annual estimate is obtained by summing up 26 parcels, corresponding to the 26 two-week periods in the year.

The annual baseline RRAD is 3 in MCMA, or an average of 0.115 every two-week period. Concentration levels were provided by SEDUE (the observed average was 0.14,[14] while the maximum one-hour standard is 0.11 PPM). Using the specification of equation (4.2) assuming $c = 1$, b equals 6.883 so that the expected annual change in the number of RRAD = 6.4 million, or 0.69 per adult, which corresponds to 23% of the present level of RRAD.

In equation (4.2) RRAD is measured in terms of bed-disability days, school loss days, and just restriction of activity that does not fully impair the two above. Since it is not possible to determine the percentage of each of these in the regression analyses, we assume that there is a productivity loss of 50%.[15] Excluding suffering and medication to treat minor RRAD, *the estimated annual benefits associated with reduction of current average levels of ozone pollution to the legislation standard in* MCMA are US$102 million.

Lead

Lead in air has been shown to have a strong correlation with blood lead levels associated with neurological damage in children and with high blood pressure in adults (see figure 4.1). In infants and children, absorption of lead can be via mouthing, air inhalation, and ingestion of food. Almost all the lead deposited in the respiratory tract is absorbed. Because children inhale a proportionally higher daily volume of air per weight measure than adults, they are more susceptible to lead in ambient air. In a population sample of children in Mexico City, the main determinant of blood lead

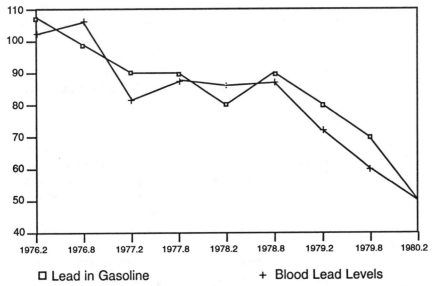

□ Lead in Gasoline   + Blood Lead Levels

Figure 4.1.   Total lead used in gasoline, per six-month period, and blood levels. Source: U.S. NHANES II Survey, after EPA (1985).

level (BLL) was the place of residency, suggesting that lead absorption through air inhalation is the major source of poisoning (SdeS 1991). Nearly 95% of the gasoline in MCMA still contains lead.

The estimates here are almost entirely based on EPA (1985), considered the major publication on the issue, but with some estimates and parameters out of date. Dose-response relations between lead concentration in air and health effects are not straightforward with simple econometric representations: they often involve thresholds and have not been quantified in a rigorous manner.

Children's treatment.   We assumed that all children with BLL above 25 μg/dl require a screening test. Those with BLL above 35 μg/dl have to undertake an EDTA testing, which requires a day in hospital plus follow-up tests and physicians' visits. According to EPA (1985), the most serious cases require an expensive treatment—chelation. The estimated population of children (under 18 years old) in MCMA is 7.65 million; the percentage in each category above (SdeS 1991) is estimated at 29% and 3%, thus 2.25 million screening tests and 230,000 EDTA tests are required. Chelation therapy is only required for approximately 1% of all children (also based on EPA 1985).

Data on hospital, medication, and treatment costs are unavailable in Mexico. We had to adjust the information of these costs in the United States to Mexican conditions. We adjusted the cost estimates presented in EPA (1985) from 1985 US$ to 1990 US$ using CPIs and based on scattered data assumed the hospital costs in the United States to be 15 times higher than in Mexico. Multiplication of incidence by the the respective treatment cost lead to a total estimated costs for children's treatment of US$60 million.[16]

Compensatory education.   Studies show that 20% of children with BLL above 25 μg/dl have lower cognitive development and require supplemental education for an average period of three years. This applies particularly to those children with BLL above 40 μg/dl. There is also evidence suggesting that, "on average, BLL of 30 to 50 μg/dl result in a 4 point decrement in IQ, and that lead levels of 50 to 70 μg/dl would reduce IQ by roughly 5 points" (EPA 1985 *apud* De la Burde and Choate 1975; Rummo et al. 1979). Figures 4.2, 4.3, and 4.4 show, respectively, the relationships between mean cell hemoglobin (MCH) and BLL after being adjusted for a number of significant variables,[17] and the correlations between BLL, (full) IQ, and

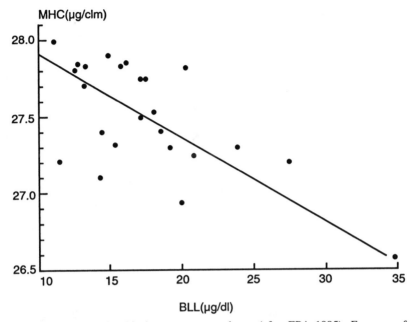

FIGURE 4.2.   Relationship between MCH and BLL (after EPA 1985). For ease of display, each point represents an average of about 100 children with consecutive BLL.

agility, the latter two having been made in Mexico City. All relationships apply only to children.

I made the conservative assumption that a three-year supplemental education would be required for those children with BLL above 40 μg/dl (140,365 children in Mexico City fall in this group). Using the average annual cost of education per child in Mexico City of US$153 produces a total cost in compensatory education of US$21.5 million.[18]

Hypertension in adults.   A relationship that a 1 μg/m³ increase in the concentration of lead in the air will result in an average increase of 2 μg/dl in BLL of adults (and between 3 and 5 μg/dl in children) has been proposed in USAID (1990) *apud* EPA (1986). Based on Mexican data (Rothenberg et al. 1990), we estimated a 3 μg/dl change in BLL. It has also been proposed that a 1% change in BLL leads to a 0.8% change in the probability of blood pressure being greater than 90 mm Hg (above which a person is considered to be hypertense—EPA 1985). This means that the elasticity of

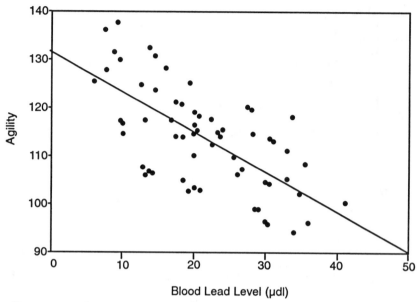

FIGURE 4.3.   Correlation of BLL and (full) IQ in 109 children in Mexico City (after SdeS 1991)

the probability of being hypertense to the lead concentration in air can be determined if the average BLL in the population is known. We made the conservative assumption (in this case by increasing it) that the average male adult population BLL was 15 μg/dl (SdeS 1991 and Rothenberg et al. 1990). The total number of cases of hypertension in MCMA has been estimated at 321,270. Also, because the harmful effects from lead on blood appear not to present threshold levels (that is, even below legislation standards there are negative health effects), we considered the effects of 1.37 μg/m³ (the 1990 average concentration). Computation with all these parameters lead to an estimated reduction of 70,422 cases of hypertension in MCMA.

According to EPA (1985), i) people with hypertension see a physician because of high blood pressure an average of 3.27 times per year: using the estimate of US$20 per visit gives a total annual cost in Mexico City of US$4.6 million; ii) the same population is forced to remain in bed an average of 0.41 days per year: considering the daily wage of US$32 gives a total cost of US$925,000; iii) 30% of the hypertense population needs medication: assuming an annual cost of US$100 (half of that in the United States) gives a total cost of US$2.1 million; finally iv) there was a relation

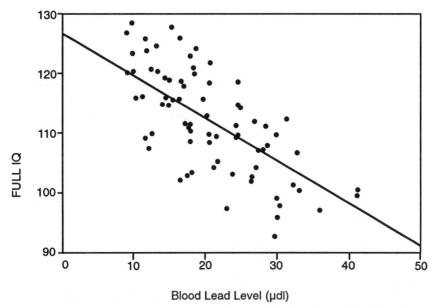

FIGURE 4.4.   Correlation of BLL and agility in 109 children in Mexico City (after SdeS 1990).

between the number of hospital bed-days of 0.058 per person per year due to hypertension alone: using this same statistic to the Mexican case would give 4,084 hospital bed-days per year in Mexico City which, for a daily cost of US$50, gives a total value of US$205,000. Adding up all components, the total estimated costs due to hypertension morbidity in Mexico City is US$7.85 million.

Myocardial infarctions (MI).   The reduction of hypertension is less important than the indirect benefits in the form of reduced cardiovascular disease associated with elevated blood pressure levels. It is estimated that 60% of MI occur in people with blood pressure greater than 90 (based on Framingham Study, McGee el al. 1976 *apud* EPA 1985, plus some simple adjustments and estimates). Since the elimination of lead from air would lead to a 21.9% reduction in the probability of blood pressure being greater than 90, there would be an expected reduction of 13.1% in the number of MI (0.219 x 0.6). According to the *Anuario Estadistico* (SdeS 1988) there were 3,794 MI in Mexico City in 1990. Thus an estimated 498 cases of MI would be eliminated.

The costs associated with treatment of MI are also based on EPA (1985) "converted" to the Mexican case. Costs associated to deaths were estimated as for particulates (human capital approach). The total estimated costs associated to myocardial infarctions is thus US$40 million.

The total annual estimated health costs associated to lead atmospheric pollution in Mexico City are US$125 million.

Adding up the costs associated to the three major air pollutants, the total estimated health costs from atmospheric pollution in MCMA is roughly US$1.1 billion.

Mining of Underground Waters and Pricing [19]

Water Supply to Mexico City Metropolitan Area (MCMA)

Since the middle of the past century, water supply to MCMA has partly relied on pumping underground waters. In the 1960s, in order to reduce the effects of mining of these waters, alternative sources were sought, particularly surface waters outside the valley. The most important source was the waters from the Rio Lerma basin, which is 200 meters below MCMA. Attempts to prohibit the opening of new wells failed, and the city's water supply could not match the massive growth of the city's population. In the 1980s, the formidable amount of 4 m³/sec began to be pumped from the Cutzaman region, 1,000 meters below MCMA. The pumping requirements are 86 GWh (gigawatt-hours) per year; Tecoluca, the next site, will demand 120 GWh.

The current total demand for water in MCMA is 56 m³/sec. About 15% of consumption comes from surface waters, with the remaining 85% from underground waters. The current deficit is 20 to 27 m³/sec, which corresponds to roughly 500 million cubic meters per year. These 500 million m³ correspond approximately to an additional average height of 0.5 meter per year. The average pumping height today is 80 meters.

One of the major potential effects from lowering the water table is the potential subsidence of terrain, which has been eight meters or more in the historical part of town. The costs implied by harm to infrastructure can be formidable. However, the information available on these effects is limited; the costs are not accounted for in this exercise.

The other type of cost is the long-run opportunity cost of water in MCMA. Rather than attempting to estimate these costs, however, a more elementary calculation is necessary, and that is the difference between the marginal social and private costs of supplying water in MCMA. "This is a typical developing country phenomenon where many prices are administered for social and economic purposes" (Pearce 1990). *The estimates here are not social cost estimates.*

In the Valley of Mexico, marginal cost of water supply is MEX$4,500 (all costs on a per cubic meter basis). On a volume basis, 82% of water goes to households for domestic consumption, 10% to industry, and the remaining 8% to agriculture for irrigation. Average prices are MEX$2,850 for households, MEX$4,000 for industry, and zero for agriculture. Sixty% of households pay according to their consumption (that is, have a meter); the remaining 40% pay on average a little more (15–20%; CNA, personal information). The average price is thus MEX$2,900, so that the difference between marginal social cost and price is MEX$1,600/m^3. Multiplying by the annual consumption of 1.8 billion m^3 gives *an annual subsidy of* MEX$2.88 trillion or US$1 billion.

Irrigation Waters

The subsidies to water consumption in MCMA can be compared to those given to farmers for irrigation in agriculture. There are three major potential environmental effects from such subsidies, all applying to the case of groundwaters. The first is when the amount pumped is greater than the average recharge of the aquifer. This leads to an irreversible reduction of reservoirs. Bajio, Central, and North-Central Mexico present this problem. The second is the intrusion of salty waters in the interface of the coastal aquifers, due to a lowering water table. This implies an irreversible lack of sweet water in the coastal aquifer. This may be the case in both North and South Baja California. Finally, excessive irrigation water use can cause waterlogging and salinization of soils: subsidies clearly provide an incentive to such excessive use. This applies to all regions in Mexico. An estimated 100,000 hectares of agricultural land in Mexico are saline due to excessive use of irrigation waters (out of a total of 600,000 hectares of soils affected by some kind of salinity effects).

Information is scarce for most parameters. The irrigated area in Mexico is 6 million hectares; 2 million hectares are irrigated with underground waters. Based on a few standard parameters,[20] the implicit subsidy of US$82/hectares/year multiplied by the 2 million hectares gives a total annual subsidy of US$164 million. These subsidies refer to provision of water; the costs of bringing water from alternative sites are not estimated here.

Health Impacts of Water Pollution and Solid Waste

Gastrointestinal diseases—namely enteric and diarrheal diseases—represent one of the most serious health problems in developing countries and still are the number one cause of infant mortality in many of them, including Mexico. Such health problems are essentially a consequence of interrelated environmental and socioeconomic problems, such as lack of sanitation, ingestion of contaminated foodstuff, and lack of education, which leads to poor hygienic practices.

The original intention here was to quantify the health costs associated to water pollution in both urban and rural areas and, independently, the health costs associated with the disposal of solid and toxic waste. To a large extent the two problems are linked because both surface and underground waters can be contaminated if rain waters percolate through residues. The fact that the major health effect from the two problems is the same—gastrointestinal diseases—makes it extremely difficult to determine the origin of a particular disease. It is impossible to attribute a child's case of diarrhea to either contact and mouthing of solid wastes or to drinking of contaminated waters. Thus the health effect, rather than the environmental problem, is analyzed here.

Water Pollution

In the 1970s, 11 surface water basins classified as the most polluted served 59% of population, while the 164 least polluted served only 6% of the population. Water treatment capacity covers 17.5% of total discharges from point sources (28 m^3/sec), in 60 industrial plants and 193 municipalities. However, only 15 m^3/sec (9%) were actually treated. Out of 30 locations identified in the Plan Nacional Hidraulico, 19 had coliform contamination.

By 1986, 72% of the total population had access to water supply—82% in urban areas and 49% in rural areas. As to sewage system, 65% had access to these facilities in urban areas and only 11% in rural areas. In total, 22.5 million people had no access to safe water and about 40.7 million lacked sewerage services. Even for those who have access to piped water, the quality is not always satisfactory: only 20% of the municipal systems (for medium and large cities) have a reliable chlorination system.

Solid Waste Disposal

In 1986, total municipal wastes amounted to 32.5 million tons; one third of this amount were not properly disposed of. Production of waste in MCMA is around 11 million tons/day of which 80% was collected (60% in other urban areas). Industrial wastes total 133 million tons, of which 5 million tons are hazardous and 15 million tons require special disposal. Most are mining residues. Toxic wastes are indiscriminately mixed with municipal wastes, and operation of solid waste disposal systems is deficient in most municipalities.

Contamination of Irrigation Waters

The large-scale reuse of untreated domestic sewage waters for irrigation has been commonplace in Mexico since the early 1900s, and often occurs without effective sanitary controls. This practice may pose substantial health risks for farm workers and for the population consuming agricultural products from such areas. Lago Texcoco and the irrigation districts surrounding Mexico City—Tula valley, where wastewaters irrigate some 90,000 hectares, are the major areas with contamination (there are plans to extend such irrigated area to 250,000 hectares in the next few years). Edible crops from these reuse sites have been found to be contaminated with fecal coliform, and evidence from toxic contamination of groundwater has recently been identified. High rates of parasitosis tend to be associated with uncontrolled reuse, and outbreaks of enteritis, other diarrheal diseases, typhoid, and hepatitis are suspected to have been caused by raw sewage irrigation of vegetables.

Cost Estimates

Mortality. According to SdeS (1990), intestinal diseases (*infeccion intestinal mal definida*) are still the number one cause of mortality in Mexico, with a rate of 32.8 per 100,000 people in 1990 (total 28,000 deaths). The same rate for children under age 1 is roughly 500 (12,500 deaths), while for children between 1 and 4 it is 70 (5,600 deaths). Death rates for the other age groups were estimated proportionally to the number of cases of the disease in each group (the incidence of diarrheas is essentially the same for the other age groups—SdeS 1990).

Two alternative scenarios were considered. The first is based on current mortality rates: we applied the same criterion as for air pollution, namely an annual salary of US$7,700 and a 5% annual discount rate. As to life expectancy, we used 40 years for children below age 19, 30 years for people in age group 20–39, 20 years for those in age group 40–50, and 10 years for the others. *Total estimated costs would be US$3.6 billion.* This excludes all suffering and pain and any tentative treatment (mitigation) cost.

The other scenario assumes that oral rehydration therapy (ORT) will completely eliminate deaths from diarrhea. This scenario essentially estimates the mitigation costs associated to such deaths. However, it does not include the costs of ensuring such universal use of ORT, namely the educational effort: such costs are almost impossible to be estimated. We also do not attempt to compare them with water treatment (control) costs. Nevertheless, the estimate gives an indication of the benefits associated with the mitigation effort. Health costs associated to scenarios in which oral therapy produces intermediate effects can be evaluated based on the two scenarios presented here.

The possibility that ORT could completely eliminate deaths from diarrhea does not appear unrealistic. Countries where conditions are likely to be worse than in Mexico have shown dramatic reductions in the rates of diarrhea-related child mortality. "An estimated 4 million youngsters under age 5 worldwide succumb to the disease each year, accounting for more than a quarter of the 14 million annual deaths in that age group. ORT now saves a million small children annually. No one, adult or child, would die of diarrhea if only every family in the world knew how to prepare and deliver some form of ORT. The ingredients needed for an adequate formulation can be found in virtually every household" (Hirschhorn and Greenough III 1991).

In the case of Mexico, ORT has not proved so effective, probably because of inadequate administration coupled with lack of knowledge on the beneficial effects of the therapy, or even its own existence (Latorre et al. 1990). The costs of the therapy are approximately US$1 plus administration.[21] "A child with diarrhea may need to be spoon fed more than half a liter of solution each day, in sessions spaced as little as three minutes apart, for five to seven days" (Hirschhorn and Greenough III 1991). Administration is estimated at US$12 (average of three daily wages of US$4, which is more than the minimum wage in Mexico, assuming that ORT administration does not require any qualification of the person administering the serum). Additionally, since ORT does not stop diarrhea, but only prevents dehydration, we added an estimated treatment cost of US$3 per case. Applying the figures (US$16 per case) to all 28,000 annual lethal cases would lead to an estimated cost of US$448,000.

Morbidity.   In 1990, the number of nonlethal cases of diarrhea in Mexico was 3.36 million (SdeS 1991). Of these cases, 60% were children under age 14 and adults over age 65. For both these age groups we assumed: (a) the necessity to treat all cases and to (b) apply ORT to 50% of the total number of cases (both costs described above); and, (c) that 5% of all cases require laboratory analyses at an average cost of US$20 each. Total costs for those age groups are estimated at US$20 million. For the other age groups we assumed the necessity to treat all cases and to apply ORT to 20% of the cases. We additionally assumed that productivity effects are not significant. Total treatment costs are estimated at US$8.5 million. *Total morbidity costs associated to diarrheal diseases in Mexico are estimated at US$30 million.*

Acknowledgments: This paper is a shorter version with few modifications of a paper with the same title written for the Bank's PRE Policy Research Working Paper Series (number 824, January 1992).

I am grateful to Sweder van Wijnbergen, Antonio Estache, Gunnar Eskeland, and Hans Binswanger for their help in preliminary discussions and later comments. Special thanks to Allan Krupnick for his extensive comments and suggestions. John Dixon, Robert Anderson, Nancy Birdsall, Jan Böjo, and Ronaldo Serôa da Motta also provided helpful comments.

Any views expressed or errors made are my responsibility. John McIntire provided parameters for the estimates on soil erosion, and José Simas for those on irrigation waters. Many thanks to Rebecca Hall, who helped me with the calculations and a number of parameters.

NOTES

1. In the case of health effects, the incidence of problems is related to the exposure rather than to ambient concentration of pollutants. Models that attempt to determine exposure of individuals to pollutants require a considerably larger volume of information. For the population at large, it is questionable whether the results differ significantly.

2. The condition is that the average utility of consumption exceeds the marginal utility, a condition that holds for all increasing, concave utility functions as long as an individual's consumption exceeds subsistence quoted in Braden and Kolstad (1991). See also Conley (1976).

3. It is clear that damage costs depend on the control measures adopted by the polluting firms or agents (the control costs which are not dealt with here). They also depend on the level of abatement. This is usually calculated taking the legislation standard as the "desired" level, see calculations below.

4. The regression coefficient for maize was -0.0091, with the rate of erosion of 8.48 ton/acre; this lead to an average yield loss of 0.077 bushels/acre, which represented 4% of the average yield of 1.97 bushels/acre/year. The same procedure was applied to the other crops.

5. The procedure is almost compulsory given the lack of models relating effects of soil erosion on agricultural productivity in developing countries, but is certainly not new here. Farming practices, mechanization, soil types, and physical properties, among other parameters, influence such effects. See Pagiola (1993).

6. The trend yield growth (with erosion), which is observable, was 3.45% for maize, -0.52% for soybeans, and 10.95% for wheat. The trend yield growth without erosion is equal to (1 + loss from trend yield growth) × (trend yield growth with erosion), where the losses from trend yield growth are the percentages observed in the United States. The figures were provided by John McIntire (personal communication).

7. US$500 million if the discount rate were 10 percent.

8. In a similar exercise conducted for Denver, Colorado, the estimated annual value for reducing (to Federal Legislation standards) particulate matter soiling and improving visibility was *17 percent higher* than the corresponding estimated values of morbidity and mortality for Ozone and particulate matter together (Chestnut and Rowe 1988).

9. The benefits (or costs) associated with different levels of pollution—typically, the incidence of diseases—are a function of the desired change in the level of pollution. To estimate the costs stemming from a certain level of pollution, it is therefore necessary to consider the difference between that level and the one that causes no health effects. Such level of air quality may be zero pollutant concentration level (in the case of lead) or the legislation environmental standard (all other pollutants).

10. Controlled variables used in the reference are sex, age, education, chronic health condition, race, marital status, income, annual mean temperature, occupational status, and number of sick paid days. Coefficients for WLD are 0.004 and for RAD is 0.009 (average of six years of observations).

11. A more recent result by Ostro has been used in NERA (1990), where a 1 $\mu g/m^3$ change in FP yields a 0.028 change in RRADs per person, irrespective of baseline RRAD. In the Mexican case, this would lead to a 0.034 change in RRAD (3 x 0.0114), which is NERA's high range estimate. We attain to the original work, even though it produces a 20% higher estimate.

12. Change in relation to the point where there are no health effects. As discussed earlier, this is the concentration legislation standard for fine particles.

13. American estimates based on willingness to pay place such values between US$500 thousand and US$10 million; using the ratio between the two countries' per capita GNPs—roughly 10—to compare U.S. and Mexico figures, our estimate appears conservative. We can also compare our estimates for Mexico with equivalent U.S. figures by applying the same human capital approach to the U.S., and this can be simply obtained by dividing wages in the two countries. Since the typical hourly wage in

metropolitan areas in the United States is roughly US$100 and in Mexico US$20, we see again that our estimates are on the conservative side.

14. We had data for the June/90–February/91 period, thus 15 2-week periods. For every period, we took the difference between the average concentration (measured in daily 1-hour maximum) and the standard to evaluate the expected number of RRAD lost. Additionally, if the average were below the standard there would be a decrease in the number of RRAD, so that in such cases we considered the observed average equal to the standard, leading to no change in RRAD.

15. This may be a large estimate, but it partly compensates for the benefits arising for asthmatics, which are not included here.

16. As noted earlier, since there is indication that even minimal concentrations cause harmful health effects, the estimates do not relate to legislation standards, but to zero concentration levels.

17. The variables were age (under 2, 2–4, and 4–6), race, sex, degree of urbanization, family income, serum albumin, dietary calcium, dietary calories, serum copper, dietary carbohydrates, dietary fat, serum iron, blood lead, dietary phosphorous, dietary protein, transferring saturation, dietary vitamin C, and serum zinc. Sample size was 1,967 children.

18. The total expenditure in education for children in Mexico was US$5.5 billion in 1990. Assuming that expenditures were uniformly distributed throughout the country, the estimated expenditure in Mexico City was US$5.5 billion multiplied by the population of Mexico City in relation to the rest of the country, which is roughly 17 million over 80 million, or 21 percent. Thus the estimated annual cost of education per child in Mexico City is US$153. Multiplying by three years (discounting at 5 percent p.a.) and multiplying by the 140,365 cases gives the figure presented in the text—US$21.5 million.

19. Mining the resource here means exploiting it in an unsustainable basis, so that the amount pumped out is larger than the recharge.

20. Average water diversion 9,000 m³/hectare/year, average pumping depth 50 meters, an energy cost to farmers of US$28 mills/kwh and a marginal cost of US$61 mills/kwh. Such estimated parameters lead to a power demand of 1 Kw per hectare and of 2,500 kwh of energy per hectare per year. Thus the marginal cost of irrigation is US$152/hectare/year, while the average cost to farmers is US$70/hectare/year.

21. Estimated costs vary between US$0.17 to more than US$10. The US$1 estimate used here may still be an overestimate (Martines et al. 1991).

REFERENCES

Alt, K., C. T. Osborn, and D. Colacicco. 1989. "Soil Erosion: What Effect on Agricultural Productivity?" Washington, D.C.: USDA, Economic Research Service, *Agricultural Information Bulletin,* No. 556.

Bartik, T. J. 1988. "Evaluating the Benefits of Nonmarginal Reductions in Pollution Using Information on Defensive Expenditures." *Journal of Environmental Economics and Management* 15:111–127.

Bentkover, J. D., V. T. Covello, and J. Mumpower. 1985. *Benefits Assessment: The State of the Art*. Dordrecht, Netherlands: D. Reidel.

Bojö, J., K.-G. Mäler, and L. Unemo. 1990. *Environment and Development: An Economic Approach*. Netherlands: Kluwer Academic Publishers.

Braden, J. B. and C. D. Kolstad, eds. 1991. *Measuring the Demand for Environmental Quality*. Netherlands: Elsevier Science Publishers.

Brajer, V., J. V. Hall, and R. Rowe. 1991. "The Value of Clean Air: An Integrated Approach." *Contemporary Policy Issues* 9:81–91.

Chestnut, L. G. and R. D. Rowe. 1988. "Ambient Particulate Matter and Ozone Benefit Analysis for Denver." Boulder: RCG/Hagler, Bailly, Inc., report prepared for the U.S. Environmental Protection Agency.

Crosson, P. R. and A. T. Stout. 1983. *Productivity Effects of Cropland Erosion in the United States*. Washington D.C.: Resources for the Future.

de la Burde, B. and M. S. Choate Jr. 1975. "Early Asymptomatic Lead Exposure and Development at School Age." *Journal of Pediatrics* 87:638–642.

Diaz, F. G. 1987. "Debt Accumulation and Distorted Growth Through Subsidized Public Sector Prices." Report to U.K. Economic and Social Research Council and the World Bank.

EPA (Environmental Protection Agency). 1985. "Costs and Benefits of Reducing Lead in Gasoline: Final Regulatory Impact Analysis." Washington, D.C.: USEPA.

—— 1986. "Air Quality Criteria for Lead." Cincinnati: Environmental Criteria and Assessment Office, Vols. 1–4, EPA 600/8–83/028dF.

Evans, J., T. Tosteson, and P. L. Kinney. 1984. "Cross-Sectional Mortality Studies and Air Pollution Risk Assessment." *Environment International* 10:55–83.

Ferris, B. G. Jr. 1978. "Health Effects of Exposure to Low Levels of Regulated Air Pollutants: A Critical Review." *Journal of Air Pollution Control Association* 28:482–497.

Freeman, A. M. III. 1982. *Air and Water Pollution Control*. Toronto: Wiley.

Harrington, W., A. J. Krupnick, and W. O. Spofford, Jr. 1991. *Economics and Episodic Disease: the Benefits of Preventing Giardiasis Outbreak*. Washington, D.C.: Resources for the Future.

Hirschhorn, N. and W. B. Greenough III. 1991. "Progress in Oral Rehydration Therapy." *Scientific American* 264:50–56.

Hoehn, J. P. and A. Randall. 1989. "Too Many Proposals Pass the Benefit Costs Test." *American Economic Review* 79:544–551.

Just, R. E., D. L. Hueth, and A. Schmitz. 1982. *Applied Welfare Economics and Public Policy*. Englewood Cliffs, N.J.: Prentice-Hall.

Kleinman, M. T., S. D. Colome, and D. E. Foliart. 1989. *Effects on Human Health of Pollutants in the South Coast Air Basin*. South Coast Air Quality Management District/California State University Fullerton Foundation.

Krupnick, A. J. and A. Alicbusan. 1990. "Estimation of Health Benefits of Reduction in Ambient Air Pollutants." Washington, D.C.: World Bank, Environment Department, Divisional Working Paper No. 11.

Krupnick, A. J. and R. J. Kopp. 1988. *The Health and Agricultural Benefits of Reductions in Ambient Ozone in the United States*. Washington, D.C.: Resources for the Future, Discussion Paper QE88–10.

Latorre, F. G., V. C. Ayala, J. I. Rosales, G. B. Guimaraes, and J. L. B. Fernandez. 1990. *Factores de Riesgo en la Mortalidad Infantil por Diarreas;* Sintesis Executiva, SE-18/90. Mexico: Instituto Nacional de Salud Publica.

Martines, J., M. Phyllips, and R. G. A. Feachem. 1991. *Diarrheal Disease; Health Sector Priority Review,* Washington, D.C.: World Bank, Population and Human Resources Department.

McGee, D. and T. Gordon. 1976. *The Results of the Framingham Study Applied to Four Other U.S.-based Epidemiologic Studies of Coronary Heart Disease.* Washington, D.C.: National Institutes of Health.

McIntire, J. and C. Shaw. 1991. Soil and Water Conservation Sector Review; Revised Initiating Memorandum/Issues Paper. World Bank, mimeo.

NERA (National Economic Research Associates, Inc.). 1990. "Benefits of the 1989 Air Quality Management Plan for the South Coast Air Basin: a Reassessment." Cambridge, Mass.

Nichols, A. L. and R. J. Zeckhauser. 1986. "The Dangers of Caution: Conservatism in Assessment and the Mismanagement of Risk." In K. Smith, ed., *Advances in Applied Micro-Economics* 4:55–82.

Oskaynak, H. 1985. "Health Effects of Airborne Particles." Cambridge: Energy and Environmental Policy Center, John F. Kennedy School of Government, Harvard University.

Ostro, B. D. 1983. "The Effects of Air Pollution on Work Loss and Morbidity." *Journal of Environmental Economics Managememt* 10:371–382.

—— 1987. "Air Pollution and Morbidity Revisited: A Specification Test." *Journal of Environmental Economics Management* 14:87–98.

Pearce, D. W. 1991. "Public Policy and Environment in Mexico." In S. van Wijnbergen and S. Levy, eds., *Mexico in Transition: Towards a New Role for the Public Sector.* Washington, D.C.: World Bank.

Portney, P. R. and J. Mullahy. 1986. "Urban Air Quality and Acute Respiratory Illness." *Journal of Urban Economics* 20:21–38.

Rothenberg, S. J., I. A. P. Guerrero, E. P. Hernandez, L. S. Arrieta, S. C. Ortiz, D. S. Carcamo, J. F. Ortega, and S. Karchmer. 1990. "Fuentes de Plomo en Embarazadas de la Cuenca de Mexico." *Salud Publica de Mexico* 32:632–643.

Rummo, J. H., D. K. Routh, N. J. Rummo, and J. F. Brown. 1979. "Behavioral and Neurological Effects of Symptomatic and Asymptomatic Lead-Exposure in Children." *Archives of Environmental Health* 34:120–124.

Samet, J. M., Y. Bishop, F. E. Speizer, J. D. Spengler, and B. G. Ferris. 1981. "The Relationship Between Air Pollution and Emergency Room Visits in an Industrial Community." *Journal of Air Pollution Control Association* 31:236–240.

Schwartz, J. and A. Marcus. 1986. "Statistical Reanalysis of Data Relating to Air Pollution During London Winters 1958–72." Washington, D.C.: U.S. EPA. Working Paper.

SdeS (Secretaria de Salud). 1988a. *Anuario Estadistico.* Mexico.

—— 1988b. *Encuesta Nacional de Salud.* Mexico: Direccion General de Epidemiologia.

—— 1990. "Informacion Epidemiologica Sobre Enfermidades Diarreicas." Districto Federal, Mexico: Consejo Directivo del Programa Nacional de Enfermidades Diarreicas.

—— 1991. "Estado Atual de la Vigilancia e Investigación Epidemiológica de los Danos a la Salúd por Efecto de la Contaminación Ambiental en la Ciudad de México." Districto Federal, Mexico: Dirección General de Epidemiologia.

Smith, V. K., ed. 1984. *Environmental Policy Under Reagan's Executive Order: The Role of Benefit-Cost Analysis.* Chapel Hill: University of North Carolina Press.

USAID (U.S. Agency for International Development). 1990. "Ranking Environmental Health Risks in Bangkok, Thailand." Washington, D.C., USAID Working Paper, Vols. 1 and 2.

Whittemore, A. S. and E. L. Korn. 1980. "Asthma and Air Pollution in the Los Angeles Area." *American Journal of Public Health* 70:687–696.

FIVE

Health Costs Associated with Air Pollution in Brazil

Ronaldo Serôa da Motta
and Ana Paula Fernandes Mendes

The intensified process of urbanization and industrialization under way in Brazil over the past few decades has contributed considerably to a rapid drop in air quality in the country's major urban centers, made worse by a lack of integrated measures controlling land use and settlement. The priority assigned to fostering growth in certain sectors of the economy and the lack of controls developed by society have led to the use of high-risk procedures and products that at times run counter to environmental security standards.

As the dynamics of the Brazilian economy are concentrated in a few major centers, metropolitan populations have been the principal victims of air pollution. Although this varies in intensity, depending on the characteristics of each region, neither its form nor its effects diverge to an appreciable extent.

Curiously enough, although the polluted air of Brazil's main urban and industrial centers unquestionably causes serious problems for human health, there are few epidemiological surveys highlighting these effects. Studies carried out in a few countries[1] already spotlight a positive association between high rates of pollution and the incidence of certain specific diseases. Notwithstanding, in order to fulfill the purposes of this study, it was deemed necessary not only to analyse the relationship between mortality and air pollution, but also to measure the economic costs caused by loss of physical welfare.

Thus, in order to formalize the relatonship between air pollution and mortality rates, an attempt is made also to estimate dose-response functions in relation to air pollution and its effect on respiratory diseases and ischemic heart diseases. Section 2 presents the estimated dose-response functions. To do this, a specific study was carried out for the municipality of São Paulo, where air quality is a reasonably serious problem and there are thus long and accurate series of air quality measurements and well-documented mortality rates. Based on these functions, Section 3 tests the validity of the coefficients estimated for measurement of the mortality rates in the municipalities of Rio de Janeiro, Belo Horizonte, and Cubatão. These municipalities were selected principally because of the availability of data on the concentration of pollutants and mortality rates. It is also well known that Rio de Janeiro, São Paulo, and Cubatão are urban centers with levels of air pollution higher tnan any other place in Brazil. Section 4 presents the health care costs associated with air pollution. The final Section discusses the results obtained and compares them with equivalent estimates drawn up for water pollution presented elsewhere.

ESTIMATION PROCEDURES: A POOLING STUDY FOR SÃO PAULO

The intention of this study, in analysing the quality of the air in the Municipality of São Paulo, is focused on measuring the level of exposure of individuals to the pollutants discharged into the atmosphere. However, in order to define air quality levels, this analysis should not be restricted to sources of production. Air quality can change, basically in function of meteorological conditions that determine the degree to which the pollutants are diluted. Only on the bases of this interaction is it possible to estimate the impact of air pollution on human health.

Additionally, other factors not associated with air quality influence mortality rates, including: nutritional standards, educational levels, smoking, age and sex. In this study it was possible to introduce only the educational level variable, which it is hoped will also give some indication of nutritional standards. Age and sex were not introduced as 1991 population census data on this particular variables was not available. Nor was it possible to introduce the effects of smoking.

In order to formalize the relationship between air pollution and morality rates, initially a dose-response function was estimated for respiratory system diseases that, in accordance with the International Health Classification, aggregate (a) acute bronchilitis and bronchitis; (b) pneumonia; (c) grippe; (d) chronic, nonspecific bronchitis, emphysema and asthma; (e) bronchoectasia; and (f) other lung diseases.

Data on mortality rates were obtained from death certificates processed by the SEADE Foundation,[2] containing information broken down by district and subdistrict for the period 1983–1991. These data were selected on the basis of the subdistrict of residence recorded on the death certificates. This source also provided information on the average educational levels of residents by subdistrict. In the case of child mortality (under fifteen years of age) the educational level of the mother was used. On the basis of these educational levels, it was possible to calculate an index education (IE) that estimated the percentage of the population resident in each subdistrict with elementary (up to four years) schooling or none at all. As expected, the districts considered more affluent—Ibirapuera and Cerqueira César—had the lowest illiteracy rate. An attempt was made to use this information as an independent variable representing by proxy all the various social and economic differences in the subdistricts.

The group of social and economic variables also included the parameter hospital beds (H.BEDS), meaning the number of general and specialized hospital beds by sanitary district and subdistrict in São Paulo. Since 1991 population census data on district and subdistrict population was not available, the demographic indicator—the resident population—by this local situation and sex was estimated using linear annual average rates based on data from 1980 and 1991 population on total municipal population.

Another group of independent variables—the air quality parameters—was estimated on the basis of the Air Quality Bulletins issued by CETESB. PM10 represents the concentration of inhalable particulate matter, SO2 the sulfur dioxide concentration, 03 the ozone concentration, CO the carbon monoxide concen tration, and NO2 the nitrogen dioxide concentration.

In temporal terms, a quarterly distribution was estimated on the basis of a quarterly division (Jan.–March; April–June; July–Sept.; Oct.–Dec.) of daily air quality reports. The temporal aggregation of the observations is justified by the relatively low number of deaths when distributed by subdistrict per day. By opting for quarterly distribution, this analysis sought to follow the seasons and climatic changes in order to capture the meteorological differences during the course of the year. Thus, in order to complete the set of independent variables selected for the proposed model, a third group of variables was defined, composed of TEMP—average minimum daily temperatures and UR—average relative humidity.

Because of the limited number of stations monitoring the entire set of pollutants analyzed, initially a regression (Function 1) was prepared, analyzing the relationship between mortality and air pollution, only with regard to the concentration in the atmosphere of two of the five pollutants selected: inhalable particulate matter and sulfur dioxide, which had a larger number of observations. Function 2 was developed, covering the sample with data on CO, NO2 and O3.

Function 1: PM10 and SO2

With the dependent variable R representing the number of persons suffering from respiratory diseases, a linear regression was developed, relating R to social and economic variables, air quality parameters, and meteorological indicators.

This regression was composed of 295 observations for the districts and subdistricts in the municipality of São Paulo with air quality monitoring stations: Cambuci, Cerqueira César, Ibirapuera, Jabaquara, Lapa, Moóca, Nossa Senhora do O, Penha, Santana, Santo Amaro, and Sé. The results of the regression are presented in table 5.1.

With regard to the social and economic variables, it was noted that both POP and H.BEDS are reliably nonzero at a 95% confidence interval. The negative sign assumed by the estimated parameter for H.BEDS confirms the hypothesis that the districts most lacking in hospital facilities are those

TABLE 5.1
Function 1: PM10 and SO2

R^2	0.9182	
Intercept	2.596683	
Air pollution		
PM10	0.06634	(2.304)
SO2	0.04754	(1.499)
Social/economic factors		
POP	0.000189	(51.02)
H.BEDS	−0.003247	(−2.392)
IE	5.6298	(0.753)
Meteorological factors		
TEMP	−1.5441	(−4.999)
UR	0.1915	(1.039)

NOTE: The figures in parentheses correspond to t-test(s).

where the number of deaths from respiratory disease is most marked. On the other hand, the positive sign of the POP shows a directly proportional relationship between the number of deaths and population growth. With regard to IE, although a positive trend was noted in the association between the level of education and the dependent variable, it cannot be stated categorically that people wtih lower levels of education necessarily die more frequently from respiratory diseases, as coefficients estimated were not significant at the same confidence interval.

In terms of the air pollution parameters, very different behavior was noted for PM10 and SO2. At a 95% confidence level, only the PM10 coefficient is appreciably different from zero. Assessing the quality of the air in the light of the limits set to protect the health and welfare of the population, it is noted that in the case of SO2, a target was set in 1981 for 1986 for the total control of emissions of this pollutant. However, by mid 1984 the situation was already under control in almost the entire municipality of São Paulo, meaning that the concentrations of SO2 at all monitoring stations were below the primary standard of $80\mu g/m.^2$ Primary air quality standards are established to give the concentration of pollutants at which human health becomes adversely affected.

With regard to meteorological variations, it was noted that temperature was an important determinant in the degree of dilution of pollutants in the atmosphere. For instance, during the quarters corresponding to the colder seasons of autumn and winter, the quality of the air grew worse and concomitantly increased respiratory diseases. For both effects the negative value of the TEMP variable was confirmed. The relative humidity—UR— factor did not vary appreciably from zero, although a positive trend appeared linking quarters with higher relative humidity to deaths from respiratory diseases. The methodology of this study ensures that the relationship between temperature and respiratory diseases is not included in air pollution coefficients. As climatic conditions affect the dilution levels of pollutants in the atmosphere, a certain synchrony is observed between the two data series. This is why this study is so emphatic about differentiating in the model the relative importance of each of the two groups of variables.

Also worthy of note is the fact that the regression presented a high R^2 of 91.82%. The other tests were also consistent, such as the Durbin-Watson test at 1.824, whose value suggests lack of serious problems with autocorrelation.

Function 2: CO, NO2, and O3

As already described, monitoring data are available for the other pollutants—CO, O3, and NO2—only from the Jabaquara, Sé, and Moóca stations. As the data series behave differently in each district, there is evidence that this is an excessively small sample. Nevertheless, the lack of spatially more diversified information on the concentration levels of these pollutants justifies the presentation of Function 2 (table 5.2).

Comparing Functions 1 and 2, it is noted that, at 95% confidence, the regressors IE and UR are not appreciably different from zero, although in both cases they present a positive relationship with the mortality rate for diseases of the respiratory system. With regard to Function 2 specifically, the socioeconomic indicator of Hospital Beds was also not appreciably different from zero at the same confidence interval. In the case of Function 2, this result should be strongly biased by the fact that one of the three districts (Sé) had no hospital beds on record during the entire period analysed.

Nevertheless, the main purpose of the study of Function 2 is to obtain air pollution estimators. The limited number of stations monitoring carbon monoxide, ozone and nitrogen dioxide reduced considerably the Function 2 sample—108 quarterly observations. The results of the regression reveal an appreciable association between the concentration of ozone in the atmosphere and deaths from respiratory system disease. This was not confirmed in the case of carbon monoxide and nitrogen dioxide. Neither of these pollutants were appreciably different from zero at the 95% confidence level.

In sum, based on the two functions presented above, it is possible to

TABLE 5.2
Function 2: CO, NO2 and O3

R^2	0.8494	
Intercept	21.892534	
Air pollution		
O3	0.049833	(2.183)
Social/economic factors		
POP	0.000138	(23.438)
Meteoreological factors		
TEMP	-1.24953	(-4.289)

NOTE: The figures in parentheses correspond to t-test(s).

draw some important conclusions. First, as regards air pollution, it was noted that both inhalable particulate matter and ozone reduced lung capacity, aggravating respiratory disease and even leading to death. It was not possible to note this for sulfur dioxide, carbon monoxide and nitrogen dioxide. The levels observed of sulfur dioxide show that all the stations complied with the standard established by Brazilian law, which could justify the low significance of this pollutant in Function 1. In its turn, in the case of carbon monoxide, people who are more sensitive to this pollutant are traditionally those with circulatory or cardiovascular problems, which are not specifically defined in the dependent variable R of Function 2. Finally, with regard to nitrogen dioxide, although Function 2 does not confirm a positive significant association between R and NO2, this is considered a strong irritant that can lead to symptoms similar to emphysema. In this respect, it is admitted that insofar as nitrogen dioxides are the precursors of ozone formation, their effects on the respiratory system are already indirectly estimated in the O3 coefficient.

A Study of Elasticity

The question that now arises is that of the expected percentage reduction in mortality rates, given a reduction in the concentration of an air pollutant. For this purpose it would be interesting to interpret the coefficients estimated as elasticity terms, and compare them with preceding works. Unfortunately this cannot be done with the result encountered in Thomas (1985), which also covers Rio de Janeiro, as this latter study did not provide information sufficient to estimate elasticity.

On the other hand, the elasticity figures obtained in Function 1 are close to those noted in the classic study by Lave and Seskin (1977), which estimates that a drop of 1% in pollution, represented by total particulate matter and SO4, results in a reduction of 0.12% in the mortality rate of the smsas (Standard Metropolitan Statistical Areas) in the United States for 1969.

An outline presented in Ostro (1992) also reveals that the results of Function 1 are significantly close to those summarized by this author. The bibliographical review suggests that a variation of 10 $\mu g/m^3$ of inhalable particulate matter implies an average variation of 1.24% in the mortality rate due to respiratory system diseases. Through a line of thought similar to that applied to Function 1, a variation of 1.62% is obtained in the mortality rate, which is around the average for the upper confidence levels of the works mentioned by Ostro (1992). This result is thus not far from other international estimates and also confirms the hypothesis that the level of pollution by particulate matter in São Paulo is among the sources of damage to human health.

Through the Function 1 coefficients, an estimate may be made of the elasticity between deaths due to respiratory disease and the concentrations of inhalable particulate matter and sulfur dioxide: 0.14 for PM10 and 0.049 for SO2; as well as the joint elasticity of the two pollutants—0.19. Taking all the stations together reveals that the levels of sulfur dioxide have been dropping over time. Remaining at the low levels encountered and with the observed downward trend in this pollutant, the problem of SO2 concentration in the São Paulo metropolitan area is on its way to being solved.

Notwithstanding the evident differences in the samples, caused not only by their inclusion of different counties, but principally because they introduce completely different spatial divisions, the elasticity of the inhalable particulate matter obtained in Function 1 for São Paulo is not appreciably higher than that found in North America, which is 0.08 for total particles in suspension (inhalable and noninhalable); it is worthwhile recalling that while the concentration of total particulate matter in São Paulo averages 140.40 μg/m^{3,3} in the SMSAs it is found to lie at a relatively lower level of around 95.58 μg/m^3, although both are well above the primary national air quality standard of 80 μg/m^3.

Continuing with this elasticity calculation, it can be estimated that the proportion of deaths due to pollution in São Paulo is considerably higher than the levels laid down under Brazilian law. For instance, while the primary standard is 50 μg/m^3, the level of PM10 concentration in São Paulo averages out at 89.3784 μg/m^3. A drop in this average pollution level to 50 μg/m^3 would represent a drop of 44.05%, which could avert the death of 6.37% of patients who today die of respiratory diseases. In comparative terms, and based on the original study by Lave and Seskin, a drop of 88% in the SO4 concentration and a drop of 58% in particulate air pollutants would be reflected in a reduction of around 7% in the SMSA mortality rates.

Based on Function 2, it is also possible to calculate the elasticity of ozone. All the measurement stations indicate that this pollutant exceeds both the one hour standard (160 μg/m^3) as well as the so-called alert level of 200 μg/m$^{3\cdot}$ In accordance with this calculation, it is estimated that a reduction of 1% in the ozone concentration would produce a drop of some 0.23% in the mortality rate due to respiratory system diseases. There are few studies in this field that refer to the relationship between respiratory sustem diseases and 03 concentrations. Portney and Mullahy (1986) carried out a survey of the effects of ozone on morbidity due to respiratory problems. Their conclusions point to a positive, significant association between O3 and RRADS (restricted activity days) due to respiratory system problems—principally in the case of adults. This association was also confirmed for mortality, as may be noted through observation of Function 2.

URBAN AIR POLLUTION IN BRAZIL: AN OVERVIEW

In order to give a general overview of urban air pollution in Brazil, an analysis was initially made of the air quality parameters and their impact on respiratory system diseases in São Paulo, as noted above. Although problems caused by deterioration in air quality have already appeared in various parts of Brazil, they are most clearly in evidence in the Greater São Paulo Metropolitan Area. The largest metropolis in Brazil, both by population and built-up area, São Paulo is also among the largest urban centers in the world, with a fairly well-developed industrial park as well as a large fleet of vehicles in circulation. For this and other reasons, São Paulo is currently faced with very serious environmental problems.

However, although using São Paulo as a case study, most of the previous analysis could be generalized. Therefore, in order to test the representativity of Function 1 in terms of urban air pollution in Brazil, respiratory system disease mortality rates were estimated for other municipalities: Rio de Janeiro, Belo Horizonte, and Cubatão, based on table 5.1. The lack of long series on concentrations of 03, CO and NO2 prevented the application of Function 2.

Municipality of Rio de Janeiro

Monitoring of air pollution concentration in the municipality of Rio de Janeiro is undertaken by FEEMA—the environmental protection agency in the state of Rio de Janeiro.

In order to estimate the death rate for respiratory diseases in São Paulo, based on the function developed for São Paulo, an analysis was made of the pollution levels at 10 stations in the municipality of Rio de Janeiro— Benfica, Bonsucesso, Centro, Copacabana, Ilha do Governador, Irajá, Maracana, Méier, Rio Comprido, and Santa Cruz—taking as a reference the administrative regions relative to each of these stations, respectively: São Cristóvão, Ramos, Zona Central, Copacabana, Ilha do Governador, Irajá, Tijuca, Méier, Rio Comprido, and Santa Cruz.

Applying the São Paulo function to the municipality of Rio de Janeiro, 1,252 deaths are estimated, as shown in table 5.3, while official data record a total of 1,273 deaths for this year, a difference of only 2% between the estimated and official data.

Municipalities of Cubatão and Belo Horizonte

As emphasized above, the problem of air pollution is more serious in São Paulo and Cubatão than in any other part of Brazil. Inter-regional differences are very clear. To illustrate these differences, it would be interesting to compare the average concentrations of total and inhalable particulate matter for the municipalities mentioned.[4]

High levels of air pollution noted in Cubatão have led to international notoriety as the Valley of Death.[5] However, the concentration of pollutants in Vila Parisi, the industrial area of Cubatão, is not representative of the municipality as a whole. Today, pollution data can be analysed for the various regions of the municipality, showing that problems appear in varous ways, and that the urban area, where the Centro station is sited, is appreciably different from the industrial area, with an air quality that is even better than in some districts of the São Paulo Metropolitan Region.

TABLE 5.3

Estimated Deaths from Respiratory Disease in Urban Areas in Brazil

Year	Municipality	Number of Deaths		(y)/(x)
		Official	Estimate	
1984	Rio de Janeiro[a]	1273	1252	0.98
1988	Cubatão	45	49	1.09
1988	Belo Horizonte	1159	1294	1.12
1989	São Paulo[b]	1708	1740	0.92

NOTE: Using the dose-response function estimated for São Paulo for the following diseases: acute bronchiolitis and bronchitis; pneumonia; grippe; chronic, non-specific bronchitis, emphysema and asthma; bronchoectasia; and other lung disease.
[a]São Cristóvão, Ramos, Zona Central, Copacabana; Ilha do Governador, Irajá, Tijuca, Méier, Rio Comprido, and Santa Cruz.
[b]Cambuci, Cerqueira César, Ibirapuera, Jabaquara, Lapa, Moóca, Nossa Senhora do Ó, Penha, Santana, Santo Amaro, and Sé.

Obviously, this statement is not designed to minimize the problems of the Vila Parisi industrial area, where air pollution figures have in the past reached extraordinarily high levels; today they are lower but still give rise to much concern.

According to table 5.4, it was possible to size the differences in the pollution levels recorded in the urban and industrial areas of Cubatão, at the Centro and Vila Parisi stations respectively. The concentration levels for inhalable particulate matter for inhalable particulate matter recorded in Vila Parisi and the municipalities of São Paulo and Rio de Janeiro are also not comparable. In the case of Belo Horizonte, for the years under observaton, concentration levels for total particulate matter were almost below the primary standards (50 $\mu g/m^3$). At the Mangabeiras and Horto Florestal stations—the only stations in operation in Belo Horizonte during 1988—the average annual concentration was respectively 46 $\mu g/m^3$ and 62 $\mu g/m^3$.

In 1981, the automatic air quality monitoring network began operations in Cubatão, under the administration of CETESB. Installation of this network as it is today was completed only in 1984, at three points: Centro, Vila Parisi and the Vila Nova district. Among the pollutants encountered in the Cubatão area, particulate matter is that found with the greatest intensity. Based on table 5.5, it may be stated briefly that appreciable reductions have already occurred in the concentration of inhalable particulate matter at the Centro staion downtown, and despite violations of the daily standard of 150

TABLE 5.4

Concentration of Inhalable Particulate Matter (PM10)
(annual arithmetic average; unit = $\mu g/m^3$)

	Rio de Janeiro	São Paulo	Cubatão		
			Vila Parisi[a]	Centro[b]	Vila Nova[c]
1985	57	86	173	65	110
1986	57	83	165	53	−(5)
1987	44	98	151	55	−(5)
1988	61	107	116	69	110
1989	51	98	115	54	119
1990	51	116	90	58	99
1991	49	71	147	67	72

[a] Station located in the Vale do Mogi, Cubatão.
[b] Station located in downtown Cubatão.
[c] Station located in the Vila Nova district.

TABLE 5.5

Inhalable Particulate Matter (PM10), Cubatão 1981–1990

(unit = $\mu g/m^3$)

Year	Centro		Vila Parisi	
	Max. daily[a]	AAA[b]	Max. daily[a]	AAA[b]
1981	357	117	([c])	([c])
1982	243	117	411	168
1983	306	108	475	131
1984	216	56	567	186
1985	514	65	519	173
1986	186	53	409	165
1987	201	55	466	151
1988	257	69	409	116
1989	173	54	319	115
1990	200	58	438	90

[a] Maximum daily amount measured in year.
[b] Annual arithmetic average.
[c] Not measured.

$\mu g/m^3$, the annual standards are close to compliance (50 $\mu g/m^3$). At Vila Parisi, consistent reductions are noted with regard to both daily maximums and annual averages, but these reductions are still far from bringing current concentrations into line with standards.

Working along lines identical to those developed for Rio de Janeiro, the respiratory disease mortality rates were also estimated for the municipalities of Belo Horizonte and Cubatão, as well as their relationships with air pollution by inhalable particulate matter. The results of table 5.3 seem to confirm the application of the São Paulo dose-response function in other municipalities. In 1988 the Ministry of Health recorded some 45 deaths in Cubatão[6] and 1,159 in Belo Horizonte. With the dose-response function, estimates would lead to, respectively, 49 and 1,294 deaths due to respiratory system diseases. Through this statistical exercise it may be concluded that the dose-response function estimated initially for the municipality of São Paulo is also applicable to other municipalities with differing levels of air quality.

Health Costs

In the methodology adopted to estimate health costs associated with air pollution, it was considered that these costs would be, on the one hand, a foregone output resulting from missed work days and the premature death of persons suffering from respiratory system diseases and, on the other, the output made feasible were the expenditures incurred through the treatment and diagnosis of these diseases to be channeled into other activities. In order to estimate this foregone output, it is necessary to determine the mortality rate curve for respiratory disease that is strictly related to air pollution. To do this, as discussed previously, it is necessary to develop a dose-response function that allows the determination of the respective incidence indicator for each year and municipality analysed. It is on the basis of this indicator that hospital costs and foregone output were estimated. These estimates refer to more recent years than the calculations obtained from the data base—1989 for São Paulo, 1988 for Cubatão, and 1984 for Rio de Janeiro. In the case of Belo Horizonte, the concentration levels recorded for particulate matter are not far from the legal standards, and thus do not justify calculating health costs.

It is important to note that there is no single general method for measuring health costs associated with air pollution. The choice of a specific method means that the health costs are calculated on the basis of specific parameters of the loss of welfare to the detriment of others. In the case of this study, the estimated figures make no reference to the loss of welfare caused by respiratory diseases with regard to discomfort, pain and other restrictions. To incorporate these parameters, other methods should be selected in order to determine individual preferences for improved health.[7] This is unfortunately beyond the scope of this study.

Table 5.6 presents figures on deaths from respiratory disease associated with air pollution, calculated by level of education, with the applicaton of the dose-response estimated previously for the cities of São Paulo, Rio de Janeiro, and Cubatão. The differentiation by educational level will act as a proxy for income levels in the calculation of health costs presented below.

Hospital Costs

In order to calculate hospital costs, the cost of each hospitalization resulting in a death was multiplied by the number of deaths associated with air

TABLE 5.6

Number of Deaths by Educational Level

Educational Level	Rio de Janeiro 1984	Cubatão 1988	São Paulo 1989
No schooling	7	6	24
Basic schooling	16	9	40
Secondary schooling	11	9	45
University degree	6	5	30

NOTE: The diseases studied are: acute bronchiolitis and bronchitis; pneumonia; grippe; chronic, non-specific bronchitis, emphysema and asthma; bronchoectasia; and other lung diseases.

pollution (see table 5.7). It was initially necessary to estimate the average number of hospitalizations per death on the basis of SINTESE[8] data which consolidates data on government medical care in Brazil. The SINTESE statistical system also provided average cost of hospitalization for respiratory system diseases (table 5.7).

Table 5.7 shows, in 1989 dollars, that for only the eleven districts analyzed—Sé, Santana, Moóca, Cambuci, Ibirapuera, Nossa Senhora do O, Jabaquara, Lapa, Cerqueira César, Penha, and Santo Amaro—hospital costs for 1989 in São Paulo reached some US$785,000, while for the ten administrative regions in Rio de Janeiro—São Cristóvão, Ramos, Zona Central, Copacabana, Ilha do Governador, Irajá, Tijuca, Méier, Rio Comprido and Santa Cruz—in 1984, this figure was not over $151,000. How-

TABLE 5.7

Hospital Costs per Death and Total

Year	Municipality	Deaths Associated with Air Pollution	Hospital Cost per Death	Total Hospital Cost
1984	Rio de Janeiro[a]	40	3,775	151,000
1988	Cubatão	29	4,896	142,000
1989	São Paulo[b]	139	5,647	785,000

[a]São Cristóvão, Ramos, Zona Central, Copacabana, Ilha do Governador, Irajá, Tijuca, Méier, Rio Comprido, and Santa Cruz.
[b]Cambuci, Cerqueira César, Ibirapuera, Jabaquara, Lapa, Moóca, Nossa Senhora do Ó, Penha, Santana, Santo Amaro, and Sé.

ever, in the case of Cubatão there are some methodological differences. It was admitted that the average concentrations of inhalable particulate matter at the three stations—Centro, Vila Parisi and Vila Nova—is representative of the entire municipality. In addition, the data imported from SINTESE are not broken down by municipality. This being the case, the information on São Paulo State were used as a proxy for Cubatão. In these terms, the estimated amount was US$142,000 for 1988. Because data were unavailable, no reference was made to the percentage of workers' wages spent on medicines or laboratory examinations when not provide by the natural medical care systems.

Morbidity

Loss due to morbidity is the foregone output of people who die from air pollution. This figure is reached through the ratio between the length of hospital stay in the case of deaths associated with air pollution and the average income of these people, estimated for each educational level in order to include the differences in income for each death.

The loss of working days was estimated on the basis of the average value of the length of hospitalization for respiratory system diseases determined by the SINTESE system. The average income of the economically active population was obtained from the household Surveys in accordance with educational levels. Table 5.8 shows that in the case of São Paulo for example, in 1989 and in current dollars, this income varied from US$1,092 and $6,959, in accordance with educational levels, while in São Paulo in 1984 this varied from $710 for illiterates to $5,713 for university graduates, as shown in table 5.8.

Data from SINTESE do not take into account deaths taking place outside

TABLE 5.8
Real Income (1989 US$)

	São Paulo	Rio de Janeiro
No schooling	1,092	710
Basic schooling	1,744	1,243
Secondary schooling	3,062	2,434
University degree	6,959	5,713

SOURCE: National Domicile Sampling Survey

government health-care system hospitals. In order to correct this underestimate, a conversion factor of 2.319212 was adopted, an estimate based on Ostro (1992), which determined the ratio between the number of hospitalizations and the number of consultations at emergency centers, health care costs and out-patient clinics.

The figures determined for foregone output due to morbidity or the number of workdays missed in Rio de Janeiro and São Paulo was respectively $65,000 and $351,000. For Cubatão this cost was $71,000.

Mortality

In order to estimate the health care costs caused by the impact of air pollution on mortality, Human Capital Theory was used, assuming that the value of life or a "statistical life" is equivalent to the present value of the future output generated by the individual who dies prematurely of respiratory disease. The foregone production due to premature death results from the product of the number of deaths associated with air pollution estimated on the basis of Function 1, and the value of this lost human capital. In order to represent this concept algebraically, the formula given below is based on that defined by Ridker (1967), expressed in the following manner

$$HCVx = \frac{\Sigma\ (Px)_{1n} \cdot (Px)_{2n} \cdot (Px)_{3n} \cdot Yn}{(1+r)^{n-x}}$$

where:
$HCVx$ is the present value of the future income of a person aged x;
$(Px)_{1n}$ is the probability of this person being alive at age n;
$(Px)_{2n}$ is the probability of this person being in the workforce at age n;
$(Px)_{3n}$ is the probability of this person being employed at age n;
Yn is the output expected at age n; and
r is the discount rate.

The $(Px)_1$ probability, which represents life expectancy, was estimated on the basis of the *Mortality Tables by Age* published in the 1980 Demographic Census. This variable reflects the probability of a person aged n being alive at the age $n+t$, where t varies from 1 to 85. It was arbitrarily assumed that this probability drops to nil when the individual reaches 85 years of age.

The probability $(Px)_2$ was also estimated on the basis of demographic data, observing the participation of the economically active population by age group and educational level. The $(Px)_3$ refers to the average unemployment rate for the economically active population.

Two figures were tested for the discount rate: 5% and 15%. The value of Yn is the same as that adopted for the calculation of morbidity, meaning the income of the economically active population in accordance with educational levels (see table 5.3).

According to the Theory of Human Capital, premature death of young children does not cause a loss of future output, as no investments have been made in education and vocational training. The lack of these investments offsets the future loss of output, as wages represent the return on these investments. This has been one of the strongest criticisms of this type of measurement. However, for the estimatory purposes of this study, the present value of future output associated with children was considered, since children are very vulnerable to the diseases being studied, as shown in figure 5.1. On the other hand, values estimated for old people were very low due to this low income flow, although they are also very vulnerable.

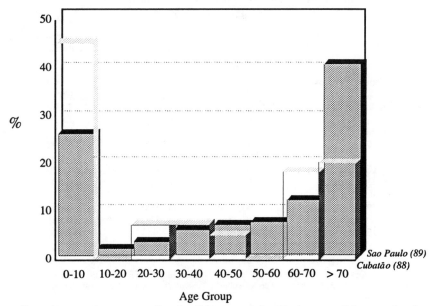

FIGURE 5.1.   Age at mortality for Cubatão and São Paulo, mortalities associated with respiratory disease. Source: Ministry of Health.

As shown in figure 5.1, in the case of respiratory system diseases, the mortality rate curves are different for São Paulo and Cubatão. In Cubatão, for example, almost 45% of deaths occur in persons aged under ten years, while in São Paulo this does not exceed 30%. In compensation, for older age groups—the over-70s—this distribution is inverted, being more concentrated in São Paulo.

In order to give a general overview of the health care costs associated with air pollution in Brazil, the figures in table 5.9 give total estimates for morbidity, mortality and those directly associated with air pollution for the municipalities of São Paulo, Rio de Janeiro and Cubatão:

As shown in table 5.9, the per capita health care costs associated with air pollution are somewhat different for each municipality. In Cubatão, at a discount rate of 5%, the estimated totals weigh up to ten times more on the local resident population than in the municipality of São Paulo, and some fifty times more than on the population of Rio de Janeiro.

TABLE 5.9

Total and Per Capita Healthcare Costs Associated with Air Pollution (1988 US$)

	São Paulo (1989)	Rio de Janeiro (1984)	Cubatão (1988)
Hospital costs	785,000 (0.36)	151,000 (0.08)	142,000 (1.65)
Morbidity	351,000 (0.16)	65,000 (0.03)	71,000 (0.82)
Mortality			
$r = 5\%$	1,073,000 (0.49)	201,000 (0.10)	725,000 (8.38)
$r = 15\%$	514,000 (0.23)	101,000 (0.05)	297,000 (3.44)
Total			
$r = 5\%$	2,210,000 (1.00)	417,000 (0.22)	939,000 (10.85)
$r = 15\%$	1,650,000 (0.75)	317,000 (0.17)	511,000 (5.90)

NOTE: Amounts in brackets are the per capita costs estimated in relation only to the population of places where the measurements of pollutant concentrations were used to calculate the total costs.

FINAL CONSIDERATIONS

The set of data presented in table 5.9 provides excellent input for reflections on the behavior of health care costs in the urban and industrial areas of Brazil, providing important indicators to guide pollution control and action programs.

First, based on the proposed methodology, an analysis may be made of the inter-municipal health care costs through calculation of foregone output due to premature death, or more specifically through the statistical life concept. Dividing foregone output due to mortality[9] by the number of deaths associated with pollution by inhalable particulate matter, an average measure of the "statistical life" is reached. In accordance with this calculation, in 1989 dollars, the estimated average statistical life was US$ 7,714 for São Paulo in 1989 and $5,029 for Rio de Janeiro in 1984, while for Cubatão this figure reached $25,002 in 1988.

This marked difference between the statistical life value in São Paulo and Cubatão may be justified by the distribution of the deaths by age groups as shown clearly in figure 5.1. As already noted, the highest mortality rate from respiratory diseases in Cubatão is in the 0-to-10 year age group, where the present value os future income is comparatively large. This contrasts with São Paulo, where the deaths are concentrated mainly among the over-70s.

The procedures established in Serôa da Motta et al. (1992) for estimating the health care costs linked to water pollution[10] are similar to those used in this study. In order to analyze health care costs associated with air and water pollution, estimates of the statistical life value and total per capita costs were used as the parameters of comparison. Based on the urban population of Brazil affected by the negative effects of household water pollution (Serôa da Motta et al. 1992) an average life value of US$19,550 was estimated, in 1989 dollars and with a 5% discount rate. As shown in table 5.10, this figure is higher than the average amount noted in the case of air pollution, which reaches an average of only $6,843 for São Paulo, Rio de Janeiro, and Cubatão.

This amount shows that in general terms, the health care costs associated with premature death are more alarming when associated with water pollution. Only in particularly critical situations such as the case of Cubatão is this apparently not confirmed. The same conclusions are noted in terms of the per capita costs, as shown in table 5.10. It is estimated, based on Serôa

TABLE 5.10
Healthcare Costs Associated with Domestic
Water and Air Pollution in Brazil (1989 us$)

	Statistical Life (us$/death)	Per Capita Cost (us$/inhabitant)
Water	19,550	2.97
Air	6,843	0.84

SOURCE: Water Pollution, Serôa da Motta et al. (1992)
NOTE: Average costs among the populations studied in São Paulo,
Rio de Janeiro and Cubatão.

et al. (1992), that the total costs associated with domestic water pollution cost each person in Brazil's urban population an average of us$2.97. This figure is also higher than the average per capita cost of air pollution, which is $0.84, as shown in table 5.10. It is noted that the average national figures for air pollution are over-estimated, as the municipalities analysed are those with the highest concentrations in the country.

In sum, although the health care costs associated with air pollution are appreciable, they seem to hover at considerably lower levels than those for water pollution. Additionally, the estimates given here clearly indicate that an air pollution control policy should first be drawn up and its priority rating should be ranked against other urgent environmental problems.

Acknowledgments. A Portuguese version of this chapter was presented in Pesquisa e Planejamento Econômico *25(1), 1995. See also Mendes (1993) for more details on the econometric aspects of this study.*

We are very grateful to John Dixon, World Bank–LATEN for his support, comments, and valuable suggestions during the research period. We thank Leonardo Bandeira Rezende for his participation in the econometric exercises, Cláudio Soares de Sousa and Renata Soares for assisting with data collection and analysis, and Vitor Pêgo Hottum for computer support. Armando Castelar Pinheiro has also contributed with valuable comments on the econometric exercises. We wish to express our gratitude to Antônio de Castro Bruni of CETESB and Roberto Men Fernandes of the Brazilian Ministry of Health for their always prompt data assistance. We also recognize the valuable data base provided by the SEADE Foundation.

NOTES

1. See Lave and Seskin (1977) and Ostro (1992) among others.

2. Fundação Sistema Estadual de Análise de Dados; State Data Analysis System Foundation.

3. Through a "Comparative Study of Measurements of Dust in Suspension in the Atmosphere" carried out by the Large Volumes Sampling Method and the B Radiation Attenuation Method, it was possible to extract the correlations between total particulate matter and inhalable particulate matter for Greater São Paulo.

4. In the case of Rio de Janeiro and Belo Horizonte, there is only monitoring of total particulate matter. In order to estimate the concentration of inhalable particulate matter, it was necessary to apply a conversion algorithm researched by CETESB, where PM = 1.28 × PM10 + 26.

5. See, for example, Findley (1988).

6. In order to apply the São Paulo dose-function response to the Municipality of Cubatão, the data for temperature and relative humidity in the town of Santos were used.

7. See, for example, Pearce and Markandya (1987) for a survey in the relevant literature in these issues.

8. Integrated Strategic Series Statistical Treatment System—SINTESE—Sistema Integrado de Tratamento Estatístico de Séries Estratégicas.

9. For the purposes of the proposed calculation, it was decided to use the 5% discount rate.

10. This study estimated the services and environmental losses derived from the use of water resources by urban families between 1970 and 1990.

REFERENCES

CETESB. 1991. *Relatório da Qualidade do Ar em São Paulo, 1990*. São Paulo.

Findley, R. W. 1988. "Pollution Control in Brazil." *Ecology Law Quarterly* 15:1–68.

Greene, W. H. 1990. *Econometric Analysis*. New York: Macmillan.

Griliches, Z. 1986. "Economic Data Issues." In Z. Griliches and M. Intrilligator, eds., *Handbook of Econometrics*, vol. 3. Amsterdam: North Holland.

IBGE. several years. *Censo Demográfico*. Rio de Janeiro: Instituto Brasileiro de Geografia e Estatística.

—— several years. *PNAD: Pesquisa Nacional por Amostra de Domicílios*. Rio de Janeiro: Instituto Brasileiro de Geografia e Estatística.

Lave, L. B. and E. P. Seskin. 1977. *Air Pollution and Human Health*. Baltimore: John Hopkins University Press.

Mishan, E. 1981. "The Value of Trying to Value a Life." *Journal of Public Economics* 15:133–137.

Ostro, B. 1992. "The Health Effects of Air Pollution: A Methodology with Applications to Jakarta." Washington, D.C.: World Bank, mimeo.

Pearce, D. and A. Markandya. 1987. "Appraisal of the Economic Value of Environmental Improvement and the Economic Cost of Environmental Damage." London: Dept. of Economics, University College.

Portney, P. R. and J. Mullahy. 1986. "Urban Air Quality and Acute Respiratory Illness." *Journal of Urban Economics* 20:21–38.

Ridker, R. G. 1967. *Economic Costs of Air Pollution: Studies in Measurement.* New York: Praeger.

Serôa da Motta, R. et al. 1993. "Perdas e Serviços Ambientais do Recurso Agua para Uso Doméstico." Rio de Janeiro: IPEA Discussion Paper.

Thomas, V. 1985. "Evaluating Pollution Control: The Case of São Paulo, Brazil." *Journal of Development Economics* 19:133–146.

SIX

Managing the Transition to Sustainable Development: The Role for Economic Incentives

Thomas H. Tietenberg

There is nothing more difficult to carry out, nor more doubtful of success, nor more dangerous to handle, than to initiate a new order of things. For the reformer has enemies in all who profit by the old order, and only lukewarm defenders in all those who would profit from the new order. The lukewarmness arises partly from fear of their adversaries who have law in their favor; and partly from the incredulity of mankind, who do not truly believe in anything new until they have had actual experience of it.
Machiavelli The Prince *(1513)*

In 1989 the Operations Evaluation Division of the World Bank published an analysis of the results of 335 World Bank agricultural and forestry projects in the tropics. The report noted severe environmental impacts had emerged some 5 to 15 years after completion in a disturbingly large number of the projects. These impacts were so severe that the projects to were not able to achieve their economic objectives. Undermining the natural resource base caused the short-term goals and long-term goals to be incompatible. Similar statements could have been made about other development projects.

THE SUSTAINABILITY VISION

All nations have been given an endowment of environmental and natural resources. Used properly these resources can provide sustainable increases in living standards to both this generation and those yet to come. Yet virtually all countries, including my own country (the United States), are violating the sustainability principle both by using existing technologies inappropriately and by continuing to rely on technologies which were appropriate in the past, but which are ill-suited for the future.

Some have chosen to suggest that technology itself is the cause of the problem and that the repudiation of technology is the solution (Commoner et al. 1971). I am not among them. It is true that many traditional forms of development have, in the glare of hindsight, proven to be myopic and excessively exploitative; rather than living off the "interest and dividends" from our endowment of environmental and natural resources (which economists refer to as "natural capital"), they destroy the principal. Sustainable forms of development represent a departure in that they are able to raise the living standards of the current generation without destroying the environmental and natural resource base on which all economic activity ultimately depends. The threat to sustainable development is not modern technology per se, but the conditions under which those new technologies are created and used.

But change is never easy. Many individuals and institutions currently have a large stake in maintaining the status quo. The principle of inertia applies to politics as fully as to physical bodies; a body at rest will tend to stay at rest unless a significant outside force is introduced. Changing economic incentives can provide that force.

I would like to share two principles with you, principles which, if implemented, could play a significant role in facilitating the transition to sustainable forms of development. In discussing these principles I will also share some ideas on how they can be implemented in developing countries.

The Full Cost Principle

According to the "full cost" principle, all users of environmental resources should pay their full cost. Though this sounds rather obvious, implementing this principle would represent quite a change from traditional practice. Most environmental resources are undervalued either due to ignorance about their true cost or improper incentives in the decision making processes responsible for determining how the resource is to be used.

Applying the full cost principle would send a strong signal that the environment is a scarce, precious resource and should be treated accordingly. Products produced by manufacturing processes which are environmentally destructive would become relatively more expensive; those produced by environmentally benign production processes would become relatively cheaper.

The transition to a more sustainable economic system depends upon the development of new technologies and upon much greater levels of energy efficiency than are currently being achieved. Those transitions will not occur unless the prevailing economic incentives support and encourage them. Once the full cost principle was implemented innovators would focus on developing environmental benign technologies rather than environmentally destructive ones, because environmentally benign technologies would be cheaper to use and therefore more attractive to potential adopters.

Implementing the full cost principle would end the implicit subsidy that all polluting activities have received since the beginning of time. When the level of economic activity was small, the corresponding subsidy was also small and therefore probably not worthy of political attention. Since the scale of economic activity has grown, however, the subsidy has become very large indeed; ignoring it leads to significant resource distortion.

The full cost principle is similar to, but not the same as, the "polluter pays" principle being applied in the OECD nations. The polluter pay principle usually is applied only to industries; the full cost principle would be applied to all emitters, including homeowners and automobile owners.

How could the full cost principle be implemented? One step would be to systematically include environmental costs in national income accounting and in government investment project evaluation. Since that is the primary focus of the session which follows this one, I shall not dwell on it here. I will, however, point to the fact that the literature on valuing environmental resources in developing countries is growing rapidly.[1]

Government investment projects would not be the only impacted area. Other policies would be affected as well. One aspect of fiscal policy which is receiving increasing attention in Europe is the potential for shifting the burden of taxation from taxes on labor and capital to taxes on emissions or on the extraction of natural resources. By raising the cost of acquiring capital and supplying labor, traditional taxes have an unintended discouraging effect on these particular activities. Since the transition to new economic activities will require considerable investment and the active cooperation of the labor force, discouraging investment or labor supply may well be counterproductive.

Taxes on capital and labor could be reduced without reducing revenue by introducing compensating increases in taxes on commodities which affect the environment. Common candidates include taxes on materials that enter the waste stream or on resources which have been underpriced because their environmental costs have been successfully transferred from the polluters to the victims. Packaging taxes, severance taxes on minerals or forests, production taxes on toxic substances, effluent or emission taxes on pollutants injected into the air or water and taxes on fossil fuels are a few of the examples that have been discussed.

In one recent application of this principle in the United States per unit fees have been imposed on polluters based upon the emission levels authorized by operating permits. The revenues from these fees is designed to fund the administrative costs associated with monitoring and enforcement of pollution control regulations. Forcing polluters, rather than taxpayers, to bear this cost represents another step in the process of imposing the full cost of pollution on those who emit it.

Implications for the legal system would flow from the full cost principle as well.[2] Both international and domestic laws should permit full recovery for damage caused by environmental incidents. Not only should the contaminated site be restored insofar as possible, but those suffering demonstrable losses should be fully compensated.

Making explicit environmental costs that have been hidden is only one side of the coin; the other is eliminating inappropriate subsidies. Subsidies which are incompatible with the full cost principles should be eliminated. Another policy instrument that has the virtue that it can raise revenue while restructuring incentives involves removing subsidies that stimulate behavior that encourage short-term gains at the expense of long term gains.

The tendency is to assume that political inertia protects all subsidies, but that need not be the case. Subsidies can be and have been removed. In Indonesia for example according to work by Robert Repetto pesticide subsidies had reached 82 percent of the retail price by 1985. Panayotou (1991) has shown the excessive use promoted by these subsidies was resulting in negative economic returns. The FAO even concluded that the heavy doses of pesticides had encouraged the rise of pests that were immune to these pesticides.

In November 1986 President Suharto issued a decree banning 57 brands of pesticides, 20 of which were heavily subsidized, and the country embarked on a policy of integrated pest management. Three planting seasons later the FAO reported a 90% reduction in pesticide use and a rise in the average yield of from 6.1 tons per hectare to 7.4 tons per hectare.

Another avenue worth pursuing is using what I call quasi-regulatory structures. One such area involves the use of insurance as an alternative to traditional regulatory structures (Holderness 1990; Katzman 1988; Kehne 1986). When environmental incidents occur and a cleanup is required, the full cost principle suggests that the responsible party should pick up the tab. One problem with this is that many organizations may not have the assets to do the job right. Insufficient assets to cover the damage poses two problems: (1) the resulting cleanup may not be adequate and (2) the responsible party may not have an adequate incentive to act with appropriate caution since they can get off the hook for considerably less than the damage caused.

Insurance can provide a solution to both problems. The assets of insurance groups are large. Furthermore to hold down their costs they have an incentive to provide some monitoring of premium-paying clients and the clients have an incentive to support this monitoring as long as it lowers insurance costs.

Let me provide one example of how this approach is working in maritime shipping. Shippers depend on insurance companies to help them deal adequately with the risk of maritime accidents. When on those relatively rare occasions when cargoes and ships are lost, the resulting financial burden can be staggering. By spreading the risk over time and among shippers the financial burden is made manageable.

But insurance companies do more than simply spread the risk; they also play an active role in promoting cost-justified measures to reduce that risk. When the risks get high, premiums rise and insurance companies begin to encounter significant resistance from purchasers. To maintain their market they look for ways to reduce premiums without reducing profits. The obvious approach is to reduce costs.

Insurance companies have traditionally actively promoted safety measures which hold premiums down. Inspections of premises and practices are common when a substantial amount of insurance is involved. Following the inspections specific recommendations are forwarded to the purchaser on how premiums could be reduced by adopting certain practices. Companies that adopt safe practices face lower premiums, while companies taking fewer precautions face higher premiums.

The premium structure represents only one means insurance companies have at their disposal to assure voluntary compliance with safety standards. Another is defining the boundaries around what risks are covered and what risks are not.

Perhaps the best way to explain this point is with an example. Due to their special ecological sensitivity and navigational risk, certain areas have been designated "areas to be avoided." Yet this designation does not mandate navigational practices; it merely serves as a guideline. Compliance, when it occurs, is voluntary.

Insurance companies, however, encourage voluntary compliance by including the designation in their definition of covered risks. Any ship having an accident in an "area to be avoided" is not covered by insurance. Taking the risk of entering such an area voids the coverage. As a result ship owners take on a significant self-insured risk in entering those areas. Due to the actions of the insurance companies, deviating around these areas now makes a good deal of economic sense.

THE CARRYING CAPACITY PRINCIPLE

The second principle of sustainable development I want to share with you is the carrying capacity principle. The development process faces physical limits that it must anticipate and accommodate. Both the capacity of the environment to absorb pollution and the capacity to supply depletable resources such as energy and minerals are finite. Ecosystems can tolerate only so much abuse before they change, sometimes in dramatic and unanticipated ways.

How can these limits be integrated smoothly into a sustainable development plan? Let me briefly share some ideas.

Overstressed Renewable Resources

The exploitation of renewable resources is one of the traditional areas where modern technologies have been most maligned. For example, modern technologies of finding, detecting, and catching fish have been responsible for a degree of overfishing never before possible. For the first time modern technologies have made the extinction of commercially attractive species a real possibility. Even if the level of exploitation unleashed by these technologies does not threaten extinction, excessively depleted fisheries require an enormous amount of harvesting effort merely to make a reasonable income.

The source of the problem from an economic perspective is that most fisheries are treated as a common property resource with free access. No individual has an incentive to preserve the stock. Any unilateral efforts to conserve the stock will be self-defeating because others can simply harvest proportionately more. Free access common property resources are systematically overexploited and population levels are drawn well below efficient levels.

The typical response to the problem of fisheries overexploitation has been to ban the modern technologies, which are seen as the source of the problem. But this is short sighted. If the population could be restored, the modern harvesting technologies provide a wonderful opportunity to provide good incomes to those harvesting the fish, by reducing the effort required. Technology bans merely raise harvesting costs and require fishermen to expend a great deal more effort than necessary to earn their income. Is it possible to solve the overexploitation problem while using modern technologies to reap the benefits those technologies could confer?

It is.[3] Consider the case of New Zealand. Some particularly desirable fish species in New Zealand were being seriously overfished because of an unfortunate confluence of two trends. Not only was the number of fishermen seeking to exploit the fishery increasing, but modern fishing technologies gave them an unprecedented power to harvest the sea's bounty. Rather than simply banning modern harvesting technology, the traditional approach, they wanted simultaneously to use it while first restoring and then maintaining the stock of fish.

While the need to reduce the amount of pressure being put on the population was rather obvious, how to accomplish that reduction was not at all obvious. Although it was relatively easy to prevent new fishermen from entering the fisheries, it was harder to figure out how to reduce the pressure from those who had been fishing in the area for years or even decades. Because fishing is characterized by economies of scale, simply reducing everyone's catch proportionately wouldn't make much sense. That would simply place higher costs on everyone and waste a great deal of fishing capacity as all boats sat around idle for a significant proportion of time. A better solution would clearly be to have fewer boats harvesting the stock. That way each boat could be used closer to its full capacity without depleting the population. Which fisherman should be asked to give up their livelihood and leave the industry?

The economic incentive approach addressed this problem imposing catch quotas on fishermen for which they had to pay an annual fee. The revenues derived from this fee were used to buy out fishermen who were willing to forego any future fishing for the species in jeopardy. Essentially each fisherman stated the lowest price that he or she would accept for leaving the industry; the regulators selected those who could be induced to leave at the lowest price, paid the stipulated amount from the tax revenues, and retired their licenses to fish for this species. It wasn't long before a sufficient number of licenses had been retired and the population was protected. Because the program was voluntary, those who left the industry only did so when they felt they had been adequately compensated. Meanwhile those who paid the fee realized that this small investment would benefit them greatly in the future as the population recovered. A difficult and potentially dangerous pressure on a valuable natural resource had been avoided by the creative use of an approach that changed the economic incentives.

Additionally this resource is now protected and the most up to date technologies are encouraged. Whereas new fishing technologies were previously viewed as the source of the problem, now they are the source of rising incomes. Economic policies which could have the unintended effect of destroying this resource as long as it remained vulnerable will no longer pose a threat.

REDUCING THE CONFLICT BETWEEN GROWTH AND DEVELOPMENT

Economic incentives can not only be used to reduce the conflict between economic development and environmental protection, they can become the means by which economic development becomes the vehicle by which greater environmental protection is achieved (Tietenberg 1990; Dudek and Palmisano 1988). In the mid 1970s several geographic regions in the United States found themselves in violation of the ambient air quality standards, which had been designed to protect human health. At that point the law provided that new industries would not be allowed to move into these areas if they added any more of the pollutant responsible for the standard being violated. Since even those potential entrants adopting the most stringent control technologies would typically add some of the pollutant, this was a serious political blow to mayors eager to expand their employment and tax base. How could they allow economic growth while assuring that air quality would steadily improve to the level dictated by the ambient standard?

To respond regulators adopted the economic incentive approach known as the "offset policy." Under this policy firms already established in these polluted areas that chose to voluntarily control their emissions more than required under the prevailing regulations would be allowed to have those excess emission reductions certified as "emission reduction credits." Once certified their operating permits would be tightened to assure that the reductions were permanent. These emission reduction credits could then be sold to new firms seeking to move into the city providing that the acquiring firm bought 1.2 emission reduction credits for each 1.0 units of emissions added by the new plant. Air quality improved every time a new firm moved into the area.

Though definitive data are not available, several estimates suggest that some 2,000 to 2,500 offset transactions have taken place. With this policy the confrontation between economic growth and environmental protection was diffused. New firms were not only allowed to move into polluted cities, but they became one of the main vehicles for improving the quality of the air. Economic growth facilitated, rather than blocked, air quality improvement.

Working with Inefficient Regulations

At times it may seem that only serious structural changes will begin to harmonize short-term and long-term goals. And given that serious structural changes are frequently impossible, the task appears hopeless.

But that is not necessarily the case! Working within an existing regulatory framework is sometimes possible even when the regulations are quite inefficient. Political inertia frequently prevents the preferred solution— structural reform which eliminates the inefficient regulations. Therefore it is comforting to note that it is possible to get results even when the feasible menu is severely restricted.

An example of this point involves an application of the trading concept to water conservation in arid regions. In some parts of the United States well-intentioned regulations had an unintentional side-effect—they discouraged water conservation even when water is scarce. In essence the regulations don't allow those conserving the water to recover any of the costs associated with conservation by transferring the conserved water to others willing to pay for it, so the incentive to conserve is lost.

On January 17, 1989, a historic agreement was negotiated between a growers association, a major user of irrigation water, and the Metropolitan Water District (MWD) of California, a public agency that supplies water to the Los Angeles area (Taylor 1990). Under that agreement the MWD will bear the capital and operating costs, as well as the indirect costs (such as reduced hydro power), of a huge program to reduce seepage losses as the water is transported to the growers and to install new water-conserving irrigation techniques. In return they will get all of the conserved water. Everyone gains. The district gets the water it needs at a reasonable price; the growers get virtually the same amount irrigation benefits as they got before without being forced to bear large additional expenditures they would be difficult to pass along to consumers.

Moving Toward Energy Sustainability

One industrialized country innovation which has been transplanted to a developing country setting involves demand management strategies for electric utilities.[4] The growth in electricity demand triggers a need to build more plants. New plants typically mean more pollution. The need for these plants would be eliminated or at least deferred if much better use could be made of the existing capacity. In virtually every country of the world the existing capacity is not being used efficiently. This means that we could be getting a lot more value from the existing capacity.

One area where this is clearly true is in lighting. New light bulbs have been developed which provide as much light as traditional bulbs using a fraction of the electricity. The problem in the developing country context is the high initial cost of these bulbs. How can people afford to buy them?

A new project in India shows how this problem can be solved. The local utility will sponsor a program to place these compact fluorescent bulbs in a large number of Bombay residences despite the high ($11.00) cost.

Here is how it works. The utility will lease the bulbs to residential customers for about $0.25 a month. These lease payments, when spread over four years will repay the (interest-free) cost of the bulbs. Each month the new light bulbs will reduce residential light bills by more than $0.25. Over their eight-year lifetime it is estimated that these new bulbs will save the Indian economy at least six times their purchase price in avoided capital investments for peak power generation. Furthermore the electricity conserved in Bombay will be made available to several India states on the Western grid currently suffering from power cuts, brownouts and drops in frequency during evening peak demand hours.

Everyone wins. The utility has to build fewer power plants and has fewer dissatisfied customers. Residential customers have the same amount of light for less money. Western India has a better, more reliable power supply.

Global Warming and Development

Some carrying capacity limits function at the global, rather than the national or local, level. As the scale of economic activity has proceeded steadily upward, the scope of environmental problems triggered by that activity has transcended both geographic and generational boundaries. Whereas the nation state used to be a sufficient form of political organization for resolving environmental problems, that may no longer the case. Whereas each generation of humans used to have the luxury of being able to satisfy its own needs without worrying about the needs of those generations to come, that is no longer the case either.

A creative use of policy instruments could, for example, institutionalize and regularize a system for sharing the costs of meeting global pollution control goals. As the Eastern European countries take hesitant steps toward market economies and Third World countries seek to provide a higher standard of living for their people, most observers believe that the ability of these nations to pay for substantial improvements in environmental control is questionable. Some sort of cost sharing arrangements between the western industrialized nations and these other nations is seen as one possible resolution of this conflict.

The level and form of any such cost sharing arrangements, however, are usually not clearly specified. By the appropriate choice of policy instruments, much of this cost sharing could be handled by normal market forces.

One example which received a good deal of attention at the Earth Summit is the potential use of transferable carbon entitlements to attack global warming (see UNCTAD 1992; Barrett 1990; Shelling 1992). Market-based economic incentive strategies would offer industrialized nations the opportunity to receive more environmental improvement per dollar spent and would offer the less industrialized nations the opportunity to receive financial help in their efforts to reduce pollution. Both would share in the resulting improvement in the global environment.

Is such an approach a pipe dream? I don't believe so because it can be designed to evolve slowly over time. And the joint implementation procedures outlines in the Climate Convention provide an appropriate starting point. The initial steps will necessarily be small as the parties will be hesitant to undertake large commitments.

Under this approach carbon dioxide emission entitlements would be assigned to a signatory nations with deadline for achievement. Signatory nations would be free to trade or lease these entitlements with other signatory nations. Signatory nations would also be able to secure offsetting reduction from nonsignatory countries are long as the reductions were certified.[5]

Regardless of the initial allocation of permits, the trading which would subsequently take place would provide the means for the control of greenhouse gases to be accomplished cost-effectively. This is a particularly important feature when, as is the case with controlling the gases contributing to global warming, concerns about fairness and affordability preclude simple solutions such as equal proportional reductions. Even very complex international allocations of the control responsibilities which are sensitive to a host of individual country concerns can be fully compatible with achieving the desired emission target at the lowest possible cost.

Because transferable entitlement systems allow the issue of who will pay for control to be separated from who will undertake control, they allow distributional and cost-effectiveness goals to be pursued simultaneously. They also facilitate technology transfer by providing a means for cost-sharing and risk-sharing. Cost-sharing and risk-sharing can be achieved even for very limited versions of transferable entitlement systems. In the United States now, for example, some sulfur oxide control equipment manufacturers have indicated a willingness to install the pollution control equipment free of charge, taking only the sulfur oxide allowances in return. In this way the recipient utility incurs neither a financial burden nor a financial risk; the equipment supplier is willing to accept both by accepting the allowances as payment. It is not difficult to imagine equipment manufacturers striking a similar deal with developing countries should a transferable carbon dioxide entitlement system be implemented.

IMPLEMENTING CHANGE

The challenge comes in implementing these policies. How can we proceed from concept to implemented policy in the developing country context? Let me sow a few ideas on some new strategies for instituting change when bureaucracy is smaller and has fewer resources to work with than in the industrialized nations.

Let's first tackle the problem of how to enforce pollution control regulations when bureaucracies are too small or too underfunded to do an effective job of monitoring and enforcement. One strategy is to use innovative penalty structures so that the cost of noncompliance is raised sufficiently even with limited enforcement activity that compliance becomes the cost-minimizing strategy. Two different strategies have been invoked. The first is to change the structure of noncompliance penalties and the second is privatize some of the routine enforcement activities traditionally delegated exclusively to public agencies.

Penalty structures can be manipulated in many ways. First the penalties for noncompliance can be increased. Higher penalties tend to offset to some degree the noncompliance incentives associated with infrequent enforcement. Another strategy being used in the United States is to complement monetary civil penalties with criminal penalties for selected environmental crimes (Cohen 1992; Segerson and Tietenberg 1992). Even the threat of incarceration turns out to provide a significant incentive. Finally, enforcement resources can be targeted more effectively on the most egregious polluters. For example, one strategy is to subject polluters to a rather low level of scrutiny until they have been caught in repeated noncompliance. Once a pattern of persistent failure to comply has been established, the firms are subjected to much more intense scrutiny and harsher penalties. Knowing that this treatment awaits persistent offenders turns out to provide an enormous incentive to comply and thereby avoid being labeled as a repeat offender, even in the face of infrequent monitoring.

Private environmental groups can, and have, also become important players in the total institutional mix. It was a private group that negotiated the first successful debt-for-nature swap. In the United States, for example, private groups are now allowed to enforce U.S. environmental laws by undertaking so-called citizen suits. When they win, which is very frequently, not only their court costs are reimbursed, but their attorney fees are reimbursed as well. Adding a private component expands the enforcement capability of the government tremendously. Research that I and a colleague have conducted on private enforcement suggests that it can be even better than public enforcement in some areas such as dealing with pollution from public facilities (Naysnerski and Tietenberg 1992).

Economists from developing countries have often expressed to me the view that their countries have limited resources for environmental enforcement and that enforcement staffs face irresistible pressures to engage in corrupt practices. In principle private enforcement provides a partial solution to each of these problems. By breaking the public monopoly on enforcement private enforcers can circumvent the constraints imposed by limited public funds and can limit the incentives for corruption by eliminating the guarantee of immunity a corrupt enforcer could otherwise provide.

This approach is currently being used in India for the 500 megawatt Dahanu Thermal Power project, the authorities in charge of pollution control plan to distribute to local communities and NGO's summaries in nontechnical language of the results of environmental monitoring. Communities can then check emissions against the legal standards and seek redress in the courts if necessary.

Skeptics are likely to suggest that public awareness of noncompliance is not a sufficient condition for compliance. That may be true, but it is also true that the power of public awareness should not be underestimated. In the United States, for example, many toxic air pollutants had not been regulated prior to the passage of the 1990 Clean Air Act Amendments. The Emergency Planning and Community Right-to-Know Act of 1986, however, required some 20,000 plants to report annual emissions of 320 potentially carcinogenic chemicals. These reports were then made available to the public. Publicized by newspapers and environmental groups, they became a rallying point for action. Even before the discussions about increasing the regulation of these substances became serious, businesses were beginning to make significant reductions in toxic emissions to counter the adverse publicity.

This tide of environmental policy innovations has produced some rather striking changes in the way environmental risks are managed by both public and private organizations. It has now become cheaper to anticipate problems than to react to them once they have occurred. Reducing waste has become a preferred solution to simply capturing it before it is released into the environment. Even captured waste has to be disposed of somewhere!

To accommodate these new organizational approaches for controlling environmental risks organizational structures have changed (Schmidheiny 1992). Once relegated to a remote part of the organizational chart and consulted only rarely, environmental risk managers are now a central part of operational decision-making in many corporations. They are consulted on design, production techniques, and input choices to name a few. Corporations such as 3M have discovered that as soon as they began systematically integrating environmental concerns into their operating decisions, they could actually save money. Once they started looking for environmentally benign ways to produce their product they found them. In many cases these new ways proved not only to be better for the environment, but to cost less. Surprisingly the evidence in the United States suggests that sustainable approaches to development are frequently as cheap as unsustainable approaches or result in rather mild increases in costs. The notion that only the rich can afford a healthy environment does not seem consistent with the historical experience.

While economic incentive approaches to environmental control offer no panacea, they frequently do offer a practical way to achieve environmental goals more flexibly and at lower cost than more traditional regulatory approaches. That is a compelling virtue.

Acknowledgment. An earlier and somewhat expanded view of these and related principles can be found in Tietenberg (1991).

NOTES

1. For a recent review of this literature see Munasinghe (1992), Dixon (1990), and Braden and Kolstad (1991).
2. For a detailed treatment of this point see Tietenberg (1992).
3. I am focusing on regulatory solutions. In some cases, however, it is possible for users of a common property resource to develop informal rules to ration access. While these rules may not achieve all of the benefits of a regulatory solution they are sometimes sufficient. See Ostrom (1990).
4. Information supplied by Dr. Asok Gadgil of Lawrence Berkeley Lab.
5. The details of the proposed certification, monitoring and enforcement procedures, and institutions as well as a detailed description of how a full-blown permit system might evolve from current arrangements can be found in Tietenberg and Victor (1994).

REFERENCES

Barrett, S. 1990. "The Problem of Global Environmental Protection." *Oxford Review of Economic Policy* 6:68–79.
Braden, J. B. and C. D. Kolstad, eds. 1991. *Measuring the Demand for Environmental Quality.* New York: Elsevier.
Cohen, M. 1992. "Criminal Penalties." In T. H. Tietenberg, ed., *Innovation in Environmental Policy: Economic and Legal Aspects of Recent Developments in Environmental Enforcement and Liability,* pp. 75–108. Cheltenham, UK: Edward Elgar.
Commoner, B., M. Corr, and P. J. Stamler. 1971. "The Causes of Pollution." *Environment* (April).
Dixon, J. 1990. *Economics of Protected Areas: A New Look at Benefits and Costs.* Washington, D.C.: Island Press.

Dudek, D. J. and J. Palmisano. 1988. "Emissions Trading: Why Is This Thoroughbred Hobbled?" *Columbia Journal of Environmental Law* 13:217–56.

Munasinghe, M. 1992. *Environmental Economics and Valuation in Development Decisionmaking.* Washington D.C.: World Bank, Environment Working Paper No. 51.

Holderness, C. G. 1990. "Liability Insurers as Corporate Monitors." *International Review of Law and Economics* 10:115–129.

Katzman, M. T. 1988. "Pollution Liability Insurance and Catastrophic Environmental Risk." *The Journal of Risk and Insurance* 55:75–100.

Kehne, J. 1986. "Encouraging Safety Through Insurance-Based Incentives: Responsibility for Hazardous Wastes." *Yale Law Journal* 96:403–427.

Naysnerski, W. and T. Tietenberg. 1992. "Private Enforcement of Environmental Law." *Land Economics* 68:28–48.

Ostrom, E. 1990. *Governing the Commons: The Evolution of Institutions for Collective Actions.* Cambridge UK: Cambridge University Press.

Panayotou, T. "Economic Incentives in Environmental Management and Their Relevance to Developing Countries." In D. Eröcal, ed., *Environmental Management in Developing Countries,* pp. 83–126. Paris: OECD.

Schmidheiny, S. 1992. *Changing Course: A Global Business Perspective on Development and the Environment.* Cambridge, Mass.: MIT Press.

Segerson, K. and T. Tietenberg. 1992. "Defining Efficient Sanctions." In T. H. Tietenberg, ed., *Innovation in Environmental Policy: Economic and Legal Aspects of Recent Developments in Environmental Enforcement and Liability,* pp. 53–73. Cheltenham, UK: Edward Elgar.

Shelling, T. C. 1992. "Some Economics of Global Warming" *The American Economic Review* 82:1–14.

Taylor, R. E. 1990. *Ahead of the Curve: Shaping New Solutions to Environmental Problems.* New York: Environmental Defense Fund.

Tietenberg, T. H. 1990. "Economic Instruments for Environmental Regulation." *Oxford Review of Economic Policy* 6:17–33.

—— 1991. "Managing the Transition: The Potential Role for Economic Policies." In J. Matthews, ed., *Preserving the Global Environment: The Challenge of Shared Leadership,* pp. 187–226. New York: Norton.

Tietenberg, T. ed. 1992. *Innovation in Environmental Policy: Economic and Legal Aspects of Recent Developments in Environmental Enforcement and Liability.* Cheltenham, UK: Edward Elgar.

Tietenberg T. H. and D. Victor. 1994. "Tradeable Permits for Controlling Global Warming: Implementation Issues." Paper presented at the American Economics Association meetings in Boston, January.

UNCTAD (United Nations Conference on Trade and Development). 1992. *Combating Global Warming: Study on a Global System of Tradeable Carbon Emission Entitlements.* New York: United Nations.

SEVEN

Ecological Economics: Creating a Transdisciplinary Science

Robert Costanza

Ecological economics (EE) is a *transdisciplinary* approach to environmental sciences that examines the interdependent relationships between ecological and economic systems as well as between mounting global environmental, population, and economic development problems. The overall goal is to sustain both ecological and economic systems by identifying ways that local and short term goals and incentives (like local economic growth and private interests) can be made consistent with global and long term goals (like sustainability and global welfare). Ultimately, sustainability depends on our ability to develop an equitable economic system that values both cultural and biological diversity, and makes it in everyone's interest to protect natural capital.

This paper: (1) summarizes the state and goals of this emerging transdisciplinary field, with respect to issues of sustainability; (2) provides a working agenda for research, education, and policy development for the coming decade; and (3) provides some guiding principles and recommendations for policies to achieve these goals. Some recommendations for operationalizing these concepts are: (1) to establish a hierarchy of goals for local, national, and global ecological economic planning and management; (2) to develop better regional and global ecological economic modeling capabilities that illustrate the range of possible outcomes of our current activities; (3) to identify mechanisms, such as prices and other behavioral incentives, of taking into consideration long run, global ecological costs, *including uncertainty*; and (4) to develop policies that prevent further decline in the stock of *natural capital.*

AN ECOLOGICAL ECONOMIC WORLD VIEW

There is increasing awareness that our global ecological life support system is endangered, and that economic decisions made by individuals on the basis of local, narrow, short-term criteria can produce disastrous results globally and in the long run because they exclude environmental and social costs. Disastrous results have already occurred for approximately 40% of the world's population who do not have access to an adequate amount of food, safe and sufficient supplies of water, secure shelter, and access to education and health care (WHO 1992), and who, in general, are disproportionately affected by environmental degradation. There is also increasing awareness that traditional economic and ecological models and concepts fall short in their ability to deal with these problems.

EE is a *transdisciplinary* field of study that addresses the relationships between ecosystems and economic systems in the broadest sense. These relationships are central to many of humanity's current problems and to building a sustainable future, but are not well covered by individual scientific disciplines.

By *transdisciplinary* we mean that EE goes beyond the boundaries of individual scientific disciplines and tries to integrate and synthesize many different disciplinary perspectives. One way it does this is by focusing more directly on the problems, rather than the particular intellectual tools and models used to solve them, and by ignoring arbitrary intellectual turf boundaries. No discipline has intellectual precedence in an endeavor as important as achieving sustainability. While the intellectual tools we use in this quest are important, they are secondary to the goal of resolving critical environmental problems and managing our use of the planet. Focusing on tools and techniques is analogous to being "a person with a hammer to whom everything looks like a nail." Rather we should consider the task, evaluate existing tools' abilities to handle the job, and design new ones if they are ineffective. EE uses the tools of conventional economics and ecology as appropriate, although the need for new tools may emerge where the coupling of economics and ecology is not possible with existing ones.

How Is EE Different from Conventional Approaches?

Just as the whole is more than the sum of its parts, EE differs from the individual disciplines of economics and ecology in terms of the importance it attaches to environment-economy interactions as well as links between different scales of space and time.

Figure 7.1 illustrates one aspect of the relationship; the domains of the different subdisciplines. The upper left box represents the domain of "conventional" economics, the interactions of economic sectors (like mining, manufacturing, or households) with each other. The domain of "conventional" ecology—the interactions of ecosystems and their components with each other—is in the lower right box. The lower left box represents inputs from ecological sectors to economic sectors, i.e.,the use of renewable and nonrenewable natural resources by the economy. This is the usual domain of *resource* economics and environmental impact analysis. The upper right box represents the "use" by ecological sectors of economic "products." The products of interest in this box are usually unwanted by-products of production and the ultimate wastes from consumption. Pollution and its mitigation, prevention and mediation is the usual domain of *environ-*

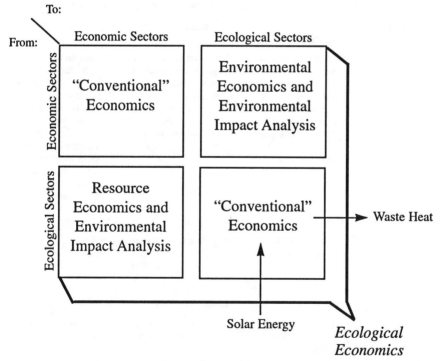

FIGURE 7.1.   The domains of conventional economics, conventional ecology, environmental and resource economics, and ecological economics.

mental economics and environmental impact analysis. EE encompasses and transcends these disciplinary boundaries by focusing on the entire web of interactions between economic and ecological sectors, and by viewing the human economy as part of a larger whole.

Table 7.1 presents some of the other major differences between EE and conventional economics (CEcon) and conventional ecology (CEcol). The basic world view of CEcon is one in which individual human consumers are the central figures. Their tastes and preferences are taken as given and are the dominant, determining force. The resource base is viewed as essentially limitless due to technical progress and infinite substitutability; EE takes a

TABLE 7.1

Comparison of "Conventional" Economics and Ecology with Ecological Economics

	"Conventional" Economics	"Conventional" Ecology	Ecological Economics
Basic world view	Mechanistic, static, atomistic	Evolutionary, atomistic	Dynamic, systems, evolutionary
	Individual tastes and preferences taken as given and the dominant force. The resource base viewed as essentially limitless due to technical progress and infinite substitutability	Evolution acting at the genetic level viewed as the dominant force. The resource base is limited. Humans are just another species but are rarely studied.	Human preferences, understanding, technology and organization coevolve to reflect broad ecological opportunities and constraints. Humans are responsible for understanding their role in the larger system and managing it for sustainability
Time frame	Short	Multiscale	Multiscale
	50 yrs max. 1–4 yrs usual	days to eons, but time scales often define non-communicating sub-disciplines	days to eons, multiscale synthesis
Space frame	Local to international	Local to regional	Local to global
	framework invarient at increasing spatial scale, basic units change from individuals to firms to countries	most research has focused on relatively small research sites in single ecosystems, but larger scales becoming more important recently	hierarchy of scales

	"Conventional" Economics	"Conventional" Ecology	Ecological Economics
Species frame	Humans only	Nonhumans only	Whole ecosystem, including humans
	plants and animals only rarely included for contributary value	attempts to find "pristine" ecosystems untouched by humans	acknowledges interconnections between humans and rest of nature
Primary macro goal	Growth of national economy	Survival of species	Sustainability of ecological economic system
Primary micro goal	Max profits (firms) Max utility (indivs)	Max reproductive success	Must be adjusted to reflect system goals
	all agents following micro goals leads to macro goal being fulfilled. External costs and benefits given lip service but usually ignored	all agents following micro goals leads to macro goal being fulfilled.	Social organization and cultural institutions at higher levels of the space/time hierarchy ameliorate conflicts produced by myopic pursuit of micro goals at lower levels, and vice versa
Assumptions about technical progress	Very optimistic	Pessimistic or no opinion	Prudently skeptical
Academic stance	Disciplinary	Disciplinary	Transdisciplinary
	monistic, focus on mathematical tools	more pluralistic than economics, but still focused on tools and techniques. Few rewards for	pluralistic, focus on problems

more holistic view with humans as one component (albeit a very important one) in the overall system. Human preferences, understanding, technology and cultural organization all coevolve to reflect broad ecological opportunities and constraints. Humans have a special place in the system because they are responsible for understanding their own role in the larger system and managing it for sustainability.

This basic world view is similar to that of CEcol, in which the resource base is limited and humans are just another (albeit seldom studied) species.

But EE differs from CEcol in the importance it gives to humans as a species, and its emphasis on the mutual importance of cultural and biological evolution.

The concept of *evolution* is a guiding notion for both ecology and EE (see Boulding 1991). Evolution is the process of change in complex systems through selection of transmittable traits. Whether these traits are the shapes and programmed behavioral characteristics of organisms transmitted genetically or the institutions and behaviors of cultures which are transmitted through cultural artifacts, they are both evolutionary processes. Evolution implies a dynamic and adapting non-equilibrium system, rather than the static equilibrium system often assumed in conventional economics. Evolution does *not* imply change in a particular direction (i.e., progress).

EE uses an expanded definition of the term "evolution" to encompass both biological and cultural change. Biological evolution is slow relative to cultural evolution. The price human cultures pay for their ability to adapt rapidly is the danger that they have become too dependent on short-run payoffs, and thereby, usually ignore long-term payoffs and issues of sustainability. Biological evolution imposes a built-in long-run constraint that cultural evolution does not have. To ensure sustainability we may have to develop institutions that constrain short-sighted consumptive behavior, and bring the global, long-term, multi-species, multi-scale, whole systems perspective to bear on short term cultural evolution.

The issue of humans' role in shaping the combined biological and cultural evolution of the planet is of critical importance. Humans are conscious of the processes of biological and cultural evolution and cannot avoid being anthropocentric, nor can humans avoid the necessity of meeting short-term and immediate survival needs justs as all other species. However, our evolutionary and cultural heritage, as exemplified in non-market economic systems of indigenous populations, demonstrates that we also have the capacity to take a broader *biocentric* perspective that is necessary for human survival in the long run. Culture itself may be defined as a system of resource management in that it structures human relationships and interactions with the environment. What many nonmarket indigenous economic systems have in common is that they have persisted over a long period of time, are based on the precautionary principle of reducing risk through sharing and common property institutional arrangements—rather than on maximization of individual gain, and on relationships of fairness and long-term reciprocity not only among humans, but also between humans and other species, as well as other elements of the natural world.

EE acknowledges that the human system is a subsystem within the larger ecological system. This implies not only a relationship of interdependence, but ultimately a relation of dependence of the subsystem on the larger parent system. The first questions to ask about a subsystem are: how big is it relative to the total system, how big can it be, and how big should it be? These are questions of scale, which involve the macro-allocation of resources between natural and human systems, as well as between present and future uses and generations. Resolving these questions is a social and political matter that requires an institutional perspective because future values are uncertain and are not based on transactions between individuals (Martinez-Alier 1991).

EE is also unique in acknowledging the two-way linkages between scales, rather than the one-way view of the conventional sciences in which all macro behavior is the simple aggregation of micro behavior. Consequently, social organization and cultural institutions at higher levels of the space/time hierarchy may ameliorate conflicts produced by myopic pursuit of micro goals at lower levels, and visa versa. The macro goal of EE is sustainability of the combined ecological economic system. CEcol's macro goal of species survival is similar to sustainability, but is generally confined to single species and not the whole system. CEcon emphasizes growth rather than sustainability at the macro level.

Perhaps the key distinctions between EE and the conventional sciences lie in their academic stances, and their assumptions about technical progress. CEcon is very optimistic about the ability of technology to ultimately remove all resource constraints to continued economic growth. CEcol really has very little to say directly about technology, since it tends to ignore humans altogether. But to the extent that it has an opinion, it would be pessimistic about technology's ability to remove resource constraints because all other existing natural ecosystems that don't include humans are observed to be resource limited. EE is prudently skeptical in this regard. Given our high level of uncertainty about this issue, it is irrational to *bank on* technology's ability to remove resource constraints. If we guess wrong then the result is disastrous, irreversible destruction of our resource base and civilization itself. We should at least for the time being assume that technology will *not* be able to remove resource constraints. If it does we can be pleasantly surprised. If it does not we are still left with a sustainable system. EE assumes this prudently skeptical stance on technical progress.

A Hierarchy of Goals and Incentives

No complex system can be managed effectively without clear goals, and appropriate mechanisms for achieving them. In managing the earth, we are faced with a nested hierarchy of goals that span a wide range of time and space scales. Ecological systems play a fundamental role in supporting life on Earth at all scales. They form the life-support system without which economic activity would not be possible. They are essential in global material cycles like the carbon and water cycles. They provide raw materials, food, water, recreational opportunities, and microclimate control for the entire human population. In any rational system of management, global ecological and economic health and sustainability (see May, paper 1 for definitions) should be "higher" goals than local, short-term national economic growth or private interests. In this context, economic growth can only be supported as a policy goal to the extent that it is consistent with long term global sustainability.

Unfortunately, most of our current institutions and incentive structures deal only with relatively short-term, local, goals and incentives (Clark 1973). This would not be a problem if the local and short-term goals and incentives simply added up to appropriate behavior in the global long run. as many assume they do. In other words if they were *consistent* with global and long-term goals. Unfortunately, this often not the case. Individuals (or firms, or countries) pursuing their own private self-interests in the absence of mechanisms to account for community and global interests frequently run afoul of these larger goals and can often drive themselves to their own demise.

These goal and incentive inconsistencies have been characterized and generalized in many ways, beginning with Hardin's (1968) classic paper on the tragedy of the commons and continuing through more recent work on "social traps" (Platt 1973; Cross and Guyer 1980; Tieger 1980; Costanza 1987; Costanza and Schrum 1988; Costanza and Perrings 1990). Social traps occur when local, individual incentives that guide behavior are inconsistent with the overall goals of the system. Examples are cigarette and drug addiction, overuse of pesticides, economic boom and bust cycles, poverty, absence of defined property rights and lack of assurance of future access to resources, and a host of others. Social traps are also amenible to experimental research to see how people behave in trap-like situations and how to best avoid and escape from social traps (Edney and Harper 1978; Tieger 1980; Brockner and Rubin 1985; Costanza and Schrum 1988) The bottom line emerging from this research is that in cases where social traps exist, the system is not inherently sustainable, and special steps must be taken to harmonize goals and incentives over the hierarchy of time and space scales involved.

This is in contrast to natural systems, which are forced to adopt a long-term perspective by the constraints of genetic evolution. In natural systems "survival" generally equates to sustainability of the species as part of a larger ecosystem, and natural seclection tends to find sustainable systems in the long run. Humans have broken the bonds of genetic evolution by the expanded use of learned behavior our large brains allow and extending our physical capabilities with tools. The price we pay for this rapid adaptation is a partial isolation from long-term constraints and a susceptability to social traps.

Another general result of social trap research is that the relative effectiveness of alternative corrective steps is not easy to predict from simple "rational" models of human behavior prevalent in conventional economic thinking. The experimental facts indicate the need to develop more realistic models of human behavior under uncertainty which acknowledge the complexity of most real world decisions, and our limited information processing capabilities (Heiner 1983).

A RESEARCH AGENDA
FOR ECOLOGICAL ECONOMICS

An essential element of a strategy to achieve sustainability is innovative and applied research that is integrated with the policy and management process. The research agenda for EE suggested below is intended to begin the process of defining topics for future ecological economic research. The list of topics can be divided into five major parts: (1) sustainability: maintaining our life support system; (2) valuation of natural resources and natural capital; (3) natural resource accounting; (4) ecological economic modeling at local, regional, and global scales; and (5) innovative instruments for environmental management. Some background on each of these topics is given below.

Sustainability: Maintaining Our Life Support System

Sustainability has been variously construed (cf. Brown et al 1987; Pezzey 1989; WCED 1987) but a useful definition is the amount of consumption that can be continued indefinitely without degrading capital stocks—including "natural capital" stocks (cf. El Serafy 1991). In a business, capital stock includes long-term assets such as buildings and machinery that serve as the means of production. Natural capital is the soil and atmospheric structure, plant and animal biomass, etc. that, taken together, forms the basis of all ecosystems. This natural capital stock uses primary inputs (sunlight) to produce the range of ecosystem services and physical natural resource flows. Examples of natural capital include forests, fish populations and petroleum deposits. The natural resource flows yielded by these natural capital stocks are, respectively, cut timber, caught fish, and pumped crude oil.

We have now entered a new era in which the limiting factor in development is no longer manmade capital but remaining natural capital. Timber is limited by remaining forests, not sawmill capacity; fish catch is limited by fish populations, not by fishing boats; crude oil is limited by remaining petroleum deposits as well as the capacity of the environment to absorb greenhouse gasses, rather than by pumping and drilling capacity. Most economists view natural and manmade capital as substitutes rather than complements. Consequently neither factor can be limiting. Only if factors are complementary can one be limiting. Ecological economists see manmade and natural capital as fundamentally complementary and therefore emphasize the importance of limiting factors and changes in the pattern of scarcity. This is a fundamental difference that needs to be reconciled through research and debate.

In an important sense, sustainability is merely justice with respect to future generations as well as to the poor and most vulnerable members of society within our own generation, who have more direct economic dependence on natural resources, who are disproportionately affected by resource depletion and environmental degradation, and who are excluded from decisions that affect them. This includes other species, even though our main interest may be in our own species. The most obvious danger of ignoring the role of nature in economics is that nature is the economy's life support system, and by ignoring it we may inadvertently damage it beyond it's ability to repair itself. Indeed, there is much evidence that we have already done so. Several authors have stressed the fact that current economic systems do not *inherently* incorporate any concern about the sustainability of our natural life support system and the economies which depend on it (e.g., Costanza and Daly 1987; Hardin 1991; Clark 1991). Pearce (1987) discusses the reasons for the inability of existing forms of economic organization (free market, mixed, planned) to guarantee sustainability.

Sustainable "development" is distinct from economic "growth" which is an increase in quantity, and that cannot be sustained indefinitely on a finite planet. "Development," which is an improvement in the quality of life without necessarily causing an increase in quantity of resources consumed, may be sustainable. Sustainable growth is an impossibility. Sustainable development must become our primary long-term policy goal (see Ahmad 1989; Boulding 1991; Daly and Cobb 1989; and Daly 1991 for more on these ideas).

Definitions of sustainability are obviously dependent on the time and space scale we are using. Rather than trying to determine the *correct* time and space scale for sustainability we need to concentrate on how the different scales interact and how we might construct *multiscale* operational definitions of sustainability.

While acknowledging that the sustainability concept requires much additional research, the following working definition of sustainability has been developed (Costanza et al 1991):

Sustainability is a relationship between dynamic human economic systems and larger dynamic, but normally slower-changing ecological systems, in which

(a) human life can continue indefinitely,
(b) human individuals can flourish,
(c) human cultures can develop; but in which
(d) effects of human activities remain within bounds, so as not to destroy the diversity, complexity, and function of the ecological life support system.

Valuation of Ecosystem Services and Natural Capital

A prerequisite for achieving sustainability is an economic system that values natural capital and accounts for ecosystem goods and services. The first step is to determine values for them comparable to those of economic goods and services. In determining values we must also consider how much of our ecological life support systems we can afford to lose. To what extent can we substitute manufactured for natural capital, and how much of our natural capital is irreplaceable (El Serafy 1991). For example, could we replace the radiation screening services of the ozone layer which are currently being destroyed?

Some argue that we cannot place economic value on such "intangibles" as human life, environmental aesthetics, or long-term ecological benefits (Norton 1986). But, in fact, we do so every day. When we set construction standards for highways, bridges and the like, we value human life—acknowledged or not—because spending more money on construction would save lives. To preserve our natural capital, we must confront these often difficult choices and valuations directly rather than denying their existence.

Because of the inherent difficulties and uncertainties in determining values, there is no consensus on the correct approach to valuation—perhaps because different approaches reflect particular value judgments and are associated with different social and environmental implications. Historically, resources have been managed individually, for particular values, without considering how they are linked in the ecosystem and how the costs and benefits are distributed among social groups (NRC 1993). For example, forests have been valued and managed for timber resources, without considering the effects of forestry practices on fisheries and their role in regulating water flow, providing habitat for wildlife, and providing nontimber and nonmarket resources to people. Conflicts among these values and management priorities need to be resolved through informed social dialogue in which the interests of all stakeholders are represented, rather than on the basis of market behavior and partial values.

The conventional economic view defines value as the expression of individualistic human preferences, with the preferences taken as given and with no attempt to analyze their origins or patterns of long-term change. For goods and services produced with relatively few long-term impacts (like tomatoes or bread) that are traded in well-functioning markets with adequate information, market ("revealed preference") valuations may work relatively well.

But ecological goods and services (like wetland sewage treatment or global climate control) are long-term by nature, are generally not traded in markets (no one owns the air or water), and information about their contribution to individual's well-being is poor. To determine their value, economists try to get people to reveal what they would be willing to pay for ecological goods and services in hypothetical markets (cf. Bartlett 1984; Bishop 1982; Brookshire et al. 1983; Conrad 1980; Greenley et al. 1981; Randall and Stoll 1980; Randall 1986). For example, we can ask people the maximum they would pay to use national parks, even if they don't have to actually pay it. The quality of results in this method depends on how well informed people are; and it does not adequately incorporate long-term goals since it excludes future generations from bidding in the markets. Also, it is difficult to induce individuals to reveal their true willingness to pay for natural resources when the question is put directly. Contingent referenda (willingness to be taxed as a citizen along with other citizens, as opposed to willingness to pay as an individual) is superior to ordinary willingness to pay studies in this regard.

In practice, valuation, or shadow pricing of environmental functions, may require some collectively set quantitative standard. Shadow prices can then be calculated subject to the constraint represented by that standard (i.e., Hueting, 1991).

An alternative method for estimating ecological values assumes a bio-physical basis for value (cf. Costanza 1980; Cleveland et al. 1984; Costanza et al. 1989; Cleveland 1991). This theory suggests that in the long run humans come to value things according to how costly they are to produce, and that this cost is ultimately a function of how organized they are relative to their environment. To organize a complex structure takes energy, both directly in the form of fuel and indirectly in the form of other organized structures like factories. For example a car is a much more organized structure than a lump of iron ore, and therefore it takes a lot of energy (directly and indirectly) to organize iron ore into a car. The amount of solar energy required to grow forests can therefore serve as a measure of their energy cost, their organization, and hence, according to this theory, their value.

Table 7.2 shows the results of applying these two radically different approaches, one based on human perceptions (willingness to pay or WTP) and one based on biophysical production (energy analysis or EA) to the valuation of wetlands in Louisiana (Costanza et al. 1989). The striking feature is just how close the results are to each other. They can in fact be interpreted as setting the range within which the true value probably falls. The WTP method sets the low end of the range since it must ennumerate all the individual nonmarketed services of the ecosystem and develop pseudo-markets (via questionaires or observations of behavior) to evaluate each one. This process will almost certainly miss some important services. The EA method, on the other hand, assumes that all the production of the ecosystem is valuable, directly or indirectly, and to the extent that some ecosystem services are not ultimately valuable to humans it overestimates.

The point that must be stressed, however, is that the economic value of ecosystems is connected to their physical, chemical, and biological role in both the short term and the long-term, global system-whether the present generation of humans fully recognizes that role or not. If it is accepted that each species, no matter how seemingly uninteresting or lacking in immediate utility, has a role in natural ecosystems (which *do* provide many direct benefits to humans), it is possible to shift the focus away from our imperfect short-term perceptions and derive more accurate values for long-term ecosystem services. Using this perspective we may be able to better estimate the values contributed by, say, maintenance of water and atmospheric quality to long-term human well-being.

Ecological Economic System Accounting

GNP, as well as other related measures of national economic performance have come to be extremely important as policy objectives, political issues and benchmarks of the general welfare. Yet GNP as presently defined ignores the contribution of nature to production, often leading to peculiar results.

For example, a standing forest provides real economic services for people: by conserving soil, cleaning air and water, providing habitat for wildlife, and supporting recreational activities. But as GNP is currently

TABLE 7.2
Summary of Wetland Value Estimates ($1983)

Method	Per Acre Present Value at specified discount rate	
	8%	3%
WTP based		
Commercial fishery	$ 317	$ 846
Trapping	151	401
Recreation	46	181
Storm protection	1915	7549
Total	$2429	$8977
Option and existence values	?	?
EA based		
GPP conversion	6,400–10,600	17,000–28,200
"Best Estimate"	$2,429–6,400	$8,977–17,000

SOURCE: Costanza et al. (1989)

figured, only the value of harvested timber is calculated in the total. On the other hand, the billions of dollars that Exxon spent on the Valdez cleanup—and the billions spent by Exxon and others on the more than 100 other oil spills in the last 16 months—all actually *improved* our apparent economic performance. Why? Because cleaning up oil spills creates jobs and consumes resources, all of which add to GNP. Of course, these expenses would not have been necessary if the oil had not been spilled, so they shouldn't be considered "benefits." But GNP adds up all production without differentiating between costs and benefits, and is therefore not a very good measure of economic health.

In fact, when resource depletion and degradation are factored into economic trends, what emerges is a radically different picture from that depicted by conventional methods. For example, Herman Daly and John Cobb (Daly and Cobb 1989) have attempted to adjust GNP to account mainly for depletions of natural capital, pollution effects, and income distribution effects by producing an "index of sustainable economic welfare" (ISEW). They conclude that while GNP in the United States rose over the 1956–86 interval, ISEW remained relatively unchanged since about 1970. When factors such as loss of farms and wetlands, costs of mitigating acid rain effects, and health costs caused by increased pollution, are accounted for, the U.S. economy has not improved at all. If we continue to ignore natural ecosystems we may drive the economy down while we think we are building it up. By consuming our natural capital, we endanger our ability to sustain income. Although many arbitrary judgments go into the ISEW, according to Daly and Cobb it is less arbitrary than GNP as a measure of welfare. John Cobb and his group at Claremont have continued work on the index and their procedure is worth mentioning as a model for scholarly debate. Cobb sent the ISEW to a number of standard economists for criticism, offering an honorarium and contracting to publish their criticisms along with a revised version of the ISEW that would take account of their criticism, or else explain why that could not or should not be done. The result has been a fruitful interchange and better mutual understanding.

There are a number of additional promising approaches to accounting for ecosystem services and natural capital being developed (cf Ahmad 1989; El Serafy 1991; Hannon 1991; Hueting 1991; Peskin 1991; Faber and Proops 1991; and Ulanowicz 1991) and this area promises to be a major focus of research in EE. The approaches are based on differing assumptions, but share the goal of attempting to quantify ecological economic interdependencies and arriving at overall system measures of health and performance.

The economist Wassily Leontief (1941) was the first to attempt detailed quantitative descriptions of complex systems to allow a complete accounting of system interdependencies. Leontief's input-output (I-O) analysis has become a standard conceptual and applied tool in economic accounting. Isard (1972) was the first to attempt combined ecological economic system I-O analysis. Combined ecological economic system I-O models have been proposed by several other authors. as well (Daly, 1968; Victor, 1972; Cumberland 1987). Ecologists have also applied I-O analysis to the accounting of material transfers in ecosystems (Funderlic and Heath 1971; Finn 1976; Barber et al 1979; Hannon 1973, 1976, 1979, 1991; Costanza and Neill 1984; Costanza and Hannon 1989). We refer to the total of all variations of the analysis of ecological and/or economic networks as *network analysis*.

Network analysis holds the promise of allowing an integrated quantitative treatment of combined ecological economic systems. One promising route is the use of "ascendancy" (Ulanowicz 1980, 1986) and related measures (Wulff et al. 1989) to measure the degree of organization in ecological, economic, or any other networks. Measures like ascendency go several steps beyond the traditional diversity indices used in ecology. They estimate not only how many different species (or sectors) there are in a system but, more importantly, how those species are organized. This kind of measure may provide the basis for a quantitative and general index of system health applicable to both ecological and economic systems.

Another promising avenue for research in network analysis has to do with its use for "pricing" commodities in ecological or economic systems (Costanza 1980; Costanza and Herendeen 1984; Costanza and Hannon 1989). The "mixed units" problem arises in any field that tries to analyze interdependence and limiting factors in complex systems that have many different types and qualities of interacting processes and commodities. Ecology and economics are two such fields. Network analysis in ecology has avoided this problem in the past by *arbitrarily* choosing one commodity flowing through the system as an index of interdependence (i.e., carbon, enthalpy, nitrogen, etc.). This ignores the complex interdependencies among commodities and assumes that the chosen commodity is a valid "tracer" for relative value or importance in the system. This assumption is unrealistic and severely limits the comprehensiveness of an analysis whose major objective is to deal comprehensively with whole systems.

There are evolving methods for dealing with the mixed units problem based on analogies to the calculation of prices in economic input-output models. Starting with a more realistic *commodity by process* description of ecosystem networks that allows for joint products one can ultimately convert the multiple commodity description into a pair of matrices that can serve as the input for standard (single commodity) network analysis. The new single commodity description incorporates commodity and process interdependencies and limiting factor relationships in a manner analogous to the way economic value incorporates production interdependencies in economic systems (Costanza and Hannon 1989). This analysis allows a biophysical valuation of components of combined ecological and economic systems as a compliment to subjective evaluations.

In this approach, the system is conceptualized as interacting processes and commodities. A *commodity* is defined as some identifiable unit moving through the system. It can be a simple element (like carbon) or a complex structure (like plant biomass or cars) or a service (like transportation). Commodities are transformed (produced, consumed, or combined into more complex commodities) in *processes*. Biomass, for example, is produced by the photosynthetic process, which combines (consumes) water, carbon dioxide, sunlight and nutrients into plant material. Matrices that indicate the amounts of each commodity used and produced in particular processes during a specified time interval can be used to illustrate net ecological and material inputs to each process in the system as well as exports, changes in stock, and depreciation (see tables 7.3 and 7.4). Interdependence relationships or "ecological interdependency factors" (EIFs) are expressed in weighting factors, and are used to convert the quantity of commodities into commensurable units. EIFs are based on the assumption that the total inputs of each commodity to all processes are equal to the total output of each commodity from all processes.

Note that conservation holds for each commodity but not for the processes, which are each measured in different units. The total output of each commodity from all the processes which produce it (the row sum of V) is equal to the total input of that commodity to all the processes that use it (the row sum of U), including the amount of commodity that is "depreciated" or exported (r). Processes (columns in V) that contain more than one entry represent "joint products." Table 7.5 illustrates the calculation of direct and indirect uses and EIFs. Negative values reflect the significance of joint products. At the global level joint products are significant and unavoidable.

This simplified example shows the possibility of implementing global ecological economic input-output accounting as first suggested by Daly (1968). The approach allows a comprehensive treatment of the interdepen-

TABLE 7.3

Global Multicommodity Input ("Use") Matrix (**U**), Along With The Vectors For Net Export + Stock Replacement (**r**), Total Output Excluding Waste Heat (**p**), and The Net Input Vector (Sunlight, **e**)

Commodities	Urban econ. (1)	Agri-culture (2)	Natural plants (3)	Ani-mals (4)	Soil (5)	Deep ocean (6)	Surface ocean (7)	Atmo-sphere (8)	Deep geology (9)	Net output r	Total output p
Manufact. goods (1)	2.71	0.08	0	0	0	0	0	0	0	1.19	3.98
Agr. Products (2)	1.28	4.55	0	3.27	0	0	0	0	0	0	9.1
Natural products (3)	1.18	0	0	27.9	103.4	34.6	0	0	0.16	0.06	167.3
Nitrogen (4)	55	62.4	208	0	493.6	0	168	389.5	0	0	1376.5
Carbon (5)	0	8.2	147	0	0	15.6	37.2	110.3	0	0	318.3
Phosphorous (6)	12.6	28.5	1345.7	0	8.4	0	21	9.5	13	0	1438.7
Water vapor (7)	0	0	0	0	0	0	0	496100	0	0	496100
Fresh water (8)	1008	15490	51226	0	111419	0	424700	0	0	2000	605843
Fossil fuels (9)	5	0	0	0	0	0	0	0	0	-4.93	0.07
Net input (sunlight) (**e**)	0	23	227	0	0	0	606	0	0		

SOURCE: Complete references are given in Costanza and Neill (1981)

NOTE: Units are (1) Manufactured goods—$10^{12}$$/yr; (2) Agricultural products—10^{15}g dry wt/yr; (3) Natural products—10^{15}g dry wt/yr; (4) Nitrogen—10^{12}gN/yr; (5) Carbon—10^{15}gC/yr; (6) Phosphorous—10^{12}gP/yr; (7) Water vapor—Km^3/yr; (8) Fresh water—Km^3/yr; (9) Fossil fuel—10^{15}gC/yr; e. Sunlight—10^{18} kcal/yr.

TABLE 7.4

Global Multicommodity Output ("make") Matrix (V), Along with the Vector for Total Input
(Units are the same as table 7.3)

Commodities	Urban econ. (1)	Agriculture (2)	Natural plants (3)	Animals (4)	Soil (5)	Deep ocean (6)	Surface ocean (7)	Atmosphere (8)	Deep geology (9)	Total input
Manufact. goods (1)	3.98	0	0	0	0	0	0	0	0	3.98
Agr. products (2)	0	9.1	0	0	0	0	0	0	0	9.1
Natural products (3)	0	0	163.4	3.9	0	0	0	0	0	167.3
Nitrogen (4)	80	31	0	295	340.5	0	182	448	0	1376.5
Carbon (5)	5	6.1	73.6	14	46.5	15.6	49.5	108	0	318.3
Phosphorous (6)	14.2	0	0	0	241.3	1161.1	0	9.5	12.6	1438.7
Water vapor (7)	79	5931	50740	0	14650	0	424700	0	0	496100
Fresh water (8)	929	9829	0	0	98985	0	0	496100	0	605843
Fossil Fuels (9)	0	0	0	0	0	0	0	0	0.07	0.07

TABLE 7.5

Matrix $(V-U)^{-1}$ for the U and V Matrices Shown in Tables 7.3 and 7.4, Respectively

Commodities	Processes									EIF
	Urban econ. (1)	Agriculture (2)	Natural plants (3)	Animals (4)	Soil (5)	Deep ocean (6)	Surface ocean (7)	Atmosphere (8)	Deep geology (9)	(3)
Manufact. goods (1)	0.79869	0.01329	-0.00029	0.00018	-0.00112	-0.00001	0.00002	0.00002	-0.00070	190.365
Agr. products (2)	0.17925	0.21105	-0.00453	0.00281	-0.01771	-0.00013	0.00037	0.00037	-0.01112	13.997
Natural products (3)	0.07260	-0.02471	0.00916	0.00063	-0.00336	-0.00027	0.00051	0.00051	0.02249	39.158
Nitrogen (4)	-0.06323	-0.01735	-0.00619	0.00384	-0.02421	-0.00018	0.00050	0.00050	-0.01520	0.630
Carbon dioxide (5)	-0.00592	-0.03113	0.00256	-0.00020	0.00142	-0.00008	0.00052	0.00052	0.00629	57.123
Phosphorous (6)	0.11335	-0.01646	0.01109	0.00086	-0.00289	0.00119	0.00051	0.00051	0.03216	1.167
Water vapor (7)	0.28014	0.02434	0.06136	0.00070	0.09619	0.00183	0.00070	0.00070	0.15070	0.550
Fresh water (8)	0.24934	0.01992	0.05349	0.00069	0.08183	0.00159	0.00067	0.00067	0.13136	0.550
Fossil fuels (9)	57.04948	0.94962	-0.02038	0.01265	-0.07970	-0.00061	0.00165	0.00165	14.23566	96.171

NOTE: Entries in this matrix indicate the *direct* and *indirect* inputs (or outputs if negative) of the row commodities to (or from) the column processes. EIF's for the commodities based on this matrix and the direct sunlight input vector listed in table 7.3 (using equation 6) are shown as the last column on the right.

dences between ecological and economic systems and the derivation of EIFs to weight or value the products of ecological systems. EIFs can be thought of as ecological "prices" based on the production and consumption interdependencies in ecological and economic systems without requiring subjective, preference based evaluation. This is a more elaborate version of the simple energy analysis method discussed earlier for valuing wetlands.

But this approach, like all others, is limited by its underlying assumptions and the precision of the data that go into it. There is no one modeling approach that can give us all the information we need about something as large and complex as the whole biosphere. And even with the best conceivable modeling capabilities, we will always be confronted with large amounts of uncertainty about the response of the environment to human actions. Learning how to effectively manage the environment in the face of this uncertainty is critical.

Ecological Economic Modeling at Local, Regional, and Global Scales

Since ecosystems are being threatened by a host of human activities, protecting and preserving them requires the ability to understand the direct and indirect effects of human activities over long periods of time and over large areas. Computer simulations are now becoming important tools to investigate these interactions and in all other areas of science as well. Without the sophisticated global atmospheric simulations now being done, our understanding of the potential impacts of increasing CO_2 concentrations in the atmosphere due to fossil fuel burning would be much more primitive. Computer simulations can now be used to understand not only human impacts on ecosystems, but also our economic dependence on natural ecosystem services and capital, and the interdependence between ecological and economic components of the system (cf Braat and van Lierop 1985; Braat and Steetskamp 1991; Costanza et al. 1990).

Several recent developments make such computer simulation modeling feasible, including the accessibility of extensive spatial and temporal data bases and advances in computer power and convenience. Computer simulation models are potentially one of our best tools to help understand the complex, nonlinear, and often choatic dynamics of integrated ecological economic systems.

But even with the best conceivable modeling capabilities, we will always be confronted with large amounts of uncertainty about the response of the environment to human actions (cf. Funtowicz and Ravitz 1991). Learning how to effectively manage the environment in the face of this uncertainty is critical (Perrings 1987; Costanza 1987; Perrings 1989; Costanza and Perrings 1990; Perrings 1991).

The research program of EE should pursue an integrated, multiscale, transdisciplinary, and pluralistic, approach to quantitative ecological economic modeling, while acknowledging the large remaining uncertainty inherent in modeling these systems and developing new ways to effectively deal with this uncertainty (Norgaard 1989).

Innovative Instruments for Environmental Management

Current systems of regulation are not very efficient at managing environmental resources for sustainability, particularly in the face of uncertainty about long-term values and impacts (Arrow and Fisher 1974; Perrings 1987; Costanza 1989; Cumberland 1990). They are inherently reactive rather than proactive. They induce legal confrontation, obfuscation, and government intrusion into business. Rather than encouraging long-range technical and social innovation, they tend to suppress it. They do not mesh well with the market signals that firms and individuals use to make decisions and do not effectively translate long-term global goals into short-term local incentives.

We need to explore promising alternatives to our current command and control environmental management systems, and to modify existing government agencies and other institutions accordingly. The enormous uncertainty about local and transnational environmental impacts needs to be incorporated into decision-making. We also need to better understand the sociological, cultural, and political criteria for acceptance or rejection of policy instruments.

One example of an innovative policy instrument currently being studied is a flexible environmental assurance bonding system designed to incorporate environmental criteria and uncertainty into the market system, and to induce positive environmental technological innovation (Perrings 1989; Costanza and Perrings 1990; Perrings 1991).

In addition to direct charges for known environmental damages, a company would be required to post an assurance bond equal to the current best estimate of the largest potential future environmental damages; the money would be kept in interest-bearing escrow accounts. The bond (plus a portion of the interest) would be returned if the firm could show that the suspected damages had not occurred or would not occur. If they did, the bond would be used to rehabilitate or repair the environment and to compensate injured parties. Thus, the burden of proof would be shifted from the public to the resource-user and a strong economic incentive would be provided to research the true costs of environmentally damaging activities and to develop cost-effective pollution control technologies. This is an extension of the "polluter pays" principle to "the polluter pays for uncertainty as well." Other innovative policy instruments include tradeable pollution and depletion quotas at both national and international levels. Also worthy of mention is the new Global Environmental Facility of the World Bank, which is intended to provide concessionary funds for investments that reduce global externalities.

POLICY RECOMMENDATIONS

Sustainability as the Goal

We should institute a consistent goal of sustainability in all institutions at all levels from local to global. We should strive to address prevailing values and decision-making processes by increasing the awareness of institutions and persons about ecological sustainability. We should promote long-term thinking, the use of a systems approach in decision-making, and use of "ecological auditors" (i.e., trained environmental professionals) by public and private institutions whose activities affect the environment.

For example, the World Bank is an important global institution that directly affects economic policy, and has severe environmental, secondary effects, especially upon the environmental conditions of developing nations. We recommend that the bank and similar institutions require that all projects meet the following criteria: For renewable resources, the rate of harvest should not exceed the rate of regeneration (sustainable yield) and the rates of waste generation from projects should not exceed the assimilative capacity of the environment (sustainable waste disposal). For nonrenewable resources the rates of waste generation from projects shall not exceed the assimilative capacity of the environment and the depletion of the nonrenewable resources should require comparable development of renewable substitutes for that resource. These are safe, minimum sustainability standards; and once met, the bank should then select projects for funding that have the highest rates of return based on other, more traditional economic criteria.

We recognize that this policy will be very difficult at first, and that the policies will likely shift as more information is developed about managing for sustainability. However, there is a need for major institutions to not only affirm, but to operationalize the goal of sustainability, because of the global scope of their programs and because of the impact their example will provide for smaller institutions worldwide. We also recognize that goal setting is an ethical issue, and that it is absurd to ignore the normative preconditions of policy, however necessary it may be to avoid mixing normative and positive statements in analysis. Both economists and ecologists, if they want to talk about policy, must offer much more explicit ethical support for their goals, whether for sustainability or for growth.

Maintaining Natural Capital to Assure Sustainability

A minimum necessary condition for sustainability is the maintenance of the total natural capital stock at or above the current level. While a lower stock of natural capital may be sustainable, given our uncertainty and the dire consequences of guessing wrong, it is best to at least provisionally assume that the we are at or below the range of sustainable stock levels and allow no further decline in natural capital. This "constancy of total natural capital" rule can thus be seen as a prudent minimum condition for assuring sustainability, to be abandoned only when solid evidence to the contrary can be offered (Costanza and Daly, in prep). There is disagreement between technological optimists (who see technical progress eliminating all resource constraints to growth and development) and technological skeptics (who do not see as much scope for this approach and fear irreversible use of resources and damage to natural capital). By limiting total system natural capital at current levels (preferably by using higher severance and consumption taxes) we can satisfy both the skeptics (since resources will be conserved for future generations) and the optimists (since this will raise the price of natural capital resources and more rapidly induce the technical change they predict). By limiting physical growth, only development is allowed and this may proceed without endangering sustainability.

Improving Our Use of Policy Instruments

We need to use a wide variety of policy instruments including regulation, property rights, permits, marketable permits, fees, subsidies and bonds to assure sustainability. Criteria for the use of policy instruments are: equity, efficiency, scientific validity, consensus, frugality, and environmental effectiveness. We should institute regulatory reforms to promote the appropriate use of financial, legal, and social incentives. We may use market incentives where appropriate in allocation decisions. In decisions of scale individual freedom of choice must give way to democratic collective decision making by the relevant community.

Economic Incentives: Linking Revenues and Uses

We should implement fees on the destructive use of natural capital to promote more efficient use, and ease up on income taxes, especially on low incomes in the interest of equity. Fees, taxes, and subsidies should be used to change the prices of activities that interfere with sustainability versus those that are compatible with it. This can be accomplished by using the funds generated to support an alternative to undesirable activities that are being taxed. For example a tax on all greenhouse gases, with the size of the tax linked to the impact of each gas could be linked to development of alternatives to fossil fuel. Gasoline tax revenues could be used to support mass transit and bike lanes. Current policies that subsidize environmentally harmful activities should be stopped. For example, subsidies on virgin material extraction should be stopped. This will also allow recycling options to effectively compete. Crop subsidies that dramatically increase pesticide and fertilizer use should be eliminated, and forms of positive incentives should also be used. For example, debt for nature swaps should be supported and should receive much more funding. We should also offer prestigious prizes for work that increases awareness of or contributes to sustainability issues, such as changes in behavior that develop a culture of maintenance (i.e., cars that last for 50 years) or promotes capital and resource saving improvements (i.e., affordable, efficient housing and water supplies).

Ecological Economic Research

While economics has developed many useful tools of analysis, it has not directed these tools toward the thorny questions that arise when considering the concept and implementation of sustainability. In particular, we need to better understand preference formation, and especially time preference formation. We also need to understand how individual time preferences and group time preferences may differ, and how the preferences of institutions that will be critical to the success or failure of sustainability are established. We have heretofore paid too little attention to ecological feedbacks. An understanding of these will be critical to the implementation of sustainability goals, whatever they may be. We need to concentrate on the valuation of important non-market goods and services provided by ecosystems. We need to better understand the effects of various regulatory instruments that can be utilized to attain sustainability. This may require experimental testing of behavior in a laboratory context. Most importantly, we need to study how positive sustainability incentives can be employed to induce reluctant participants to lengthen their time horizons and think globally about their resource policies.

We also need to develop an ecological history of the planet (to complement the existing human economic history) that would contain trends of resource use, development and exhaustion, changes in science and technology, etc. We should promote the use (as one of a bundle of decision-making tools) of broad benefit/cost analyses that includes the consideration of all market and non-market costs and benefits.

Ecological Economics Education

Our education system is currently characterized by over-specialization and disciplinary isolation. We need to develop transdisciplinary curricula and job and academic support systems for both specialists and generalists. This needs to be combined with an emphasis on the value of general education and personal development, versus the more narrow training of professional technical specialists.

We need to develop an EE core curriculum and degree granting programs that embody the skills of both economics and ecology. This implies a curriculum with some blending of physical, chemical and biological sciences and economics. Within this curriculum quantitative methods are essential, but they should be problem directed rather than just mathematical tools for their own sake.

There is a need to develop a capacity for experimentation that provides EE with a solid empirical base which is built upon creative and comprehensive theory. We need to develop extension programs that can effectively transfer information among both disciplines and nations.

We should promote at all levels education that weaves together fundamental understanding of the environment with human economic activities and social institutions, and promotes research that facilitates this interweaving process. Particularly, awareness by the media of the common benefits of sustainability should be promoted to insure accuracy in reporting, and the media should be encouraged to utilize opportunities to educate others through mechanisms such as special reports and public service announcements. We should promote education of broadly-trained environmental scientists, whose jobs will be to provide on-going environmental assessment as an input to the decision-making processes of various institutions.

Institutional Changes

Institutions with the flexibility necessary to deal with ecologically sustainable development are lacking. Indeed many financial institutions are built on the assumption of continuous exponential growth and will face major restructuring in a sustainable economy. Many existing institutions have fragmented mandates and policies, and often have not optimally utilized market and non-market forces to resolve environmental problems. They have also conducted inadequate benefit/cost analyses by not incorporating ecological costs; used short-term planning horizons; inappropriately assigned property rights (public and private) to resources; and not made appropriate use of incentives.

There is a lack of awareness and education about sustainability, the environment, and causes of environmental degradation. In addition, much environmental knowledge held by indigenous peoples is being lost, as is knowledge of species, particularly in the tropics. Institutions have been slow to respond to new information and shifts in values, for example concerns about threats to biodiversity or the effects of rapid changes in communications technologies. Finally, many institutions do not freely share or disseminate information; do not provide public access to decision-making; and do not devote serious attention to determining and representing the wishes of their constituencies.

Many of these problems are a result of the inflexible bureaucratic structure of many modern institutions. Experience (i.e., Japanese industry) has shown that less bureaucratic, more flexible, more peer-to-peer institutional structures can be much more efficient and effective. We need to de-bureaucratize institutions so that they can effectively respond to the coming challenges of achieving sustainability.

Acknowledgment: An earlier version of this article appeared in 1991 in Structural Change and Economic Dynamics *2:335–357. Sylvia Tognetti is responsible for portions of the current text.*

REFERENCES

Ahmad, Y. J., S. El Serafy, and E. Lutz, eds. 1989. *Environmental Accounting for Sustainable Development: A UNEP-World Bank Symposium.* Washington, D.C.: World Bank.

Arrow, K. J. and A. C. Fisher. 1974. "Environmental Preservation, Uncertainty, and Irreversibility." *Quarterly Journal of Economics* 55:313–319.

Barber, M., B. Patten, and J. Finn. 1979. "Review and Evaluation of I-O Flow Analysis for Ecological Applications." In J. Matis, B. Patten, and G. White, eds., *Compartmental Analysis of Ecosystem Models,* vol 10 of *Statistical Ecology.* Bertonsville, Md.: International Cooperative Publishing House.

Bartlett, E. T. 1984. "Estimating Benefits of Range for Wildland Management and Planning." In G. L. Peterson and A. Randall, eds., *Valuation of Wildland Benefits.* Boulder, Colo.: Westview Press.

Bishop, R. 1982. "Option Value: An Exposition and Extension." *Land Economics* 58:1–15.

Boulding, K. E. 1991. "What Do We Want to Sustain?: Environmentalism and Human Evaluations." In R. Costanza, ed., *Ecological Economics: the Science and Management of Sustainability.* New York: Columbia University Press.

Braat, L. C. and I. Steetskamp. 1991. "Ecological Economic Analysis for Regional Sustainable Development." In R. Costanza, ed., *Ecological Economics: The Science and Management of Sustainability.* New York: Columbia University Press.

Braat, L. C. and W. F. J. van Lierop. 1985. "A Survey of Economic-Ecological Models." Laxenburg, Austria: International Institute for Applied Systems Analysis.

Brockner, J. and J. Z. Rubin. 1985. *Entrapment in Escalating Conflicts: a Social Psychological Analysis.* New York: Springer-Verlag.

Brookshire, D. S., L. S. Eubanks, and A. Randall. 1983. "Estimating Option Prices and Existence Values for Wildlife Resources." *Land Economics* 59:1–15.

Brown, B. J., M. E. Hanson, D. M. Liverman, and R. W. Merideth, Jr. 1987. "Global Sustainability: Toward Definition." *Environmental Management* 11:713–719.

Clark, C. W. 1973. "The Economics of Overexploitation." *Science* 181:630–634.

——— 1991. "Economic Biases Against Sustainable Development." In R. Costanza, ed., *Ecological Economics: The Science and Management of Sustainability,* pp. 319–330. New York: Columbia University Press.

Cleveland, C. J. 1991. "Natural Resource Scarcity and Economic Growth Revisited: Economic and Biophysical Perspectives. In R. Costanza, ed., *Ecological Economics: The Science and Management of Sustainability,* pp. 289–317. New York: Columbia University Press.

Cleveland, C. J., R. Costanza, C. A. S. Hall, and R. Kaufmann. 1984. "Energy and the United States Economy: A Biophysical Perspective." *Science* 255:890–897.

Conrad, J. M. 1980. "QuasiOption Value and the Expected Value of Information." *Quarterly Journal of Economics* 94:813–820.

Costanza, R. 1980. "Embodied Energy and Economic Valuation." *Science* 210:1219–1224.

—— 1987. "Social Traps and Environmental Policy." *BioScience* 37:407–412.

—— 1989. "What Is Ecological Economics?" *Ecological Economics* 1:1–7.

Costanza, R., ed. 1991. *Ecological Economics: The Science and Management of Sustainability.* New York: Columbia University Press.

Costanza, R. and H. E. Daly. 1987. "Toward an Ecological Economics." *Ecological Modeling* 38:1–7.

—— 1992. "Natural Capital and Sustainable Development." *Conservation Biology* 6:37–46.

Costanza, R. and B. M. Hannon. 1989. "Dealing with the 'Mixed Units' Problem in Ecosystem Network Analysis." In F. Wulff, J. G. Field, and K. H. Mann, eds., *Network Analysis of Marine Ecosystems: Methods and Applications,* pp. 90–115. Heidelberg: Springer-Verlag.

Costanza, R. and R. A. Herendeen. 1984. "Embodied Energy and Economic Value in the United States Economy: 1963, 1967, and 1972." *Resources and Energy* 6:129–163.

Costanza, R. and C. Neill. 1981. "The Energy Embodied in the Products of the Biosphere." In W. J. Mitsch, R. W. Bosserman, and J. M. Klopatek, eds., *Energy and Ecological Modeling,* pp. 745–755. New York: Elsevier Scientific.

—— 1984. "Energy Intensities, Interdependence, and Value in Ecological Systems: A Linear Programming Approach." *Journal of Theoretical Biology* 106:41–57.

Costanza, R. and C. H. Perrings. 1990. "A Flexible Assurance Bonding System for Improved Environmental Management." *Ecological Economics* 2:57–76.

Costanza, R. and W. Shrum. 1988. "The Effects of Taxation on Moderating the Conflict Escalation Process: An Experiment Using the Dollar Auction Game." *Social Science Quarterly* 69:416–432.

Costanza, R., H. E. Daly, and J. A. Bartholomew. 1991. "Goals, Agenda, and Policy Recommendations for Ecologcal Economics." In R. Costanza, ed., *Ecological Economics: The Science and Management of Sustainability.* New York: Columbia University Press.

Costanza, R., S. C. Farber, and J. Maxwell. 1989. "The Valuation and Management of Wetland Ecosystems." *Ecological Economics* 1:335–361.

Costanza, R., F. H. Sklar, and M. L. White. 1990. "Modeling Coastal Landscape Dynamics." *BioScience* 40:91–107.

Cross, J. G. and M. J. Guyer. 1980. *Social Traps.* Ann Arbor: University of Michigan Press.

Cumberland, J. H. 1987. "Need Economic Development be Hazardous to the Health of the Chesapeake Bay?" *Marine Resource Economics* 4:81–93.

—— "Public Choice and the Improvement of Policy Instruments for Environmental Management." *Ecological Economics* 2:149–162.

Daly, H. E. 1968. "On Economics as a Life Science." *Journal of Political Economy* 76:392–406.

——1991. "Elements of Environmental Macroeconomics." In R. Costanza, ed., *Ecological Economics: The Science and Management of Sustainability,* pp. 32–46. New York: Columbia University Press.

Daly, H. E. and J. B. Cobb, Jr. 1989. *For the Common Good: Redirecting the Economy Toward Community, the Environment, and a Sustainable Future.* Boston: Beacon.

Edney, J. J. and C. Harper. 1978. "The Effects of Information in a Resource Management Problem: A Social Trap Analog." *Human Ecology* 6:387–395.

El Serafy, S. 1991. "The Environment as Capital." In R. Costanza, ed., *Ecological Economics: The Science and Management of Sustainability.* pp. 168–175. New York: Columbia University Press.

Faber, M. and J. L. R. Proops. 1991. "National Accounting, Time, and the Environment: A Neo-Austrian Approach." In R. Costanza, ed., *Ecological Economics: The Science and Management of Sustainability,* pp. 214–243. New York: Columbia University Press.

Farber, S. and R. Costanza. 1987. "The Economic Value of Wetlands Systems." *Journal of Environmental Management* 24:41–51.

Finn, J., 1976. "The Cycling Index." *Journal of Theoretical Biology* 56:363–373.

Funderlic, R and M. Heath. 1971. "Linear Compartmental Analysis of Ecosystems." Oak Ridge Natl Lab, ORNL-IBP-71–74.

Funtowicz, S. O. and J. R. Ravetz. 1991. "A New Scientific Methodology for Global Environmental Issues." In R. Costanza, ed., *Ecological Economics: The Science and Management of Sustainability,* pp. 137–152. New York: Columbia University Press.

Hannon, B. 1973. "The Structure of Ecosystems." *J. Theor. Biology* 41:535–46.

—— 1976. "Marginal Product Pricing in the Ecosystem." *J. Theor. Biology* 56:256–267.

—— 1979. "Total Energy Costs in Ecosystems." *J. Theor. Biology* 80:271–293.

—— 1991. "Accounting in Ecological Systems," in R. Costanza, ed., *Ecological Economics: The Science and Management of Sustainability,* pp. 234—252. New York: Columbia University Press.

—— 1968. "The Tragedy of the Commons." *Science* 162:1243–1248.

—— 1991. "Paramount Positions in Ecological Economics," in R. Costanza, ed., *Ecological Economics: The Science and Management of Sustainability,* pp. 47–57. New York: Columbia University Press.

Heiner, R. A. 1983. "The Origin of Predictable Behavior." *American Economic Review* 75:565–601.

Hueting, R. 1991. "Correcting National Income for Environmental Losses: a Practical Solution for a Theoretical Dilemma." In R. Costanza, ed., *Ecological Economics: The Science and Management of Sustainability,* pp. 194–213. New York: Columbia University Press.

Isard, W. 1972. *Ecologic-Economic Analysis for Regional Development.* New York: Free Press.

Leontief, W. 1941. *The Structure of American Economy, 1919—1939.* New York: Oxford University Press.

Martinez-Alier, J. 1991, "Ecology and the Poor: A Neglected Dimension of Latin American History." *Journal of Latin American Studies* 23:621–39.

Norgaard, R. B. 1989. "The Case for Methodological Pluralism." *Ecological Economics* 1:37–58.

Norton, B. G. 1986. "On the Inherent Danger of Undervaluing Species." In B. G. Norton, ed., *The Preservation of Species.* Princeton: Princeton University Press.

NRC (National Research Council). 1993. *Setting Priorities for Land Conservation.* Washington D.C.: National Academy Press.

Pearce, D. 1987. "Foundations of an Ecological Economics." *Ecological Modeling* 38:9–18.

Perrings, C. 1987. *Economy and Environment: A Theoretical Essay on the Interdependence of Economic and Environmental Systems.* Cambridge University Press.

—— 1989. "Environmental Bonds and the Incentive to Research in Activities Involving Uncertain Future Effects." *Ecological Economics* 1:95–110.

—— 1991. "Reserved Rationality and the Precautionary Principle: Technological Change, Time and Uncertainty in Environmental Decision-Making." In R. Costanza, ed., *Ecological Economics: The Science and Management of Sustainability,* pp. 153–167. New York: Columbia University Press.

Peskin, H. 1991. "Alternative Environmental and Resource Accounting Approaches." In R. Costanza, ed., *Ecological Economics: The Science and Management of Sustainability,* pp. 176–193. New York: Columbia University Press.

Pezzey, J. 1989. "Economic Analysis of Sustainable Growth and Sustainable Development." Washington, D.C.: World Bank, Environment Department Working Paper No. 15.

Platt, J. 1973. "Social Traps." *American Psychologist* 28:642–651.

Randall, A. 1986. "Human Preferences, Economics, and the Preservation of Species." In B. G. Norton, ed., *The Preservation of Species.* Princeton: Princeton University Press.

Randall, A. and J. Stoll. 1980. "Consumer's Surplus in Commodity Space." *American Economic Review* 70:449–55.

Teger, A. I. 1980. *Too Much Invested to Quit.* New York: Pergamon.

Ulanowicz, R. E. 1980. "An Hypothesis on the Development of Natural Communities." *J. Theor. Biol.* 85: 223–245.

Ulanowicz, R. E. 1986. *Growth and Development: Ecosystems Phenomenology.* New York: Springer-Verlag.

Ulanowicz, R. E. 1991. "Contributory Values of Ecosystem Resources." In R. Costanza, ed., *Ecological Economics: The Science and Management of Sustainability,* pp. 253–268. New York: Columbia University Press.

Victor, P. A. 1972. *Pollution, Economy, and Environment.* Toronto: University of Toronto Press.

WCED (World Commission on Environment and Development). 1987. *Our Common Future: Report of the World Commission on Environment and Development.* Oxford, UK: Oxford University Press.

Wulff, F., J. G. Field, and K. H. Mann. 1989. *Network Analysis of Marine Ecosystems: Methods and Applications.* Heidlberg: Springer-Verlag.

EIGHT

Carrying Capacity as a Tool of Development Policy: The Ecuadoran Amazon and the Paraguayan Chaco

Herman Daly

The remaining sparsely inhabited portions of the world (polar regions, deserts, tropical rainforests) have been "saved for last" for good reason. They are difficult to inhabit and have low average carrying capacity for human activities. Sparse populations are all that have ever been sustainably supported by the ecosystems of such areas. The concept of carrying capacity is an indispensable tool for planning the rational use of these areas, as has been demonstrated recently by Fearnside (1986) and earlier by Ledec et al. (1985). The present note aims to supplement these two works by showing how in two specific cases even very simple and crude estimates of carrying capacity can have significant policy implications.

For humans the calculation of carrying capacity is far more complex than for other species. Other species have "standards of living" that are constant over time (animals and plants do not experience economic growth, although consumption may vary over the life cycle). Also they have relatively uniform "standards of living" (i.e., per-capita resource consumption levels) throughout their populations at a given point in time (no class inequality, with a few exceptions such as social insects whose class structure is genetic rather than social). And the technologies of other species are also relatively constant-genetically given endosomatic technologies that have coevolved with the environment and are consequently well-adapted to it. Furthermore the level of international or inter-ecosystem "trade" among animals is relatively constant and limited. For humans these four constants become variables. The calculation of human carrying capacity requires, therefore, some assumptions about: (1) living standards, (2) degree of equality of distribution, (3) technology, and (4) extent of trade. As these four variables change carrying capacity will change. But the concept remains useful because these four variables do not change discontinuously, unpredictably, or beyond all limits. There is inertia and there are ultimate limits.

One need not and should not try to prove that the Ecuadoran Amazon or the Paraguayan Chaco will never support more than x people. Never is a long time. It is sufficient for policy purposes to argue that it is very unlikely that within the next generation (25 years) Amazonia could support more than x people living at the average Ecuadoran standard, using known technologies available to Ecuador, assuming Ecuadoran patterns of wealth distribution, and paying for all imports to the region with current exports from the region. A similar statement holds for the Paraguayan Chaco.

Is it possible to make a back-of-the-envelope, order-of-magnitude calculation of "x" as specified in the preceding paragraph? It is argued below that this is indeed possible, and that for the two regions under consideration very important conclusions for development policy follow from a simple comparison of carrying capacity with population projected over a generational time frame. Ecuador will be considered first, the Paraguayan Chaco second.

THE ECUADORAN AMAZON

A simple approximation to an extreme upper bound of carrying capacity for the Amazonian region can be gotten by assuming that all of Amazonia could have the same population density as Ecuador as a whole. Amazonia has about 132,000 km² and Ecuador as whole has a population density of 30 persons per km². This gives 3,960,000, or roughly 4 million people as an estimate (overestimate) of "x" in the preceding paragraph.

How many people might the Amazon be required to support in the next generation? At the current 2.8% growth rate the population of Ecuador will double from 10 million to 20 million in 25 years (one generation). The rural areas of the *sierra* and the *costa* are already experiencing net emigration due to demographic pressure, ecological deterioration and droughts. Aside from the cities this leaves only the Amazon as the area of net immigration. Five provinces in the *sierra* and *costa* (Bolivar, Chimborazo, Loja, Manabi, and Carchi) have actually experienced population decline (net emigration greater than natural increase) between 1972 and 1982 (Landázuri and Jijón

1988). Just the additional ten million natural increase represents 2.5 times the extreme upper limit of Amazonian carrying capacity! Even if one were to count nonrenewable petroleum reserves as a part of Amazonian carrying capacity it would make no difference in the fundamental dilemma since these reserves will be depleted in less than 10 years, and proven plus probable reserves in less than 20 years, assuming 1988 annual extraction rates (World Bank 1988).

In the face of such a population increase any policy of protecting the Amazon by limiting colonization is doomed to failure. How can any government tell millions of poor people that their survival is less important than the survival of trees and birds and undiscovered species? Even if one believes that ethically it is better to save carrying capacity than individual lives, it would still be politically impossible to resist such colonization pressures. And the poor might well reason that if conservation is worth more than their lives then it is also worth more than the wealth of the rich. Demands for redistribution would increase. The rich, knowing their own interests, will also urge opening of the Amazon to temporarily post pone the pressure for redistribution. With 10 million extra people in the next 25 years there is no hope for saving the Ecuadoran Amazon from destruction, nor of avoiding a great deal of misery.

The above is the foreseeable outcome of present trends projected one generation. This outcome is well within the expected lifetime of the average Ecuadoran now living. What policies might avoid such an impasse?

Consider the following outline of an alternative scenario.

1. Serious and radical birth control policy, beginning with family planning incentives, but eventually moving to real population control. Perhaps it would be possible to cut the increase from 10 to 5 million in the next 25 years, and then down to zero growth in the following generation. Even with strong efforts this will take time.

2. To buy time to bring about population control, and to absorb the unavoidable increment of at least 5 million, strive to increase carrying capacity by:

(a) land reform: use best agricultural land for food crops rather than cattle. Human carrying capacity can be increased by eating lower on the food chain, and by using the best valley land for agriculture and the hillsides for grazing—the opposite of the present pattern. Intensification of agriculture (irrigation) may offer some scope for raising carrying capacity as well.

(b) redistribution—redirect resources to vital consumption and away from luxury. High sumptuary taxes with revenues invested in production of basic goods would be one way of doing this.

(c) reinvest petroleum rents and other nonrenewable surpluses in renewable resource development: reforestation, land reclamation, fisheries, etc. In general seek to balance the rate of depletion of nonrenewables with the rate of creation of renewable substitutes.

(d) exploit that part of Amazonia that is suited for sustainable agriculture, fishing, gathering, ecoturism, and scientific research.

Such a radical program could only be carried out by a nation that clearly perceived its alternatives as national survival versus national liquidation. That is clearly not he perception of the government of Ecuador, or of the majority of its citizens. Even the leading environmental organizations in Ecuador, dedicated to preserving biodiversity in the Amazon, have evaded taking any serious stand on the population issue. Yet in 25 years Ecuador will be another Haiti if present trends are allowed to continue. Not only does the Ecuadoran government not realize this, neither do the multilateral development banks. A nation in the process of environmental liquidation will not be able to pay back loans at interest—it is simply not *creditworthy*. Ecuador needs some writing down of past debt, not new debt, unless the new debt is invested much more sustainably and productively than hitherto. But reduction of past debt cannot be expected as long as any part of petroleum rents are used for consumption rather than investment in renewable alternatives. Unless Ecuador sees its situation as drastic and takes radical action on its own it cannot expect radical action by others in its behalf, no matter how much the facts may justify the need to write down its international debt. Those same dire facts also justify drastic actions by Ecuador to assure its own survival. Unless economic development and finance agencies inject urgency and more vision than at present, then Ecuador is unlikely to take serious action.

Perhaps one reason Ecuador does not perceive its situation as drastic is that the development banks are eager to lend it more money. The obvious conclusion for Ecuador to draw is that since it is creditworthy in the eyes of the development banks, things could not really be so bad. The development banks think things must not be so bad because Ecuador is willing to borrow at interest and obviously considers itself creditworthy without drastic policies. Each party takes comfort from the other's optimism. Neither party has yet faced the facts.

In order to avoid facing the facts a number of thought-stopping myths and slogans are sometimes invoked. One is that the Amazon is a vast inexhaustible source of wealth and fertility—a latter-day version of El Dorado. This is simply wrong. Another is that technology will save the day. But what specific technologies (in the next 25 years) are envisioned? Nuclear power and the green revolution have proved disappointing. Biotechnology and nontraditional export bonanzas are the currently advocated technical fixes. But specifically what kinds of biotechnology could contribute specifically what kinds of products in the next 25 years? And what nontraditional exports, other than cocaine, could make a difference over this time period? Cut flowers and kiwi fruits flown to the US market will not even make a dent in the problem. And even if one believes in the colonization of outer space it will be of no help in the next 25 years.

A policy of birth control is often dismissed on the grounds that Ecuador is a Catholic Country. But so is Italy, and it has a low birth rate. The Catholic Church, although clearly an obstacle, nevertheless urges responsible parenthood, and does not deny arithmetic. Some demographic history of France and other countries. Certain economists (Julian Simon) even believe that demographic pressure is a positive force in development and therefore that population growth should be encouraged. Such myths find a ready market among policy makers unwilling to deal with the twin taboos of population control and income redistribution. But if Ecuador does not dispel these taboos it will not be a viable country, it will not be creditworthy, and loans from the development banks will not be repayable. Even the transfer represented by unpaid loans will likely do more harm than good by extending the illusion a bit longer.

Since population control is the sine qua non of sustainable development for Ecuador it is important to look at current fertility patterns to get some idea of how much scope there is for fertility reduction by voluntary means. The most salient fact about this pattern is that for women with no education average completed fertility is 6.4 births, while for women with university education it is 2.3 births. In other words the fertility of the lowest social class is almost *triple* that of the highest class (*Encuesta Demografica* 1988). This class difference is much greater than the rural-urban difference (4.1 births for urban women, 6.1 for rural), although the latter is also significant. The point of these comparisons is to show that birth control is already practiced by the upper and urban classes, and that what is lacking is a democratization of birth control—both attitudes and techniques.

The relatively high rate of reproduction of the lower class insures an "unlimited" supply of labor at low wages which promotes inequality in the distribution of income. Far from being a repressive policy birth control serves to spread to the lower classes the attitudes and practices of the upper class. It also tends to equalize the distribution of per capita income, in two ways: (1) it reduces the number of heads among which a wage must be shared in the short run, and (2) it permits the wage to rise by moving away from an unlimited supply of labor in the long run.

Of women having two children only 38% desired to have more; of women having three children only 20% desired to have more; and of women who have four children only 8.5% desired to have more. For all women on average the desired number of children is three (*Encuesta Demografica* 1988:74, 89). Yet completed fertility for all women in Ecuador averages 4.3. Some 35% of all births in Ecuador in the last 5 years were either not wanted or not wanted at that time (*Encuesta Demografica* 1988:89). Clearly the first step in population control is the voluntary elimination of unwanted fertility, which would have a significant demographic effect as well as providing a basic human right to the lower class—one that is already enjoyed by the upper class. Birth control is therefore not politically unrealistic, in spite of dogmatic opposition from both the Catholic Right and the Marxist Left.

THE PARAGUAYAN CHACO

Paraguay's greatest environmental advantage has been its small population (some 3 million in 1982, and close to 4 million today). At the current 2.5% annual rate of population growth (doubling time of 28 years, or slightly more than one generation) this advantage is rapidly disappearing. Furthermore this environmental advantage has historically been considered as an economic disadvantage. Demographic factors are exacerbated by the fact that all public lands available for colonization have been distributed. In the future land cannot be made available to some without taking it away from others. Also fractionating of land holdings into uneconomic minifundia is driven by population growth and the practice of equal inheritance.

There is very little concern about population growth. Traditionally the goal has been to increase the population by bringing in colonists to settle the land. After the disastrous War of the Triple Alliance Paraguay was left in 1875 with only about 220,000 people. It is therefore understandable that pronatalist views should still be dominant. The question for the next generation, however, is: where will the 4 million additional Paraguayans live and work? Since 98% of the population lives in the eastern half of the country, that leaves the western half (the Chaco) as the obvious place. As just mentioned land is becoming scarce in the east, and land conflicts have already become violent. Furthermore an FAO study concluded that "the agricultural frontier has already exceeded the limits of desirable development in most of the Eastern Region," and that continued expansion would be profoundly destructive of the ecosystem (*Capacidad . . .* 1979). In 1979 when this statement was written Paraguay had about 3 million people, and now has close to 4 million, all but 2% of whom still live in the east.

There are no official estimates of human carrying capacity of the Chaco, or of the east either. Government officials speak of five million or twenty million people in the Chaco of the future, and at the same time state that the agricultural future of the country is in the Chaco. They have not thought in terms of carrying capacity over the next generation. What, then, is a reasonable estimate of carrying capacity for the next generation?

An upper bound estimate can be gotten, as in the case of Ecuador by assuming the Chaco could be populated to the same density as the east. The population density of the east is 18.6 persons per km^2, and the area of the Chaco is 247,000 km^2, giving a product of 4,594,000 people. Most people agree that this is an extreme overestimate for any foreseeable future. But it serves to rule out of court any talk of absorbing more than 5 million people in the Chaco, and that is an advance over the current level of discussion.

It is possible, however, to get a much better estimate using the actual experience of colonists in the Chaco. This would have been desirable in the case of the Ecuadoran Amazon also, and would probably have led to a much lower estimate, but such information was not available. The Mennonites have the most successful colony in the Chaco. We can take the Mennonite population density and generalize that to the entire Chaco. In 1987 there were 6,650 Mennonites living on 420,000 ha giving a density of 0.0158 persons per ha. Multiplying that by 100, the number of hectares in 1 km^2, gives 1.58 persons per km^2. That density times the total area of 247,000 km^2 gives 390,260 or roughly 400,000 persons, not even half a million!

Although still crude it is obvious that the second estimate is more realistic. But the Mennonites themselves have unused land and estimate that they could support twice their present numbers if they used all their land, which they will have to do in 35 years if they maintain their 2% growth rate. So perhaps our estimate should be 800,000. Also the Mennonite standard of living, though hardly luxurious, is above the average for

Paraguay, so a few more thousands could be supported by lowering per-capita consumption levels to the national average, even though this goes against the basic notion of development.

On the other hand our calculation implicitly assumed that the Mennonites have average Chaco land when in fact it is better than average. The calculation also assumes that other settlers during the next generation could do as well as the Mennonites. This is doubtful for several reasons. First the Mennonites brought with them the peasant traditions of Europe, which are absent among Paraguayan colonos. They also had a strong community of mutual aid and support, as well as outside help from European and American Mennonites. Furthermore it took them over two generations (60 years) of hard work and sacrifice to reach their present level. All things considered, even half a million may be an overestimate, especially if ranching rather than agriculture turns out to be the best use of most Chaco land, as seems likely.

Since water rather than soil quality seems to be the limitative factor one naturally thinks of large irrigation projects as a way of increasing carrying capacity. However the Mennonites are extremely skeptical of irrigation in the Chaco because they are convinced that it would lead to salinization of the soil (raising the level of existing salt closer to the surface and within reach of plant roots).

The low population density of the Chaco makes it the 'obvious' place to put the 4 million new people. Putting them in the east would sharpen land conflicts and require redistribution. The stage is set for an expensive settlement program of the type witnessed in the Brazilian Amazon. The likelihood of failure due to ecological reasons is very high. Politically the colonization of the Chaco will probably be seen as the way to: minimize already serious land conflicts in the east; postpone dealing with population control; and maintain temporarily the mirage of progress and optimism, as well as offer a great national project to galvanize public support. Against such political advantages the sobering calculation of carrying capacity may not be very persuasive. Elements of a realistic policy for Paraguay would not be very different from those listed for Ecuador.

In both cases the simple estimate of carrying capacity has served to clarify the gravity of the situation. Although the calculations are simple and crude the inferences made from them are quite robust because the conscious tendency was to err on the high side in estimating carrying capacity. For policy purposes refined econometric models would add little to what is already obvious. What is lacking is not more exact information, but the political will to respect the ecological reasons for the historically low population density, whether in the Ecuadoran Amazon or the Paraguayan Chaco, and to limit human populations accordingly. The fact that human carrying capacity is not constant in no way removes the serious rate and magnitude contradictions over the next generation in the two cases here considered. Nor does the 'Hong Kong solution' of importing food for a dense population by exporting manufactured goods and financial services seem realistic for either the Ecuadoran Amazon or the Paraguay Chaco. For one thing the regions are remote. Also the limited niche for food importers in the world economy is rapidly filling up.

Attempting the impossible will waste unlimited amounts of resources and cause much conflict. The first rule of development policy therefore should be: "do not attempt the impossible." The first operational corollary of this rule is: "respect carrying capacity."

None of this is meant to imply that carrying capacity is only relevant to developing countries. If the United States of America had worried about carrying capacity, it would not have become so dangerously dependent on depleting petroleum reserves belonging to other nations. If the United States cannot even pass a reasonable gasoline tax to discipline unsustainable consumption, is it realistic to expect Paraguay and Ecuador to control population? Both actions may appear politically unrealistic in the short run, but not taking such actions is biophysically unrealistic in the long run, where "long run" means only 25 years.

Acknowledgment: This paper was originally published in 1990 in Ecological Economics *2:187–195.*

References

Capacidad de Uso de los Suelos, Uso Actual y Tendencias, y del Desarrollo del Sector Forestal, 1979. PNUD/FAO/SFN Doc. Trab. 20.

Encuesta Demografica y de Salud Familiar, 1987, 1988. Quito, Ecuador: CEPAR, ININMS, DHS.

Fearnside, P. M. 1986. *Human Carrying Capacity and the Brazilian Rainforest.* New York: Columbia University Press.

Landázuri, H. and C. Jijón. 1988. *El Medio Ambiente en el Ecuador.* Quito, Ecuador: ILDIS.

Ledec, G., R. Goodland, J. Kirchner, and J. Drake. 1985. "Carrying Capacity, Population Growth, and Sustainable Development." In D. Mahar, ed., *Rapid Population Growth and Human Carrying Capacity.* World Bank Staff Working Paper.

World Bank. 1988. "Ecuador: Country Economic Memorandum." Washington, D.C.: World Bank.

NINE

Green Accounting for Sustainable Development

Peter Bartelmus

Sustainable development aims at integrating environmental concerns into mainstream socioeconomic policies by making those policies accountable for their environmental impacts. Accounting for both environmental depletion/degradation and economic performance is thus a first step towards achieving this integration. At the same time, such integrated accounting permits the rigorous definition of environmentally adjusted economic indicators such as domestic product, national income, capital and capital formation, consumption and value added. Used in economic analysis, those "green" indicators could become the variables of a new "eco-nomics" (Postel 1990).

There are limits, however, in assigning monetary values to environmental costs and benefits. As shown below, such valuation becomes arbitrary with increasing distance of environmental effects from the production and consumption activities that cause them. Social *evaluation* in terms of exogeneously set standards and targets will have to replace monetary *valuation* achieved through simulating markets for nonmarketed environmental functions.

SEEA—A SYSTEM FOR INTEGRATED ENVIRONMENTAL AND ECONOMIC ACCOUNTING

As part of the revision of the System of National Accounts (SNA), the Statistical Division of the United Nations (UNSTAT) has developed methodologies for a System of integrated Environmental-Economic Accounting (SEEA) which was recently issued as an SNA handbook on *Integrated Environmental and Economic Accounting* (UN 1993). Various components of the system were tested in case studies in Mexico (van Tongeren et al. 1993), Papua New Guinea (Bartelmus, Lutz, and Schweinfest 1993) and Thailand (unpublished). It was found in these studies that environmental accounting is not only feasible but can provide, even in tentative form, a valuable information base for integrated development planning and policy.

In the absence of an international consensus on how to incorporate environmental costs and benefits in national accounts, the Statistical Commission of the United Nations requested UNSTAT to develop an SNA *satellite system* for integrated accounting rather than to modify the core system of the SNA itself. This approach was confirmed by the United Nations Conference on Environment and Development (UNCED) in its Agenda 21. On the other hand, the revised SNA (Inter-Secretariat Working Group 1993) already takes into account a number of cost and capital items of the SEEA. They include the incorporation of nonproduced tangible (natural) assets and the description of links between the SNA and environmental (satellite) accounting. Such linkage of the SEEA with the SNA is a prerequisite for a meaningful comparison of conventional economic and environmentally adjusted indicators.

The main objectives of the SEEA can be summarized as follows (Bartelmus 1992):

(a) Segregation and elaboration of all environment-related flows and stocks of traditional accounts

The segregation of all flows and stocks of assets in national accounts, related to environmental issues, permits the estimation of the total expenditure for the protection or enhancement of different fields of the environment. A further objective of this segregation is to identify that part of the gross domestic product which reflects the costs necessary to compensate for the negative impacts of economic growth, i.e., the so-called defensive expenditures (Leipert 1989).

(b) Linkage of physical resource accounts with monetary environmental accounts and balance sheets

Physical resource accounts cover comprehensively the total stock or reserves of natural resources and changes therein, even if those resources are not (yet) affected by the economic system.[1] Natural resource accounts provide thus the physical counterpart of the monetary balance sheet and flow accounts of the SEEA.

(c) Assessment of environmental costs and benefits

The SEEA expands and complements the SNA with regard to costing the use (depletion) of natural resources in production and final demand and the changes in environmental quality, resulting from pollution and other impacts of production, consumption and natural events, on one hand, and environmental protection and enhancement, on the other.

(d) Accounting for the maintenance of tangible wealth

SEEA extends the concept of capital to cover not only man-made but also natural capital. Natural capital includes, besides produced but "naturally grown" assets of agriculture, forestry, and fisheries, nonproduced natural assets of scarce renewable resources such as marine resources or tropical forests, nonrenewable resources of land, soil, and subsoil assets (mineral deposits), and cyclical resources of air and water. Capital formation is correspondingly changed into a broader concept of capital accumulation.

(e) Elaboration and measurement of indicators of environmentally adjusted product and income

The consideration of the costs of depletion of natural resources and changes in environmental quality permits the calculation of modified macroeconomic aggregates, notably an environmentally adjusted net domestic product (EDP). Discussions are presently under way about the possibility of introducing an environmentally adjusted national income (ENI) concept by accounting for further welfare effects of environmental impacts and environmental protection.

Table 9.1 illustrates the main features of the SEEA in a consolidated framework with illustrative figures. The framework consists of three groups of accounting tables. The supply and use/value-added tables describe the flows of goods and services produced and imported (table 9.1a), and their use by economic production activities and final demand, i.e., intermediate and final consumption, capital accumulation and exports (table 9.1b). The asset accounts (table 9.1c) show the stocks of economic and environmental assets at, and changes of stocks between, the beginning and the end of the accounting period.

Table 9.1 also illustrates that the asset (stock) accounts are linked to the flow accounts of the use/value added table via capital accumulation which forms an integral part of both groups of tables. The difference between this framework and conventional accounting lies in the introduction of environmental costs of depletion of natural resources and environmental degradation (largely from pollution), mirrored in the expansion of asset boundaries to include natural assets (see shaded areas in table 9.1).

The incorporation of environmental costs in production, consumption and in changes of produced and nonproduced natural assets permits the calculation of an environmentally adjusted net domestic product (EDP). The accounting identities between income (value added generated) and expenditure (for final consumption and capital formation, modified by the difference between exports and imports) allows the calculation of NDP and EDP as the difference between output and intermediate consumption and the sum of final demand categories (see appendix for the definitory equations of NDP and EDP, based on the illustrative figures of table 9.1).

PRICING THE PRICELESS: THE LIMITS OF MONETARY VALUATION

The handbook on *Integrated Environmental and Economic Accounting* applies three categories of monetary valuation to environmental assets, changes therein, and effects on human welfare therefrom. Accordingly, three different versions or modules of the SEEA are proposed. One version (IV.1) applies a *market valuation* approach which rearranges only environmental changes already contained in the asset accounts of the conventional SNA. A second version (IV.2) uses a *maintenance valuation* which estimates the costs that would have been required to keep the natural environment intact during the accounting period. The third version (IV.3) combines the market valuation of the first version with a *contingent valuation* approach in order to assess the environmental costs borne by industries with those borne by households (as welfare losses from environmental deterioration).

The three versions reflect to an increasing degree the distance of environmental processes from economic (production and consumption) activities. Problems of consistency of valuations and of data availability increase accordingly, as does the controversiality of these versions. The handbook focuses, therefore, on the first two versions as widely applicable guidelines for environmental accounting. Version IV.3 and two further versions (which extend the production boundary of the SNA) are discussed only to provide a more comprehensive review of environmental accounting approaches and their relationships with the SEEA, even if those approaches qualify more for ad-hoc modeling and research than for routine data collection.

TABLE 9.1
Framework for Integrated Environmental and Economic Accounting (Consolidated and Modified)

Assets (Table 9.1c)

Opening stocks	produced — except natural	produced — natural (biota)	nonproduced natural
	991.3	83.1	1744.4

+ (plus)

Use/Value Added (Table 9.1b)	Total	Domestic production (industries)	Final consumption — households	Final consumption — government	Capital accumulation — produced assets — except natural	Capital accumulation — produced assets — natural (biota)	Capital accumulation — nonproduced natural assets	Rest of the world exports/imports
Use of goods and services	591.9	224.0	175.0	42.5	68.0	1.4	7.3	73.7
thereof: environmental protection services	36.2	22.4	8.8	5.0				
Gross Domestic Product (GDP)		293.4						
Consumption of fixed capital		26.3			(23.0)	(3.3)		
Net Domestic Product (NDP)		267.1						

| | | Final consumption | | + (plus) Capital accumulation | | | Rest of the world |
| | | | | produced assets | | non-produced | |
Use/Value Added (Table 9.1b)	Total	Domestic production (industries)	households	government	except natural	natural (biota)	natural assets	exports/ imports
Use of natural assets (environmental costs)	(1.6)	58.9	17.1	(5.0)	5.1		(73.0)	(4.7)
Environmental adjustment of final demand (environmental costs)		17.2	(17.1)	5.0	(5.1)			
Environmentally-adjusted net Domestic Product (EDP)		191.0						
Supply (Table 9.1a)					+ (plus)			
Goods and services	591.9	517.4						74.5
Imports of residuals	(1.6)					+ (plus)		(1.6)
Revaluation and adjustment to market valuation					138.1		464.0	
Other volume changes					(25.3)	18.5	22.8	
Closing stocks					= (equals) 1149.1	94.7	2165.5	

SOURCE: Bartelmus 1992

Version IV.1 is closest to conventional accounting in identifying changes in the market value of natural assets, already accounted for in the SNA's asset accounts as "other volume changes." In SEEA, those changes are shifted from "other volume changes" into the production accounts as imputed environmental costs. As described above, these costs include the depletion of natural resources, as well as the degradation of these and other national assets from pollution and other degrading activities—to the extent that the underlying environmental impacts are reflected in changed market values of those assets. The 1993 SNA makes allowances for such changes in its asset accounts, even if actual market prices are not observed and the stock or reserve values have to be estimated by their income-generating capacity, i.e., as (discounted) "net rent" flows.

Apart from weaknesses inherent in simplified applications of this valuation,[2] this approach permits the calculation of environmentally adjusted indicators which are consistent with the market values used in most transactions of the SNA. It can be argued, however, that these costs are imputed values that have not necessarily been internalized by individual economic agents (Bartelmus 1992). Those costs have not gone through the mill of supply and demand interaction and corresponding price formation during the accounting period; their deduction from value-added generated or capital stock would create indicators that are not fully comparable to the "observed" values in conventional accounts. On the other hand, full or partial internalization of environmental costs appears to be common practice already in some of the high-risk or resource-dependent industries.[3]

The market-value approach covers only those natural assets that have an economic value. In the SNA sense these are "economic" assets that are under controlled ownership of economic agents and provide actual or potential benefits to their owners. All other national assets obtain a zero economic value. "Environmental" assets, such as air, wild land, waters and species are thus not included in SNA asset accounts. This applies also to all environmental functions of economic assets if those functions have not been reflected in the economic (market) valuation of natural assets. In order to obtain a more comprehensive picture of the changes in the value of the environment, due to losses of its environmental functions, in particular waste absorption, a maintenance cost valuation is introduced as an alternative to market valuation in the SEEA.

The maintenance valuation caters to the environmental policy principle of "accountability" for environmental impacts. It attempts to allocate the environmental depletion and degradation costs to the causing agents in application of the polluter- and user-pays principles. It thus represents a "cost-caused" valuation. In order to maintain the closeness of these costs to the economic system, and thus their measurability, the costs caused are interpreted narrowly in relation to the immediate inputs (resource use) into and joint outputs (pollutants emitted) from production and consumption processes. The possible responsibilities for those environmental impacts of final users (domestic and from other nations) are thus not accounted for, but could (and should) be further explored in appropriate models of demand-production interaction.

Such valuation introduces a certain amount of inconsistency between market values and (maintenance) costs in the SEEA—an approach that is not totally alien to the SNA. It is applied in the cost valuation of public consumption and certain other nonmarket (subsistence) activities. Maintenance costing of "keeping the environment intact" is, however, more hypothetical because an actual depletion or degradation did occur during the accounting period. It provides an indication of the social cost that *would* have to be incurred if society *would* have behaved in an environmentally neutral manner.

The function of indicators, including EDP, modified by such valuation is thus more to alert to unsustainable trends in economic growth than to provide an accurate picture of past environmental damage. Perhaps more importantly, the maintenance cost estimation permits an assessment of the level of market instruments of cost internalization (effluent charges, tradable pollution permits, or user taxes) to bring about environmentally sound and sustainable production and consumption patterns.

The contingent valuation, on the other hand, is applied to introduce a comprehensive cost-borne concept, not only by industry (through market valuation) but also by households, suffering the welfare (health, recreation, etc.) consequences of environmental impacts. Contingent valuations, based on opinion surveys of the willingness-to-pay for the avoidance of environmental hazards, have been applied with limited success in project/program-oriented cost-benefit analyses. Their usefulness in *national* accounting is doubtful due to well-known problems (free-rider problem, short-sightedness of consumers, skewed impacts according to income distribution) that accumulate at the national level.

The handbook describes the treatment of such valuation in a consistent manner within the framework of the SEEA—more to indicate the relationships with other accounting approaches (e.g., Peskin 1989) than to recommend it for general application. The main impact on accounting indicators is the modification (decrease) of private consumption, reflecting the amount private households would be prepared to sacrifice in order to avoid the deterioration of their environment.

Clearly, economic valuation of environmental effects reaches its limits when going beyond the cost/production-oriented approaches of market and maintenance valuation and attempts the (contingent) valuation of welfare effects on health, recreation or other social values. Earlier attempts at measuring economic welfare (e.g., Nordhaus and Tobin 1972) failed thus in replacing or supplementing conventional economic indicators by an index of economic welfare.

SUSTAINABLE ECONOMIC GROWTH: CONCEPT AND MEASUREMENT[4]

Sustainability is originally an ecological concept, reflecting "prudent behavior" by a predator that avoids over-exploiting its prey to ensure an "optimum sustained yield" (Odum 1971:223). In economics, the concept of "income" has been introduced as a similar "guide for prudent conduct" in spending recurrent monetary receipts (Hicks 1946). Income is defined as "the maximum value [one] can consume during a week and still expect to be as well off at the end of the week as . . . at the beginning." The purpose is "to give people an indication of the amount which they can consume without impoverishing themselves" (Hicks 1946:172).

Generalizing this notion for the whole population of a country yields a concept of national income as the amount a population can consume during a period of time without impoverishing itself. In a closed economy and at a given level of a population, the main source of national "impoverishment" is to consume physical (produced) capital without replacing it or without reserving funds for alternative investment. Such allowance for "depreciation" is common practice in the accounts of production units: it is a cost item, entering the gross value of production but being excluded from the contribution of the unit to national income, i.e., net value added.

Recent or recently discovered scarcities in natural resource supply and environmental services of waste absorption have prompted the extension of the sustainability criterion from produced capital to "natural capital." In addition to the sustainability of produced and natural capital, the sustainability of "human capital" of labor, skill and knowledge, and of "institutional capital," providing the social, legal and organizational infrastructure for economic activities and conflict resolution, could also be introduced in a comprehensive discussion of the sustainability of economic production. The notion of sustainability of human capital or labor is controversial, since it is hardly possible to distinguish sustainability of economic activities of human beings from the general sustenance of human life. The quality of human life in its many material and nonmaterial facets bears upon both, the economic contributions of human beings, and on their pursuit of noneconomic goals. Consequently, the sustainability of human life is probably better analyzed in reference to a set of standards of living or of the "quality of life," as part of a broad multi-dimensional development concept (see below).

An empirical-historical study of the role of institutions in development and environment has shown that institutions and institutional change were critical for the nature and speed of development, though not sufficient for stimulating economic growth (Adelman et al. 1992:106). However, the measurement of flows of "services" from the institutional set-up and its maintenance also poses considerable problems of conceptualization and valuation.

Therefore, *integrated environmental and economic accounting* has concentrated on produced and natural capital consumption or use. Such accounting permits to replace or supplement conventional indicators of economic performance and growth, notably GDP or NDP, by the of environmentally adjusted indicator of EDP. Focusing on the maintenance of produced and natural capital, EDP can be used to define sustainable economic growth in operational terms. Bearing in mind possibilities of extending the use of natural capital through (resource saving and environmentally sound) technological progress, resource discovery or substitution of (produced, natural or human) inputs, *sustainable economic growth* can thus be defined as

positive trend in (real) EDP (which allows for the consumption of produced and depletion and degradation of natural capital)—assuming that the allowances made can be invested into capital maintenance and taking into account that past trends of depletion and degradation can be offset or mitigated by technological progress, discovery of natural resources and changes in consumption patterns.   (Bartelmus 1992)

This definition refers explicitly to EDP. The concept of sustainable economic growth differs, however, from the definition of EDP as an essentially analytical (ex-ante) concept that anticipates resource discovery, improvement in the efficiency of resource use, technological progress or changes in lifestyles. As a consequence, observed sustainability constraints of natural resource availability and environmental (services) capacities could be relaxed in growth analysis. Such anticipations lessen the "operationality" of the above definition, requiring predictive analysis, i.e., modeling. In addition, this definition assumes that environmental cost allowances are invested (rather than consumed) so as to ensure, e.g., through substitution, importation, or rehabilitation, that the productive capacities of the economy are maintained.

Further effects of natural or man-made disasters, high inflation, indebtedness, and changes in the institutional environment or in the productivity of human capital may of course also affect the sustainability of economic growth as defined above. Allowing for produced and natural capital consumption in the above definition obtains therefore only a "more sustainable" growth concept that needs further refinement through comprehensive modeling of sustainable growth. Such models could focus on the limits in the availability of natural resource capital and the absorptive capacity of environmental media. If those limits are reached, economic policies would have to shift the focus from the "efficiency" of resource allocation to the "sufficiency" or limitation of the scale of economic growth. Sufficiency is reached at the optimal scale of economic growth where the "long-run marginal costs of expansion are equal to the long-run marginal benefits of expansion" (Daly 1991).

Uncertainties about the effects of technological progress, resource discovery and substitution possibilities, and problems of aggregating and predicting marginal cost and benefit functions cast doubts on any assessment of the closeness to such ultimate limits, both nationally and globally. As a consequence, international recommendations on the relationships between environment and development generally stress the need for continued or accelerated economic growth.[5]

Replacing conventional growth indicators such as GDP or national income by EDP or ENI and expanding the scope of key variables such as capital and capital formation to include natural capital (use) in dynamic growth modeling could provide early-warning signals about the trends and limits of sustainable economic growth. National accounts identities such as those presented in the Annex can provide the starting point for the analysis of functional relationships between output (0) and environmental costs (EC), or between EDP and capital accumulation (CA and its components).

OUTLOOK: FROM GROWTH TO DEVELOPMENT

The above concept of economic growth is production-oriented in its focus on domestic product and constraints in the quantity and quality of production factors; it reflects the "costs caused" by production and consumption. However, economic growth analysis has also used national income, usually in per-capita terms, as its main operational variable, reflecting implicitly or explicitly a more welfare-oriented approach. Especially after further modification for transfers and taxation/subsidies, disposable (national) income can be interpreted as a potential claim on the use of welfare-generating goods and services during the current or future (through saving) accounting periods.

Negative welfare effects on human health, recreation, and other cultural values from the deterioration of environmental quality are the ultimate concern of environmental protection and can be interpreted as the "cost borne" by "final" uses or users. Those costs could be deducted from national income for a more comprehensive welfare measure. For purposes of welfare-oriented economic growth analysis, the above definition of economic growth could then be reformulated on the basis of an Environmentally-adjusted National Income (ENI indicator, in absolute terms or per capita.

A number of problems in assessing welfare-oriented growth make such definition rather ambiguous. First, like any average, per-capita figures are only meaningful if assessed in the context of their distribution. Distributionary aspects are particularly relevant for the assessment of equity in economic growth and development. Inequities are conspicuously manifest in conditions of poverty and hunger as compared to those of affluence, both within and among countries. However, they cannot be readily translated into economic costs or benefits. Second, the estimation of environmental damage, related to human well-being, faces considerable measurement and valuation problems which, in general make a welfare-oriented definition of economic growth nonoperational.

Further development goals of a social, cultural or political nature are even more difficult to value in monetary terms. The general policy focus on monetary measures of economic growth has therefore been criticized by advocates of multidimensional development. Such development would have to address the whole spectrum of human needs and aspirations as part of the overall goal of improving the quality of life.[6] A comprehensive concept of development has thus to cover both quantitative and qualitative aspects of human needs satisfaction, including consumption levels or standards of living and noneconomic goals of an environmental, social, cultural, or political nature. At the same time, such development has to consider limits or constraints in the provision of need-satisfying goods, services, and noneconomic amenities. These limits include produced and natural capital constraints, thus introducing the physical counterpart of the sustainability of economic growth into development analysis.

The introduction of standards and targets in development analysis shifts the focus of sustainability from the maintenance of capital in economic growth to the examination of development programs and activities regarding their compliance with minimum (desirable) standards of living and maximum standards of natural resource use and environmental degradation. Violation of standards or nonachievement of targets reflect a development pattern that "should" not be sustained in the long run. In this sense, the relatively neutral sustainability criterion of capital maintenance is replaced by a more normative one of the "feasibility" of development programs. The issue of sustainability of development becomes thus a question of *feasibility* of development programs or *the* development program, operating within a normative framework of (exogeneously set) targets, standards, and thresholds.

Interdependences among economic activities can be described by input-output matrices of the supply of goods and services. Similar interactions have been observed between the biotic and abiotic components of ecosystems, which again interact with human activities. If all these interactions can be formulated as relationships between single processes or activities which transform any kind of means (inputs) into ends (outputs), the powerful tools of input-output and activity analysis can be applied. The latter, in particular, permits the determination of sets and levels of activities that are feasible, i.e., satisfy constraints of minimum levels of human needs satisfaction ("inner limits") and maximum levels of production capacities, resource uses, and emissions of pollutants ("outer limits") (Bartelmus 1979).

Comprehensive integration of nonmonetary variables has not been commonly applied in development planning and policies, due to conceptual as well as statistical problems. However, the deliberations at UNCED provided evidence that there is growing recognition of the need for long-term planning and policies which take into account noneconomic demographic, social and environmental variables for achieving sustained development.

Systems of (environment) statistics and indicators aim at measuring these variables in an integrative, or at least comparable, fashion. They can thus provide a synthetic picture of the state and trend of the environment and its links to human socioeconomic activities. For example, UNSTAT is actively promoting the application of methodologies of environment statistics, organized in an integrative "framework for the development of environment statistics" (FDES). The framework links social, demographic, and economic statistics with data on environmental impacts and social responses (UN 1984, 1988, 1991). In response to a request by UNCED, UNSTAT is also developing indicators in a framework that combines FDES criteria (of data production) with sustainability concerns (of data users) expressed in Agenda 21.

The desire to obtain more aggregated indices of "development" that do not only focus on economic aggregates but also on other "human" values has prompted the estimation of a "human development index" (HDI) (UNDP 1991). The HDI accounts, apart from per-capita GDP, for literacy and life expectancy and can be adjusted for distributionary aspects.

It remains to be seen if these efforts of assessing integrated and sustainable development in nonmonetary terms can prompt decision makers to formulate and implement consistent sustainable development policies, programs, and projects. Past experience, notably from the development of social indicators, suggests that physical statistics and indicators may usefully guide managerial decision in particular environmental areas but fail usually to influence broader macro-policies of growth and development.

APPENDIX: NDP AND EDP CALCULATION
IN INTEGRATED ACCOUNTING
(definitory equations and illustrative figures from table 9.1)

1. Value added based calculations

(1a) $\text{NDP} = \text{O} - \text{IC} - \text{CFC} = 517.4 - 224.0 - 26.3 = 267.1$

where NDP = net domestic product
O = gross output
IC = intermediate consumption
CFC = consumption of fixed capital

(1b) $\text{EDP} = \text{NDP} - \text{EC} = 267.1 - 76.1 = 191.0$

where EC = environmental costs

2. Expenditure (final demand) based calculations

(2a) $\text{NDP} = \text{C} + \text{CF} - \text{CFC} + (\text{X} - \text{M}) = 217.5 + 76.7 - 26.3 - 0.8 = 267.1$

where C = final consumption
CF = capital formation
X = exports
M = imports

(2b) $\text{EDP} = \text{C} + \text{CA} - \text{CFC} + (\text{X} - \text{M}) = 217.5 + 0.6 - 26.3 - 0.8 = 191.0$

where CA = capital accumulation and

$\text{CA} = \text{CF} - (\text{EC}_p + \text{EC}_{fd}) = 76.7 - (58.9 + 17.2) = 0.6$

where EC_p = environmental cost of production and

EC_{fd} = environmental cost of final demand (shifted to production)

Acknowledgment: The views expressed in this paper are my own and do not necessarily reflect an expression of opinion on the part of the United Nations.

NOTES

1. See, e.g., the Norwegian approach to natural resource accounting (Alfsen, Bye, and Lorentsen 1987) or the more complex (including *inter alia,* interactions in the biophysical environment) French "natural patrimony" accounts (INSEE 1986).

2. See Bartelmus and van Tongeren (1994) for a further discussion of two approximations of this valuation, the "net-price method" (Repetto et al. 1989) and the "user-cost allowance" (El Serafy 1989).

3. Declarations to this end have been made in most environmental meetings and conferences involving industry representatives. Examples of balance-sheet provisions for potential toxic waste clean-up are those of U.S. chemical concerns (Monsanto Co., Du Pont Co., Cyanamid Co.), amounting to between 200 and 400 million US$ at the end of 1991 (*Wall Street Journal,* March 23, 1992).

4. For a more comprehensive discussion of the concepts and measurability of sustainability in growth and development, see Bartelmus (1994).

5. For instance, the report of the World Commission on Environment and Development comes to the conclusion that "the international economy must speed up world

growth while respecting the environmental constraints" (WCED 1987:89), and Principle 12 of UNCED's Rio Declaration on Environment and Development stipulates that "States should cooperate to promote a supportive and open international system that would lead to economic growth and sustainable development in all countries, to better address the problems of environmental degration."

6. Much of the discussion around the notions of quality of life and social indicators has been on the inadequacy of a development process that concentrates on economic growth, neglecting social values of security, health, distribution of income and wealth, and environmental quality (OECD 1973:3).

REFERENCES

Adelman, I. et al. 1992. "Institutional Change, Economic Development, and the Environment." *Ambio* 12:106–111.

Alfsen, K. H., T. Bye, and L. Lorentsen. 1987. *Natural Resource Accounting and Analysis, the Norwegian Experience 1978–1986*. Oslo: Central Bureau of Statistics.

Bartelmus, P. 1979. "Limits to Development: Environmental Constraints of Human Needs Satisfaction." *Journal of Environmental Management* 9:155–169.

—— 1992. "Accounting for Sustainable Growth and Development." *Structural Change and Economic Dynamics* 3:241–260.

—— 1994. *Environment, Growth and Development: The Concepts and Strategies of Sustainability*. London and New York: Routledge.

Bartelmus, P., E. Lutz, and S. Schweinfest. 1993. "Integrated Environmental and Economic Accounting: A Case Study for Papua New Guinea." In E. Lutz, ed., *Toward Improved Accounting for the Environment*, pp. 108–143. Washington, D.C.: The World Bank.

Bartelmus, P. and J. van Tongeren. 1994. *Environmental Accounting: An Operational Perspective*. Department for Economic and Social Information and Policy Analysis, Working Paper Series No. 1. New York: United Nations.

Daly, H. E. 1991. "Elements of Environmental Macroeconomics." In R. Costanza, ed., *Ecological Economics: The Science and Management of Sustainability*, pp. 32–46. New York: Columbia University Press.

El Serafy, S. 1989. "The Proper Calculation of Income from Depletable Natural Resources." In J. Ahmed, S. El Serafy and E. Lutz, eds. *Environmental Accounting for Sustainable Development*, pp. 10–18. Washington, D.C.: World Bank.

Hicks, J. R. 1946. *Value and Capital*. 2d ed. Oxford: Oxford University Press.

INSEE (Institut National de la Statistique et des Etudes Economiques). 1986. *Les Comptes du Patrimoine Naturel*. Les collections de l'inséé, 137/138C.

Inter-Secretariat Working Group on National Accounts. 1993. *System of National Accounts 1993*. United Nations publication (sales no. E.94.XVII.4).

Leipert C. 1989. "National Income and Economic Growth: The Conceptual Side of Defensive Expenditures." *Journal of Economic Issues* 23:843–56.

Nordhaus, W. D. and J. Tobin. 1972. "Is Growth Obsolete?" *Economic Growth*. National Bureau of Economic Research, General Series 96, New York.

Odum, E. P. 1971. *Fundamentals of Ecology.* 3d ed. Philadelphia: Saunders.

OECD (Organization for Economic Co-operation and Development). 1973. *List of Social Concerns Common to Most OECD Countries.* Paris: OECD.

Peskin, H. M. 1989. "A Proposed Environmental Accounts Framework." In Y. J. Ahmad, S. El Serafy, and E. Lutz, eds., *Environmental Accounting for Sustainable Development,* pp. 65–78. Washington, D.C.: World Bank.

Postel, S. 1990. "Toward a New "Eco"-nomics." *World Watch* 3:20–28.

Repetto, R. et al. 1989. *Wasting Assets, Natural Resources in the National Income Accounts.* Washington, D.C.: World Resources Institute.

UN (United Nations). 1984. *A Framework for the Development of Environment Statistics* (sales no. E.84.XVII.12).

——— 1988. *Concepts and Methods of Environment Statistics: Human Settlements Statistics—A Technical Report* (sales no. E.88.XVII.18).

——— 1991. *Concepts and Methods of Environment Statistics: Statistics of the Natural Environment—A Technical Report* (sales no. E.91.XVII.18).

——— 1993. *Integrated Environmental and Economic Accounting.* Interim version (sales No. E.93.XVII.12).

——— Development Programme (UNDP). 1991. *Human Development Report 1991.* New York and Oxford: Oxford University Press.

van Tongeren, J., S. Schweinfest, E. Lutz, M. Gomez Luna, and G. Martin. 1993. "Integrated Environmental and Economic Accounting: A Case Study for Mexico." In E. Lutz, ed., *Toward Improved Accounting for the Environment,* pp., 85–107. Washington, D.C.: World Bank.

WCED (World Commission on Environment and Development). 1987. *Our Common Future.* Oxford and New York: Oxford University Press.

TEN

Measuring Sustainable Income: The Cases of Mineral and Forest Depletion in Brazil

Ronaldo Serôa da Motta and Peter H. May

This paper presents estimates of depreciation values for mineral and forest resources in Brazil. In doing so, it compares the results obtained from alternative estimation methods—net price and user cost—and their theoretical justifications. It is also argued that sustainability principles may be a key parameter to use in considering which method to adopt for national development planning.

The growing concern with the environment and the preservation of natural resources has placed the traditional approach emphasizing economic growth under increasing scrutiny. Despite an increasing number of efforts to measure national environment accounts, the widely disseminated expression "sustainable development" is not yet matched by a consistent corresponding concept of "sustainable income," which expresses, in economic terms, the concept of growth consonant with the availability of natural resources to fuel that growth.

The need to discern "sustainable income" is closely associated with the urgency of devising approaches to adopt the system of national accounts (SNA) to reflect use of the environment. As environmental effects of use, depletion or degradation of natural resources are not usually valued at market prices, they are not incorporated in national accounts values. The major concern of the SNA being centered on production, the activities that result in degradation and depletion of natural resources are only regarded as an economic gain; no loss is incorporated. It is thus necessary to find ways that the SNA may include the valuation of natural resource increments or losses—insofar as they represent part of society's present and future assets.

The valuation of natural resources has engendered much attention at the microeconomic level,[1] mainly from a neoclassical perspective. However, as Daly (1990:19) points out, the principal concern of microeconomics is to establish a pricing system that will guarantee an optimal allocation of a given endowment of production factors—"once prices are right the environmental problem is "solved"—there is no macroeconomic dimension."

The proposal for an environmentally sound economic development thus not only concerns how natural resources are used, but is also a matter of knowing their utilization levels. This is a basic macroeconomic issue. Any attempt to establish a procedure to estimate the impact of the use of natural resources in the SNA should derive from a theoretical justification for the concept of income. As a consequence, new ways to calculate aggregate income values should stem from the means by which natural resource depletion and degradation are treated.[2]

This study focuses on estimation of economic loss caused by depletion of mineral and forest resources in Brazil and its impact on the measurement of that nation's domestic product (GDP). In doing so, the authors establish a definition for "sustainable income" that encompasses natural resource depletion. The first section describes alternative methods used in measuring economic losses derived from depletion of natural resources. In the next section, the preliminary results regarding depletion costs of mineral and forest resources in Brazil are analyzed. The final section examines the sustainability principles that underlie depletion cost measurement.

MEASURING SUSTAINABLE INCOME

Two methods have been proposed to measure natural capital consumption in order to determine sustainable income.

Net Price Method

The net price method accounts for the physical variation of stock multiplied by the market price of the cost of the output, net of production costs, adjusted for price changes. This net price would be the same as the rent accruing to the holder of the resource and would represent, following the Hoteling lema, the present value of the portion of natural stock that is decreasing due to extraction.[3] Such a procedure deducts from gross income the total net revenue derived from the resource being extracted, assuming that this rent reflects the depreciation of the aforementioned resource. Considering that the stock of a nonrenewable resource decreases with the amount extracted during the year, the depleted amount (evaluated at current prices) could be deducted from gross income in the same way that capital consumption is deducted from value added in manufacturing activities. Gains from mining extraction are accounted for in gross product while the value of depletion is deducted from net product

Reppeto et al. (1989) and Solórzano et al. (1992) follow this procedure in evaluating the asset loss derived from oil and timber extraction in Indonesia and Costa Rica, respectively. "Economic" accounting of natural resources derives directly from accounts expressed in physical units, giving them monetary value and adjusting for stock variations. Net variations of the stock value are assigned to present additions of yearly deposits (discoveries, net revisions, growth or reproductions) minus deductions (depletion, degradation, or deforestation) plus price changes of resources during the year. Equation (1) summarizes the procedure:

$$X_{t+1}P_{t+1} = X_t p_t + (X_{t+1} - X_t)\, p^* + X_t\, (p_{t+1} - p_t) + (X_{t+1} - X_t)$$
$$(p_{t+1} - p^*) \tag{1}$$

where:
X_t is the opening stock of the resource in physical units,
X_{t+1} is the closing stock of the resource in physical units,
P_t is the rent per physical unit at the opening of term,
P_{t+1} is the rent per physical unit at the closing of term, and
P^* is the average unit rent during the term.

The following relationships can be derived from equation (1):
i) Net variation of stock:

$$X_{t+1}P_{t+1} - Xtp = (X_{t+1} - X_t)\, p^* + X_t\, (p_{t+1} - p_t) + (X_{t+1} - X_t)$$
$$(p_{t+1} - p^*) \tag{1a}$$

ii) Current net additions during the year:

$$(X_{t+1} - X_t)\, p^* = (Ad - Rd)\, p^* \tag{1b}$$

where:
   Ad represents stock additions (discoveries, revisions (net), extensions, growth, and reproduction),

Rd represents stock reductions (production, deforestation, and degradation).

iii) Revaluations:

$$Rv = X_t\,(p_{t+1} - p_t) + (X_{t+1} - X_t)\,(p_{t+1} - p^*) \tag{1c}$$

where:

$X_t\,(p_{t+1} - p_t)$ corresponds to the revaluation of opening stocks, and $(X_{t+1} - X_t)\,(p_{t+1} - p^*)$ corresponds to the revaluation of transactions made during the term.

Note that in this method, the Hoteling lema is not properly applied since it is net price, price minus average costs, and not rent, price minus marginal costs, which is considered. Use of such a proxy overestimates capital consumption since average costs are higher than marginal costs.

Moreover, when new discoveries of reserves exceed depletion levels, the final result will indicate an accumulation of natural capital instead of a depreciation.

User Cost Method

According to El Serafy (1988), depletion of natural resources cannot be conceptually regarded as depreciation since it does not involve use of fixed capital. Receipts obtained from the extraction of non-renewable resources derive from the sale of assets, a disinvestment, which cannot be regarded as value added (gross or net). That is, instead of saying that there was a "current production" of gold, it should be stated that there was an extraction. Actually, what should be deducted is the user cost which is not explicit in mineral production costs, but that should correspond to the sacrifice imposed upon future generations when the resource will be exhausted.

If all the rent is considered as capital use, then the economy's value added from exploitable resources would tend to nil. As a result, rent is usually mistaken for gross income.

To counter this tendency, El Serafy proposes maintenance of the definition of true income suggested by Hicks (1946), that is, the amount of consumption that will not harm future use. For this to be reached, a finite series of exploitation receipts anticipated to be obtained from a resource must be converted into an infinite series of true income in such a way that the current value of both is equal. That is, part of that income would be set aside regularly as an investment capable of generating a perpetual income stream equivalent to true income. This portion would be called user cost (or depletion factor) and would not be included in the GDP valuation. This user cost would then represent a "disinvestment" to be taken into consideration in capital formation in such a way that total consumption would be equivalent to true income.

Instead of provisions to maintain the value of the natural resource in its untouched state, which would be geologically and biologically impossible, investments would be made in material capital capable of generating future income flows equivalent to the natural resource under exhaustion.

In a general and simplified form the method and estimating procedures of user cost are as follows:

The exploitation of a natural resource generates a net revenue (R), which is perceived as the receipt net of the operation and capital costs. Part of (R) must be invested in such a way as to guarantee an infinite series of sustainable income (X). Thus, during exploitation $(R-X)$ is the environmental loss due to the use of the resource which should be invested in the economy, so that X can be infinitely generated.

$F(R-X)$ is the future value of the series of $(R-X)$ accumulated during the time horizon of exploration (n) according to the opportunity cost of capital (r):

$$F(R-X) = (R-X)(1+r)t = (R-X)[(1+r)_a - 1] / r \qquad (2)$$

From t_{n+1} on this accumulated capital stock will generate annual returns equivalent to the opportunity cost of capital, (r), whose present value $P(R-X)$ will be:

$$P(R-X) = F(R-X) r \, 1/d = (R-X) [(1+r)^n - 1] / d \qquad (3)$$

where d is the discount rate on consumption (intertemporal preference).

The resource's sustainable income (X) is the same as its present value, which equals the present value of the accumulated capital return, described in (3):

$$F(R-X) r / d = (R-X) [(1+r)^n - 1] / d = X / d \qquad (4)$$

By multiplying both sides of (4) by d, the result will be:

$$(R-X) [(1+r)^n - 1] = X \qquad (5a)$$

or

$$X / R = 1 - 1/(1 + r)^n \qquad (5b)$$

Therefore, for each natural resource it is possible to estimate the X/R relationship and, consequently, to determine the $(R - X)$ portion of the exploitation receipt of these resources (that is, the user cost) that should be accounted for as environmental loss, as well as the portion X that refers to the remainder of this income, which may be regarded as sustainable income. In what follows, the ratio between $(R - X)$ and the traditional GDP will be called the depletion factor.[4]

As can be noted, the user cost method is very sensitive to the opportunity cost of capital (r) and the depletion period (n). For higher values of (r) a very low user cost value can be expected. With n values higher than 100, zero or very low values of user cost are often found.

DEPLETION COSTS OF MINERAL AND FOREST RESOURCES IN BRAZIL

Minerals[5]

Depletion costs from mineral extraction were measured for Brazil using both the net price and user cost approaches. The same net revenue values were applied in both methods for each year. The opportunity cost of capital was assumed to be 15% and depletion period and stock variations determined according to measured reserve estimates.

It can be noted in table 10.1 that annual depletion costs and factors show very distinct values in comparing the two methods applied. First of all, the differences in magnitude of depletion costs are very impressive. In this respect, the net price approach indicates that depletion factors vary between − 8,954.10 and 15,815.72 percent whereas these variations in the user cost method range only from 2.11 to 13.34 percent.

In the case of minerals in Brazil, discoveries of large reserves occurred with some frequency over the past two decades which affected significantly the values obtained using the net price method. Sign changes are also traced to revaluation of reserves.

The large reserves attributed to high value added minerals such as iron, coal, bauxite and lead have also significantly reduced the calculated user costs since depletion periods (n) assume very high values.

TABLE 10.1
Sustainable Income for Mineral Extraction in Brazil
(1980 US$ billion)

| | Mineral Sector Value Added | Depletion Costs | | Depletion Factors | |
| | | User cost (r = 15%) | Net price | User cost 2/1 | Net price 3/1 |
Year	(1)	(2)	(3)	(%)	(%)
1970	2.46	0.17	-	6.73	-
1971	2.50	0.26	62.97	10.42	2521.76
1972	2.59	0.27	-232.01	10.41	-8954.10
1973	2.62	0.25	-166.67	9.46	-6370.51
1974	2.89	0.39	457.16	13.34	15815.72
1975	2.90	0.24	-95.96	8.16	-3314.62
1976	2.92	0.18	14.39	6.07	492.82
1977	2.75	0.11	-3.02	4.13	-110.04
1978	3.00	0.10	-60.20	3.32	-2007.50
1979	2.97	0.08	48.86	2.56	1643.96
1980	3.05	0.06	-10.22	2.12	-334.95
1981	3.30	0.10	32.54	2.93	986.13
1982	3.70	0.08	-59.96	2.19	-1620.78
1983	4.48	0.15	-28.90	3.30	-646.41
1984	6.02	0.46	24.19	7.62	401.89
1985	7.06	0.69	55.84	9.77	790.64
1986	7.54	0.49	-84.09	6.54	1114.76
1987	7.77	0.35	9.67	4.50	124.39
1988	8.34	0.18	-28.21	2.11	-338.15

SOURCES: Serôa da Motta and Young (1991) and Young (1992)

Forest Resources[6]

Some assumptions are needed to apply the described methods to forest resource depletion. First, it is very plausible to assume that deforestation as it occurred in Brazil has been mainly due to agricultural expansion. Therefore, forest user cost must be deducted from agricultural output. Second, when crops or pastures are established, the forest is permanently transformed, much in the way minerals are exploited. Third, without deforestation, management of the forest would enable sustainable extraction of forest products.

For this study wood and a set of extractive products[7] accounting for nearly 50% of total nontimber forest production value in Brazil were considered. To apply the user cost approach, sustainable production levels for wood were estimated as equivalent to the forest's natural growth in annual marketable timber increment. For extractive products, a sustainable production level was determined according to technical parameters for each species. Estimates were obtained over the 1970–85 period, corresponding with data availability on production and land use change.

Thus the sustainable income (X) which could take place in time t from sustainable timber extraction would be:

$$X_{jt} = [(K_{jt+1} - K_j t) \cdot g_j] \cdot P_{jt}$$

where:
j is the Brazilian vegetation zone,
K is the forest stock in wood equivalent,
g is the natural forest growth rate, and
P is the net price of exported forest products.

Depletion period (n) is given by the ratio of K_j and total deforested area in period t. The user cost value, at discount rate i, is:

$$U_{jt} = X_{jt} / (1 + i)^n$$

In the net price approach, depletion cost is given by:

$$D_{jt} = (K_{jt+1} - K_{jt}) P_{jt}$$

In the case of extractive products, g becomes the sustainable level of extraction. The production value estimated in this case is equal for both methods since the tree itself only generates value if it is standing—there is no benefit to be derived from deforestation of non-timber forest resources.

The user costs derived were then compared to the gross crop and livestock production of the land converted to agricultural purposes in each period and not to total agricultural product as was done for the net price values (table 10.2). Such a distinction was necessary since, lacking data for historical land conversion from forests to agriculture, we were limited in our estimates to sustainable production occurring in the years after 1971 resulting from agricultural conversion in the immediately preceding period. Assuming that all area previously converted was due to agricultural conversion, one may consider the ratio of user cost and converted land product as a proxy for a comparison with the entire agricultural sector.

TABLE 10.2

Sustainable Income for Agricultural Expansion in Brazil
(1980 US$ 000,000)

Year	Converted Land Agric. Value Added[a] (1)	National Agric. Value Added (2)	User Cost (5%) wood	User Cost (5%) others[b]	User Cost (5%) total (3)	Net Price wood	Net Price others[b]	Net Price total (4)	3/1	4/2
1971	135.9	10 753	13.7	4.6	18.4	6 036	4.6	6 041	14	56
1972	155.0	12 530	16.2	-	16.2	6 582	-	6 582	10	53
1973	174.0	15 441	19.3	8.2	27.6	8 167	8.2	8 175	16	53
1974	193.0	16 949	17.4	10.0	28.4	13 082	10.9	13 093	15	77
1975	250.0	18 200	22.1	10.0	32.4	16 277	10.0	16 287	13	89
1976	300.3	20 025	47.2	21.0	58.3	15 944	21.0	15 965	23	80
1977	339.9	25 292	52.5	21.7	74.2	16 780	21.7	16 802	22	66
1978	353.9	21 599	46.4	26.6	73.0	14 370	26.6	14 397	21	67
1979	368.0	22 607	45.4	36.8	82.2	13 717	36.8	13 754	22	61
1980	311.1	24 050	37.6	33.1	70.7	11 258	33.1	11 291	23	47
1981	249.4	20 591	3.0	2.3	5.3	9 084	2.3	9 086	2	44
1982	175.8	17 577	2.1	2.7	4.7	6 525	2.7	6 528	3	37
1983	182.3	22 009	1.9	3.0	4.9	6 300	3.0	6 303	3	29
1984	188.8	23 645	1.7	3.6	5.4	6 042	3.6	6 046	3	26
1985	195.3	25 473	1.0	2.7	3.7	5 136	2.7	5 139	2	20

SOURCE: Serôa da Motta and May (1993); May (1994)
[a] Value added of land converted in each year.
[b] Forest extractive products: latex, nuts, babaçu, palmito and carnaúba. Data was not available for 1972 estimates.

Observing table 10.2, one notes that the variation in magnitudes between the values derived according to each method is extremely large, although they tend to decrease in the more recent years when deforestation rates dramatically decline reflecting economic crisis. In this latter period, the slowing of agricultural conversion leads to an extension in the depletion horizon (n).

For the net price approach, total depletion cost in the mid seventies accounts for almost all national agricultural output. In the year 1975, for example, the depletion factor corresponded to 98% of all agricultural output. That is, according to this analysis, Brazil's economy in this period would have been better off without its agricultural sector. This conclusion appears rather polemical!

Using a discount rate of 5% in the user cost method, the percentage of income to be considered as depletion costs reached the maximum level in the 1975–80 period, when the depletion factor averaged 22%, rising as high as $82 million in 1979. In the 1980s, since deforestation rates were very low compared to the total forest stock, user cost values are much smaller (less than $5 million annually).

Significant variations in magnitudes of the values measured by the net price approach, such as those observed for minerals, did not occur for forest resources since stock variations in this case result from reforestation which, in Brazil, is very minor when compared to total forest area in the country.

However, it is important to make one distinction between forest and mineral resources regarding the user cost approach. Since substitutes for minerals may be anticipated, whereas for forest services and goods such substitution may prove impossible, the exponential discounting of user costs might be replaced by a logistic function. Logistic discounting as a means to represent the finite exploitation cycles of renewable resources will increase user cost estimates, thus reflecting to some degree the necessity to define limits to ecosystem encroachment.

The measurement of natural capital depreciation is not free of empirical difficulties and theoretical controversy. Apart from theoretical disputes, both methods previously discussed—net price and user cost—also reflect different views on sustainability. According to Turner (1992) and Pearce and Atkinson (1992) one may point out two broad sustainability principles: weak sustainability where man-made and natural capitals can be fully substituted, and strong sustainability where there exists a complementarity between these two forms of capital. The former allows a society to deplete its natural resource base since investment in man-made capital can replace natural losses. The latter, however, assumes that natural capital must be kept constant over time. Less strong or even weaker sustainability hypotheses are imaginable by identifying critical capital whose replacement is not viable or limited.

Based on these principles, one may recognize that the user cost approach implicitly assumes a weak sustainability hypothesis since it is accepted that the proceeds from natural resource exploitation can be used to generate in the future the same level of consumption currently enjoyed. Inversely, the net price approach implicitly assumes that no substitution is possible, therefore, all proceeds must be counted as depreciation.

Summing up, the sustainability principle must be identified, as a weak or strong hypothesis, in order to justify the approach adopted to determine sustainable income values. Such an identification implies policy choice, since the resulting measure of national product will reflect the intensity of resource exploitation deemed politically acceptable.

NOTES

1. See Pearce and Turner (1990) for presentation and discussion of a range of techniques now routinely used for valuation of environmental costs and benefits in policy analysis.
2. See a review of the literature in Peskin and Lutz (1990).
3. See Hartwick and Hageman (1991) for a discussion of Hoteling rent as an appropriate measure of natural capital depreciation.
4. In El Serafy (1988 and 1990) and Serôa da Motta (1991) the X/R factor was called a depletion factor, though they are differently derived. In practical terms the relationship adopted here from Serôa da Motta (1991) is preferable since it can be applied based on the opportunity cost of capital.
5. This case study is fully presented in Serôa da Motta and Young (1991) and Young (1992). See Young (1992) for a detailed discussion on the user cost concept.
6. A full version of this case study is presented in Serôa da Motta and May (1993) and May (1994).
7. Latex, Brazil nuts, babaçu kernels, açaí (fruit and palmito), palmito from other sources, and carnaúba wax.

REFERENCES

Daly, H. 1990. "Towards an Environmental Macroeconomics." *Revista de Analisis Economico* 5 (2).

El Serafy, J. 1988. "The Proper Calculation of Income from Depletable Natural Resources." In Y. Ahmad et al., eds. *Environmental and Natural Resource Accounting and Their Relevance to the Measurement of Sustainable Development*. Washington, D.C.: World Bank/UNEP.

Hartwick, J. M. and A. P. Hageman. 1991. "Economic Depreciation of Mineral Stocks and the Contribution of El Serafy." World Bank, mimeo.

Hicks, J. R. 1946. *Value and Capital: An Inquiry into some Fundamental Principles of Economic Theory*. London, Oxford University Press.

IBGE. 1979. *Matriz de Relaçoes Intersetoriais: Brasil 1975*. Rio de Janeiro: IBGE.

—— 1979. *Sistemas de Contas Nacionais Consolidadas: Brasil*. Rio de Janeiro: IBGE.

Keynes, J. M. 1973. *The General Theory of Employment, Interest, and Money*. London: Macmillan (The Collected Writings of John Maynard Keynes, vol. 7).

May, P. H. 1994. "Measuring Sustainability: Forest Values and Agropastoral Expansion in Brazil." In F. J. Duijnhouwer et al., eds. *Sustainable Resource Management and*

Resource Use: Policy Questions and Research Needs , pp. 139–164. Amsterdam: Netherlands Advisory Council for Research on Nature and the Environment, RMNO Publication no. 98.

Pearce, D. and R. K. Turner. 1990. *Economics of Natural Resources and the Environment.* Baltimore: Johns Hopkins University Press.

Pearce, D. and G. Atkinson. 1992. "Are National Economics Sustainable?," London: CSERGE, University College London.

Peskin, H. and E. Lutz. 1990. "A Survey of Resource and Environmental Accounting in Industrialized Countries." Washington, D.C.: World Bank, Environmental Department Working Paper 37.

Reppeto, R. et al. 1989. *Wasting Assets: Natural Resources in the National Income Accounts.* Washington, D.C.: World Resources Institute.

Serôa da Motta, R. 1991. "Uma Proposta Metodológica para Estimativas de Contas Ambientais no Brasil." Rio de Janeiro: IPEA, Relatório Interno no. 4.

Serôa da Motta, R. and P. H. May. 1993. "Perdas Ambientais Devido ao Desmatamento no Brasil." Rio de Janeiro: IPEA, Diretoria de Pesquisa.

Serôa da Motta, R. and C. E. F. Young. 1991. "Recursos Naturais e Contabilidade Social: A Renda Sustentável da Extraçao Mineral no Brasil." Rio de Janeiro: IPEA, Texto para Discussao 231.

Solórzano, R. et al. 1992. *Accounts Overdue: Natural Resource Depreciation in Costa Rica.* Washington, D.C.: World Resource Institute.

Turner, R. K. et al. 1994. "Sea Level Rise and Coastal Wetlands in the UK: Mitigation Strategies for Sustainable Management." In A. Jansson, M. Hammer, C. Folke, and R. Costanza, eds. *Investing in Natural Capital,* pp. 266–290. Covelo, Calif.: Island Press.

Young , C. E. F. 1992. "Renda Sustentável da Extraçao Mineral no Brasil." M.Sc. Thesis, Federal University of Rio de Janeiro, Instituto de Economia Industrial.

The Contributors

Peter Bartelmus is responsible for environmental and energy statistics at the Statistical Division of the United Nations in New York, where he coordinated studies in support of a methodology recently proposed by the UN for integration of environmental accounts within the System of National Accounts. He recently authored *Environment, Growth, and Development.*

Robert Costanza is Professor at the Center for Environmental and Estuarine Studies of the University of Maryland and President of the International Society for Ecological Economics. He recently co-edited *Ecological Economics: The Science and Management of Sustainability* and *Investing in Natural Capital.*

Herman Daly is Professor in the Public Affairs Program of the University of Maryland, having served as Senior Economist in the World Bank's Environment Department. Founding Officer of the International Society for Ecological Economics, Daly authored *The Steady State Economy* and, with John Cobb, *For the Common Good.*

Ana Paula Fernandes Mendes served as Research Associate at the Institute for Applied Economic Research of the Brazilian Ministry of Planning, where she studied health impacts of water and air pollution. The latter research was the basis for her master's thesis in economics at the Federal University of Rio de Janeiro.

Sergio Margulis is currently President of the Rio de Janeiro state environmental agency FEEMA. A former economist in the Environment Department of the World Bank, and researcher at the Institute for Applied Economic Research (IPEA) in Brazil, he has pioneered studies in environmental valuation and policy in Brazil, Mexico, and Central America, and has supervised preparation of Environmental Action Plans for several African nations.

Peter H. May is Professor of Ecological Economics and Agrarian Policy at the Federal Rural University of Rio de Janeiro. Co-author of *The Subsidy from Nature*, Dr. May has served as Program Officer at the Ford Foundation and as Forestry Officer at the FAO in Rome. He is President of the Brazilian Society for Ecological Economics and coordinated the "Eco-Eco Brazil Project," supported by the Rockefeller Foundation.

Jyoti Parikh is Senior Researcher of the Indira Gandhi Institute for Development Research in Bombay. She is a specialist in the economic analysis of energy, agriculture, and environment, having written *Sustainable Development in Agriculture*.

Adam Rose, Chairman of the Department of Mineral Economics of Pennsylvania State University, is a specialist in the distributive effects of public policies regarding natural resource use, having co-authored *Natural Resource Policy and Income Distribution*.

Ronaldo Serôa da Motta is senior researcher and coordinator of Environmental Studies at the Institute for Applied Economic Research (IPEA) of Brazil's Ministry of Planning, where he has undertaken a range of studies regarding environmental policy, economic valuation of natural resources, and estimates of health costs associated with pollution. He coordinated the research project "Environmental Accounts Estimates for Brazil."

Brandt Stevens is an economist at the Fuels Planning Office of the California Energy Commission in Sacramento.

Thomas H. Tietenberg is Professor of Economics at Colby College, Maine. Former President of the American Association of Environmental and Resource Economists, he recently authored *Innovations in Environmental Policy*.

Index

Abatement costs, 49, 60, 61, 63, 65, 66, 67n5; distribution of, 64; Egalitarian criterion, 65, 66; post-trading, 64, 66; Sovereignty criterion, 58, 63, 64, 68n10; *see also* Rawls' Maximin principle
Acid rain, 15, 20
Afforestation, 47
Agarwal, A., 57
Agriculture: conservative modernization of, 27; expansion as a source of deforestation, 203–5; export-oriented, 29; horizontal expansion, 27; irrigation, 91, 93, 131; soil erosion, 72, 74, 79–81
Agroecosystem maintenance, 27
Ahmad, Y. J., 149, 153
Ahuja, D., 67n3
Air pollution, 4, 5; health effects, 79, 81; health effects, costs of, 4, 5, 81, 113–20; *see also* Brazil, air pollution; Mexico, air pollution; Mexico City, air pollution; São Paulo, air pollution
Air quality, 43, 130
Air Quality Bulletins, 103
Air quality monitoring network, 111
Alicbusan, A., 77
Alfsen, K. H., 194n1
Allocations, *see* Permit allocations; Resources, allocations

Altieri, M., 27
Amazon: deforestation of, 34n7; hydroelectric generation, 30; *see also* Ecuadoran Amazon
Andersson, T., 19
Arrow, K. J., 160
Assurance bonds, 6, 160–61
Asthma, 79
Atkinson, G., 25, 33n5, 206

Barber, M., 154
Barbier, E., 33n6
Barrett, S., 49, 133
Bartelmus, P., 181, 192, 194n2
Bartlett, E. T., 150
Baumol, W., 16
Beijer Institute for Ecological Economics, 35n12
Belo Horizonte, Brazil, 110, 111, 112
Benefit-cost analysis, 23–24, 25
Bergesen, H., 67n3
Biofuels, 3, 43, 44
Biological evolution, 144
Biotechnologies, 13, 174
Bishop, R., 150
Bojö, J., 78
Bolivar, 171
Bombay, India, 132